STUDIES IN HISTORY, ECONOMICS AND PUBLIC LAW

Edited by the

FACULTY OF POLITICAL SCIENCE OF COLUMBIA UNIVERSITY

NUMBER 492

THE PRIMROSE LEAGUE 1883-1906

BY

JANET HENDERSON ROBB

THE PRIMROSE LEAGUE
1883-1906

BY

JANET HENDERSON ROBB

AMS PRESS
NEW YORK

COLUMBIA UNIVERSITY
STUDIES IN THE
SOCIAL SCIENCES

492

The Series was formerly known as
Studies in History, Economics and Public Law.

Reprinted with the permission of Columbia University Press
From the edition of 1942, New York
First AMS EDITION published 1968
Manufactured in the United States of America

AMS PRESS, INC.
NEW YORK, N. Y. 10003

PREFACE

THE Russian political scientist, M. Ostrogorski, includes a discussion of some length of the Primrose League in his well known work *Democracy and the Organization of Political Parties,* which appeared in English in 1902.[1] The present study is apparently the first attempt to describe the heyday of the Primrose League from the perspective of a later generation.

At the offices of the Primrose League in Victoria Street in London, through the courtesy of the secretary, the manuscript account of the formation of the league and the fourteen manuscript volumes of the Grand Council of the Primrose League covering the period from 1883 to 1906 were available for this study. Together with the files of the *Primrose Record,* the *Primrose League Gazette* and the *Morning Post,* these manuscript minutes, with several manuscript rolls of habitations, form the backbone of any research on the subject. Interviews with the present Dame President of Eldridge Habitation at Thornton Heath, Croyden, and with the Ruling Councillor of the Grantham Habitation at Croydon not only provided notes from local minute books but were a source of interesting reminiscences of earlier League activities and personalities.

The manuscript and the printed minutes, and the programs of the Annual Conferences of the National Union of Conservative and Constitutional Associations were consulted at the library of the National Unionist Association, as well as several rare political pamphlets of the eighties and nineties. At the Liberal Publication Department were to be found the copies of the National Liberal Federation's publication. The journal and reports of the Imperial Federation League were available at the British Museum. Various pamphlets and reports issued by the Navy League were to be found in the office of that society in London. Through the courtesy of the management of Madame

---

1 Ostrogorski, M., *Democracy and the Organization of Political Parties.* Translated from the French by Frederick Clarke, New York, 1902.

Tussaud's famous establishment in Marylebone Road, several early catalogues served to enliven some of the politics of the era. Finally, through the invitation of Mrs. Coningsby Disraeli the writer had the opportunity of attending the 56th anniversary pilgrimage to the grave of Disraeli at Hughenden on Primrose Day.

It is true that late Victorian and Edwardian England with its buoyant confidence in a future of ever increasing prosperity and ever deepening security seems sharply severed from the stresses and strains of the contemporary scene. One feels that one sees the actors of that earlier period as if through an opera glass— they move and speak excitedly but at a great distance and on a stage. Yet no one would deny that the England of today, with her paradoxes and in her strength and weakness, is peculiarly the spiritual descendant of that period when the conservatives, reaping the Home Rule harvest and capturing the new popular electorate, ruled the country for nearly two decades. The story of the Primrose League in its own way, may convey some of the vitality which contributed to victory.

It would be impossible for the author to express adequately her obligation to Professor Carlton J. H. Hayes. To his stimulating classes and seminar she owes an interest in nineteenth century British history, and to his kindness and encouragement the undertaking of this study. She is most grateful, also, to Professor J. B. Brebner for helpful criticism of her manuscript. The author was privileged in having had several discussions with the late Professor Robert C. Binkley, which served to illuminate for her certain aspects of the social history of the last century.

The writer is indebted to her friend, Mrs. Betsy Hutchison, for deft and invaluable editorial assistance, and to her friend, Miss Blanche Eliott Lockhart, for help with preliminary research in London. In conclusion, thanks are due to Miss Betty Shapin for her help in proofreading as well as for several last-minute and indispensable touches.

JANET HENDERSON ROBB

NEW YORK, N. Y.
FEBRUARY, 1942

CONTENTS

CHAPTER I

THE BACKGROUND AND ORIGIN
OF THE PRIMROSE LEAGUE

I

A HANDBOOK for Liberal Women Workers of 1885 declared,
" The existence of the Primrose League cannot be overlooked,
nor can its subtle proselytism be set aside by a sneer. We may de-
spise or condemn its ridiculous paraphernalia, its appeals to the
ignorance and frivolous vanities of women, its prostitution of
the sacred name of Charity and its persistent perversion of political principle and the facts of history. We may proclaim that,
instead of seeking to redress the wrongs and secure the individual rights of women, it indulges in vague and delusive cries
of ' The Church,' or ' The Empire,' or some other imaginary
' interest ' being in danger, knowing well that this is only throwing dust in the eyes of the unthinking, or trying to divert attention from the real reforms which are needed. The League exists, with a widespread membership and ceaseless activity. It
possesses a large revenue; it commands the patronage and support of men and women of high position and vast influence; it
is resolute, spectacular, defiant, and must be met and counter-
acted by the combined action of Liberal women, systematically
promoting political education, and exercising, by independent
and self-respecting intercourse, an enlightened and elevating
influence." [1]

The Primrose League was scarcely in the third year of its
life when this unintentional tribute was paid to it. Yet it had
already become the model of political propaganda methods, and
had begun to mobilize that great body of vaguely conservative
and definitely traditional sentiment which the old party organization of the Tories had failed to galvanize into action. It at-

1 Reid, Mrs. H. G., *Women Workers in the Liberal Cause*, 5-6.

tracted women as well as men in an era when they—women—
were beginning to be a real political force, although enfranchisement was still far in the future. It created fortresses of Tory
strength in urban districts, which Liberals until then had
claimed for their own. It maintained the Conservative power in
rural districts at a period when rural distress threatened to disrupt the old manorial system and dispel the old manorial fidelity
to the " squire " and his political outlook. It rejuvenated enthusiasm for the Empire and the Throne at a time when the
emerging social consciousness of the working class, newly enfranchised, threatened to dominate the political scene.

Modern political propaganda in England is the child of the
franchise acts of the nineteenth century. Each of the three great
Reform Acts threw a new body of voters on the register, whose
political complexion was unknown, and perhaps not very definitely established, and whose conversion became of primary interest to each of the two great parties. A long line of legislation
regulating elections and electoral practices made new demands
on the ingenuity of party leaders and called for stronger party
organization. The spread of literacy, and the multiplication
of means of communication opened up vast new channels of
propaganda. A political party could now speak directly to millions, and its opponents could answer equally directly. The
problem now emerged clearly on the political scene: How to
convince the people?

The answer involved new methods of propaganda, and new
types of political organization. The Primrose League made a
distinct contribution in this respect, but it learned much from its
predecessors of the technique of political organization in the
constituencies.

Before the first great modern reform of the franchise, British
parties had hardly existed outside the walls of Parliament. Such
expressions as " the Bedford interest " or " the Rutland interest " reflect the fact that voters were then largely personal followers of various influential noble houses. In the counties the

local landlords directly controlled the vote, or the prestige of their names did it for them. Even after the passage of the Reform Bill of 1832, both small freeholders and tenants had not shaken off that influence.

According to a witness before the Bribery Commission of 1835, it was still common for a parliamentary candidate to ask permission of a landlord before canvassing his tenants. One landlord is reported to have submitted to a candidate a questionnaire designed to ferret out his attitude on Corn Law repeal, promising to come to the polls with his tenants if the candidate's answers should prove satisfactory. In fact, as one witness before a Parliamentary Committee remarked, even at that period, " the poll book is almost a topography of the Estates." [2]

Urban districts before 1832 were no less dominated by the local nobleman or territorial magnate. Where, exceptionally, this condition did not hold, the borough often contrived to sell itself en masse or en bloc to a party.[3] Societies were reported at Bristol, whose honorary membership paid a yearly subscription of from five shillings to as high as two pounds, and which were engaged in buying freehold votes at five shillings per head.[4] Sometimes rations of " blue beef " (the Tory Party color was blue) were distributed for votes by local church wardens,—and none for those who " split " their votes.[5] According to the testimony of an officer of a Conservative Operative Society, beer was substituted at times for beef. In other cases, better prospects

2 Great Britain, *Report of the Select Committee on Bribery at Elections (Parliamentary Papers)*, 1835, VIII, 101.

3 A committee appointed by virtue of the Grenville Act of 1776 discovered a " Christian Club " in one town, ostensibly a charitable society, but in reality occupied in finding the highest bidder for the town itself at election time. *Report on Bribery*, 1835. Quoted in Ostrogorski, M., *Democracy and the Organization of Political Parties*, I, 136, note 1.

4 Great Britain, *Report of the Select Committee on Bribery at Elections (Parliamentary Papers)*, 1835, VIII, 405.

5 *Ibid.*, 407.

for local assessment, or for school rating, were dangled before the voter.[6]

Members, therefore, for most urban as well as rural areas, depended for their votes not on the favor of their constituents, but on that of the local magnates or on the skill of their own agents in buying votes. To make sure of victory a political party found it necessary at times to buy the borough itself. Only to that extent did it ever carry its activities beyond the limits of Westminster. Such party organization as existed in the boroughs dealt with purely local questions.[7]

The Franchise Act of 1832 made an important change in the form by which the voter's name was placed on the register—a change which contributed as much to the development of modern party organization as the famous franchise provisions of the Act. It was now necessary for the voter to place his name beforehand upon the register, which was under the supervision of local or of parochial officers. The responsibility for getting his name on the register thus rested on the initiative of the individual voter between elections, and if challenged he had to start proceedings himself before the presiding barrister, from whom the case might ultimately be appealed to the Court of Common Pleas.

To the natural inertia and indifference of the average voter in a democracy there was added, at that period, a total lack of training and experience in party politics. This was true of agents and candidates as well as of voters. Undoubtedly the registration fee of a shilling must have dampened some political ardor as well.

6 *Ibid.*, 404.

7 Two other kinds of constituencies should be noted: the pocket or depopulated boroughs, and the scot and lot constituencies, like Westminster and Preston, where a system of democratic party politics existed for twenty-five years before 1832. Francis Place, for instance, knew all about machine politics long before the Reform Act. See Wallas, Graham, *The Life of Francis Place*, II, *passim*.

It was natural that both Liberal and Tory leaders should hasten to form local registration societies wherever possible, in order that they might perform these essential duties for their voters. During the fourteen years between the Reform Act and the successful repeal of the Corn Laws in 1846, Liberal Registration Societies (or Liberal Associations as they were sometimes called) vied with Conservative Loyal Constitutional Societies in the task of getting their respective voters registered. The Conservative Registration Societies, affected by the general party torpor after 1832, came into the field slightly later than the Liberal Registration Societies, which were common all over England by the middle of the thirties.[8]

It was a logical step, especially in the urban districts, for the registration societies to branch out into canvassing potential voters. At the same time the larger electorate made the older and simpler forms of bribery more difficult. Peel's famous cry to his Tamworth electors in 1841 of " Register! Register! Register! The battle of the constituencies will be fought in the registration courts," was bearing fruit in both parties.

The Anti-Corn-Law League was especially active in placing voters on the register, and after its dissolution a decided decrease in the numbers on the register was noticeable.[9] In 1844 the Anti-Corn-Law League had found the registers for the most part completely neglected. In many cases they had been carelessly kept, or had fallen entirely into the hands of legal agents, or rather " into the hands and power of victorious bribers . . ." as the parliamentary testimony described it. When an Anti-Corn-Law spokesman was asked what was his organization's principal concern, he replied: " Let it be clearly understood that the whole of their attention is being given to the subject of registration in all its branches."

8 Lowell, A. L., *The Government of England*, I, 481.

9 Several Corn Law Registration Societies eventually became Liberal Registration Societies.—Ostrogorski, M., *op. cit.*, I, 151.

The evidence before a Committee of the House of Lords in 1860 showed that many Conservative Land Societies were active in creating qualified voters.[10] W. J. James testified that the Conservatives had originally been more successful in adding voters to the register, but that most of the freeholders so created had died out, many having wound up in the Court of Chancery.[11] In Marylebone a vigilant registration society was set up in 1840, but by 1860 was reported to have died out, leaving no registration society for the district.

After 1846 the movement to found registration societies experienced a slump in both parties, some societies passing out of existence and others becoming dormant. Only in those districts where the rival parties were evenly balanced or where one party for special reasons had made some enormous stride, did the local societies show vitality. A witness before the Committee of the House of Lords in 1860 testified that " whatever approach to accuracy there is in the existing register, seems to be due to the volunteer agency of political organization."

Both parties later formed central party organizations (closely watched over and directed by the respective whips) which were designed to help promote and foster local registration societies and, where no such society existed, to keep in touch with the local solicitor who was the party representative. Outvoters, peculiar to the county electoral system, were the special charge of these central party organizations.[12]

When the electorate was small, outvoters were extremely valuable to each party, and in some cases money was advanced for

10 Great Britain. *Report of the Select Committee of the House of Lords on Elective Franchise in Counties and Boroughs (Parliamentary Papers)*, 1860, XII, 209.

11 *Ibid.*, 340.

12 In the counties, outvoters were non-residents who might vote by reason of holding or leasing property in the district, and the business of securing this absentee vote was an important one in close contests. Outvoters in the West Kent division in 1858, for instance, represented 1,500 voters in a total of 9,000. It is estimated that in the fifties and sixties of the last century, these outvoters represented at least 15% of the total electorate.—Ostrogorski, M., *op. cit.*, I, 147, note 3.

special trips from France or Holland, though after 1857 payment of traveling expenses was made illegal. Conveyances, however, might be provided and the central bodies in possession of outvoting lists for the entire Kingdom found it easy to arrange for railway companies to return electors' tickets for repayment to them, and for the central organization to be reimbursed by the candidate concerned.

These central organizations were in no sense representative of the local registration societies. They were merely groups of subscribers who supplemented registration work from central headquarters. They worked closely with the London political clubs, the Carlton and the Reform, but their role as far as the choice of candidates went, was rather that of a broker between the influential local party membership and the party whip.

Party leadership in Parliament called for professional direction, and this was supplied by the party whips, who were the political descendants of the patronage secretary (originally political secretary to the Treasury) of the early eighteenth century. " It is rather a roguish office," Wilberforce remarked of the secretary, for this official's main duty up to the time of Pitt had been to supply the Government with a majority at the lowest possible figure. With the metamorphosis of patronage secretary into whip, and the improvement of the standard of political ethics in the nineteenth century, the office was relieved of its more questionable functions. The whip's chief concern was with the M. P.'s of his party; he was their executive, charged with the task of carrying out the strategy of the party leaders, and mobilizing the party members at critical moments. There was little activity on the part of the central party organization outside of St. Stephen's, but such as existed was essentially an outgrowth and an extension of the whip's office and duties. Thus until well past the mid-century point, the control was exercised from the center outwards, and the slowly growing organizations of rank and file adherents remained without a voice in party councils.

Side by side with the growth of the central party organizations arose the great political clubs, the Carlton Club and the Reform Club. They were descended from the eighteenth century coffee clubs, which had gradually taken on a political character, though casual and informal in their organization and activities.[13] During the Reform Bill agitation of 1831, a group of Tory leaders, ex-ministers, diplomats and important county leaders founded the Carlton Club. Although it set up no political committee, it was destined to have a great share in the direction of the affairs of the Conservative Party.[14] Local Tories began to mutter about its haughty meddling in local party affairs, and in the choice of candidates, but in reality before the middle of the sixties the Club had lost most of these powers to the central party association.[15] A Liberal club, the Reform Club, was founded in 1836 in imitation of the Carlton, and achieved the same prestige in Liberal party councils. But it was destined to lose even more of its political powers to the Liberal central association than did the Carlton to the Conservative central organization.

II

Thus the early and middle years of the century saw a marked consolidation of party leadership, with the reins of party control firmly in its hands. The democratic control of parties was still an issue of the future. True, both were increasing their efforts to appeal to the increasing electorate, and to organize them into a permanent following, but it was definitely a following that they were organizing, not a democratic body to whom the party leaders should be responsible.

In the meantime, the trend of the times seemed to be with the Liberals. As the party of the rising industrial interests, and the

13 Rae, W. Fraser, "Political Clubs and Party Organizations," *The Nineteenth Century*, May, 1878, III, 908. See also Aspinall, A., *Correspondence of Charles Arbuthnot*; letters 156, 162, 163 a & b, 177b, 207, 218, 223 for the origin of the Carlton Club.

14 *Ibid.*, 920.

15 Ostrogorski, M., *op. cit.*, I, 149.

champions of reform, they appealed to the growing and ever more politically awakened urban population. The Conservative Party was depending, to a dangerous extent, on the old manorial paternalism and the fidelity of the common people to their feudal leaders.

The Reform Bill of 1867 awakened both parties to a realization of the new situation. The Liberals hastened to consolidate their favorable position; the Conservatives strove to regain their old point of vantage. Under Disraeli's brilliant leadership the Conservative Party launched its appeal to the new industrial classes by opening up the many avenues of imperialism for industrial expansion. But the Liberals, doing the duty which lay nearest them, concentrated on building up their local organizations in the towns. Thus the party caucus was born, and a truly democratic form of party organization sprang into being.

The party caucus [16] (immortalized by Lewis Carroll), was first organized in Birmingham, and thus came to be known as " the Birmingham Six Hundred." It occupied popular attention throughout the seventies, and was a bone of contention almost daily in the columns of the press. The Birmingham Six

[16] Ostrogorski, M., *Democracy and the Organization of Political Parties*, I, 161-249 and *Introduction of the Caucus into England*, by the same author, in the *Political Science Quarterly*, 1893, Vol. VIII, 282-316, describe the workings of the British caucus at great length and in much detail.—Spence, Watson, H., *The National Liberal Federation*, tells the story of that organization from its commencement to the General Election of 1906, and is an authoritative account by one of the most active officials of the Federation, but it is hostile to Chamberlain and, on the whole, fails to describe or evaluate the Federation as a living organ.

See also Lowell, A. L., *Government of England*, I, 469 ff. There are many contemporary magazine articles both in praise and in condemnation of the caucus, the most useful being: Chamberlain, J., "A New Political Organization," *Fortnightly Review*, July, 1877; Crosskey, H. W., " The Birmingham Liberal Association and Its Assailants," *Macmillan's Magazine*, December, 1878; Crosskey, H. W., "The Liberal Association—the 600 of Birmingham," *Macmillan's Magazine*, February, 1877; Howell, G., " The Caucus System and the Liberal Party," *New Quarterly Magazine*, October, 1878; Rae, W. F., " Political Clubs and Party Organizations," *Nineteenth Century*, May, 1878; Wilson, E. D. J., " The Caucus and Its Consequences," *Nineteenth Century*, October, 1878.

Hundred was a system of interlocking Liberal party councils, partly elective and partly co-optative, pyramided on a wide popular base. (It was in fact somewhat reminiscent of the councils of Napoleon III). The borough was divided into wards, each ward, in public meeting, electing delegates to an Executive Committee for the whole town. These delegates to the Executive Committee in Birmingham numbered eighty, and to their number they might add thirty more of their own choice. Each ward also elected, at special meetings for the purpose, eighty delegates to a General Committee, which was the party's deliberative assembly for the whole town. This General Committee included the entire Executive Committee as well. In Birmingham this organization roughly included six hundred persons, and consequently was known as " the Six Hundred."

Within a few years Liberal organizations in other cities organized themselves along the lines of the Birmingham model. In 1877 delegates from ninety-five of these local Liberal associations gathered at Birmingham. Here a constitution, already drawn up, was approved, and the National Liberal Federation formally launched.[17] The constitution of the new federation provided for a governing body or Council composed of delegates from the affiliated caucuses.

The caucus came under heavy fire from the Tories, who accused the Liberals of importing the notorious corruption and manipulation of American machine politics into British party life. " I am not surprised that the Tories should dislike it," Joseph Chamberlain once remarked of the caucus. " I do not wonder that they feel so painfully what they unsuccessfully try to imitate. These great open popular representative associations are not at all in their line. They are alien to the spirit of Toryism." [18] Chamberlain became Mayor of Birmingham in 1873,

17 *Proceedings attending the Formation of the National Liberal Federation with the Report of the Conference*, Birmingham, May 31, 1877.

18 Newcastle-on-Tyne, June 15, 1884. See Boyd, Charles, *Mr. Chamberlain's Speeches*, I, 117.

and his fortunes were closely linked to those of the caucus for some years. He wrote in a letter to John Morley: " The Caucus is force, enthusiasm, zeal, activity, movement, popular will and the rule of the majority—Seven Deadly Sins in fact." [19]

But critics in the Liberal camp were not lacking. In November of 1877, Hartington wrote Chamberlain: "And when we come to a federation of these associations, it seems to me that it will come before long to placing the chief control and direction of the party in the hands of these men (most advanced), to the exclusion of the more moderate and easy-going Liberals. There is a good deal of the American caucus system about it, which I think is not much liked here; and though we have all been preaching organization, I think we may sacrifice too much to it."[20]

Ostrogorski describes and comments at length on the caucus, in his monumental work: *Democracy and the Organization of Political Parties*.[21] A native of Russia, and at one time a civil servant in the Tsarist bureaucracy, this author viewed the demo-

19 September 29, 1878. See Garvin, J. L., *Life of Joseph Chamberlain*, I, 262.

20 Holland, Bernard, *The Life of Spencer Compton, Eighth Duke of Devonshire*, I, 245.

21 Moissaye Ostrogorski (1854-1919) attended the *École Libre des Sciences Politiques* at Paris, where he studied under Émile Boutmy. He represented his native province of Grodno as a Constitutional Democrat in the Duma. He has been described as a " mordant but hopeful historian of the pathology of party organization in England and the United States in the nineteenth century." — Macmahon, A., article on Ostrogorski in the *Encyclopaedia of Social Sciences*. Watson Spence remarks with undue severity of Ostrogorski's work: " I have before me a ' History of the Organization of Political Parties ' in this country which simply teems with inaccuracies so far as English political organizations are concerned, and yet the casual reader may conceivably mistake it for a work of real authority." — Spence, Watson, H., *The National Liberal Federation*, 219. J. L. Garvin, in his life of Joseph Chamberlain, says of Ostrogorski's work on the Liberal caucus, that the industry in research is minute, but " not so searching are the historical reflections," and adds that Ostrogorski's *Liberal Caucus* leaves the reader with " a singular impression as of mathematics tinged with melodrama,"—I, 252.

cratic scene from an intellectual distance. His withering comment on democracy in general and its machine politics is matched only by the caustic vein of his account of the Primrose League.[22] His thesis in *Democracy and the Organization of Political Parties* was that political development under the popular franchise has been essentially the same both in England and the United States; and that Joseph Chamberlain and Aaron Burr share the shame of fastening party systems on their respective countries. Beneath his critical narrative runs a current of temperamental abhorrence of the democratic system. Yet from his vantage point, emotionally as well as geographically foreign, he probably realized what was happening in the contemporary political scene a generation earlier than many British historians.

At the opposite pole to Ostrogorski stood Lord Randolph Churchill, one of the few Tory leaders to find some good in the caucus. " The Caucus may be perhaps a name of evil sound and omen," he wrote, " in the ears of the aristocratic or privileged classes, but it is undeniably the only form of political organization which can collect, guide and control for common objects large masses of electors." [23]

Twenty years after the League was founded, an American journal observed, in a review of Ostrogorski's monumental work : " By 1886 the Tories had devised their chain of machines

---

22 Ostrogorski's study of the Primrose League in this work is the only important one of any length—*op. cit.*, I, 534-52. He acknowledges the cooperation of Mr. George Lane Fox, the temporary Vice Chancellor of the Primrose League, in obtaining information on that body. In spite of the caustic vein in which his remarks on the League are couched, the *Primrose League Gazette* concluded its review of the book: " On the whole the book is a careful account of a factor in constitutional history which has never been previously historically studied."—*Primrose League Gazette*, May, 1903, 12.

23 Churchill, W. S., *Life of Lord Randolph Churchill*, I, Appendix II, 540. It is curious that the caucus, hailed as so significant by both its friends and enemies, should have proved so ineffectual a tool for the party rank and file. At the first real test, when the issue of the Boer War split the party from top to bottom, the Liberal leaders evaded the dangerous issue, fearing to widen the breach. One might have expected the National Liberal Federation to act as a vehicle of expression for the rank and file, but its Council refused to allow a popular vote on the issue.

under the style of the Primrose League. Essentially this was and is a political machine, although its founders were shrewd enough—or simple enough, for it is not quite clear which—to give it a veneer of mediaevalism." [24]

III

The Tories were far slower than the Liberals to recognize the demands of the new trend. But Disraeli's Reform Act of 1867 awakened his party to the need of organizing the mass of new voters, most of whom could not be counted on to vote Conservative simply by tradition. They proceeded to federate their various local associations into the National Union of Conservative and Constitutional Associations. Any local Conservative organization might join by paying a fee of one guinea. At the initial meeting the Conservative societies of fifty-four towns were represented, as well as that of the University of London.[25] A ruling body, the Council, was set up, which was to have a membership in part nominated by the larger constituent bodies. From the beginning an open effort was made to put big donors to the party on the governing council. The officers of the National Union were *ex officio* members of the Council, but members of the Consultative Committee might be co-opted by the Council at will. The offices of patron and ten vice patrons were created, apparently for the purpose of identifying titled Tories with the Union of Conservative Associations.[26]

During the first five years of its existence, the Conservative Union attracted almost no public attention and some of its

24 "Diabolus ex Machina," *The Nation*, April 30, 1903, 357.

25 Only the reports of the fourth to the ninth Conferences have been printed. The remainder for this period are available in manuscript form at the office of the National Union of Conservative and Constitutional Associations, St. Stephen's Chambers, Westminister, London.

26 In 1869 Lord Derby became patron and on his death was succeeded by the Duke of Richmond. The Report of 1872 reported a total of 365 Vice Presidents (who subscribed five guineas yearly and were *ex officio* members of the Consultative Committee) of whom 66 were noblemen and 143 M. P.'s past or present.

yearly conferences were attended by less than forty delegates. In 1871 John Gorst, appointed agent of the party, became the Honorary Secretary of the Union, and a new chapter in its history opened. In 1872 it accepted office space at the London headquarters of the Central Committee of the party, and held a conference in the Crystal Palace. One speaker at the banquet of this conference, replying to a taunt of the enemy that if a Tory workman could be found he should be put in a glass case, replied, " We have found for him the largest case in England tonight." [27]

Even after the victory of 1874, however, popular interest in the National Union grew slowly. Only 47 delegates from 226 associations appeared at the Conference of 1878, and 684 Conservative associations were not even nominally affiliated with the National Union. Some efforts were made to have a more democratically composed Council, but these attempts were either tabled or postponed, and it was only after the defeat of 1880 that they bore any fruit. Until 1876 the National Union passed not one resolution of a political character, and even after that date, resolutions were merely expressions of general confidence in the party leadership, or of congratulations on its accomplishments.

The real power in the party was vested in a Central Committee, composed of the party leaders. This Committee, an outgrowth of the whip's office, had been part of Disraeli's plan for revitalizing his party's machinery. It controlled the party funds, and consolidated the leadership, but left room for a more popular organization. Cecil Parkes, one of the founders of the National Union, reminded its conference in 1873 that the Union had been organized rather as the handmaid to the party than to usurp any of the prerogatives of leadership—an explicit statement of the role which the Union was to fill in the party.

During the seventies, a large middle class Tory vote in the urban centers became noticeable; yet the composition of the

---

[27] This banquet of the National Union was notable for Disraeli's famous speech identifying his party with imperialism.

Beaconsfield Cabinet of 1874 had shown no recognition of this new Tory element. No attempt was made to make the rank and file feel themselves participants in the new glories of the Disraeli regime in realizing the magnificent dream of Empire. Here was the opportunity for the Tories to find the urban equivalent for the old manorial fidelity, and they missed it completely. The Tory rank and file was expected to cheer and to vote, while the Liberal rank and file were soldiers in the very thick of the battle.

IV

Just what part this situation played in the defeat of the Tories in the election of 1880 is a matter for speculation. But that year saw the Conservative Party in the doldrums. Beaconsfield had retired, and the new Conservative leadership—now the Opposition—was decidedly sluggish and uninspired. Lord Salisbury led the Opposition in the Lords, and Sir Stafford Northcote in the Commons. The eminently respectable, cautious and rather colorless opposition tactics of Sir Stafford were infuriating to the more full-blooded Tory warriors, and especially to a little band of insurgents who led the new wing of " Tory Democrats."

This group, which came to be known as the " Fourth Party," consisted of Randolph Churchill, John Gorst, Henry Drummond Wolff, and Arthur Balfour. Lord Randolph was the ringleader. According to Lord Rosebery, Wolff supplied the diplomacy, Gorst an encyclopædic knowledge of public affairs and a wide experience of party organization, and Balfour was " the outrigger of this frail but daring craft; he was of it for a time, but not in it." [28] By 1880 the rebel band constituted a definite political unit in the House, at once vigorously attacking the measures of the Liberal Government, and heartily chaffing the ponderous leadership of its own party. It is odd that these heretics, regarded with decided suspicion by the leaders of the Conservative Party, were destined to found the Primrose League, which was to be known for its impeccable loyalty to

28 Rosebery, Lord, *Lord Randolph Churchill,* 158-159.

Conservative leadership, no matter whither it might lead or fail to lead.

The members of the Fourth Party first came together during the Bradlaugh controversy which began in 1880. The newly elected atheist member Bradlaugh claimed his right to take his seat in the House without taking the customary oath ending with the words: "So help me God." In the pandemonium which followed—the wildest in the reign of Victoria, according to one observer—the four insurgents formed an informal alliance in attacking Bradlaugh and the tolerance of the Liberals towards him. They emerged from the fight as a recognized political entity, a kind of offensive alliance in debate, and a self-constituted Opposition to the Gladstone Government.

Sir Stafford Northcote, known as "The Goat" by the Fourth Party, was an especial butt for their criticism. As leader of the Opposition he was accustomed to sit between Smith and Cross on the front Opposition bench in the House, frequently turning from one to the other for consultation during a debate. "Marshall and Snelgrove" the counsellors were irreverently dubbed by the Fourth Party.[29]

The four were probably united less by a common political outlook than by a genuine flair for Opposition tactics. One of their favorite techniques—copied from Disraeli—was to criticize Liberal measures as too half-hearted. This method of attack was applied in the debate on the Employers' Liability Act, and notably during the passage of the Franchise Bill of 1884. A political opponent declared of these tactics that " the policy of dishing has been elevated to a high art." [30]

Churchill used the term " Tory Democracy " on the floor of the House for the first time in 1882, according to his own statement some years later. " It is democratic," he was quoted as saying " because the welfare of the people is its supreme end;

---

29 A reference to the well-known department store in London, Marshall and Snelgrove's.

30 A Plain Tory, *Tory Democracy and Conservative Policy*, 55.

it is Tory because the institutions of the country are the means by which the end is to be obtained." [31] And again: " It involves the idea of a government who, in all branches of their policy and in all features of their administration, are animated by lofty and by *liberal ideas*. That is Tory Democracy." [32] Churchill, always the most insurgent of the Fourth Party group, had some difficulty in persuading his colleagues to unite in support of Gladstone's Franchise Bill. He maintained with many inconsistencies that the " leap in the dark " [33] had committed Disraeli's party to a policy of broadening the franchise.

Winston Churchill wrote of the movement led by his father: " Tory Democracy was necessarily a compromise (perilously near a paradox in the eye of a partisan), between widely different forces and ideas." [34] Gladstone wrote Lord Acton in 1885: " ' Tory democracy,' the favourite idea on that side, is no more like the conservative party in which I was bred, than it is like liberalism. In fact less. It is demagogism, only a demagogism not ennobled by love and appreciation of liberty, but applied in the worst way, to put down the pacific, law-respecting, economic elements which ennobled the old conservatism, living upon the fomentation of angry passions, and still in secret as obstinately attached as ever to the evil principle of class interests. The liberalism of today is better in what I have described as ennobling the old conservatism." [35]

Disraeli's attitude toward the Fourth Party movement is a little obscure. During the last year of his life he received his old party lieutenant Gorst at Hughenden. It was at the close of the first session in which the Fourth Party's activities in the House had attracted public attention. Gorst wrote Churchill: " Lord

31 Quoted in a letter by Sir John Gorst to *The Times*, February 6, 1907.

32 Rosebery, Lord, *op. cit.*, 176.

33 The Franchise Bill of 1867 was referred to by Lord Derby as " a leap in the dark."

34 Churchill, W. S., *op. cit.*, II, 487.

35 Morley, John, *The Life of William Ewart Gladstone*, III, 173.

B. was in his talk anything but Goaty!" (A reference to Sir Stafford Northcote). " He generally expressed great confidence in us, thought we had a brilliant future before us, and promised to help and advise us as much as he could." [36] At another time, agreeing that Northcote represented the respectability of the party, Beaconsfield had volunteered to Gorst, " I wholly sympathize with you all because I was never ' respectable ' myself." [37] Lord Beaconsfield's biographers are inclined to think the Fourth Party rather exaggerated the enthusiasm of the elder statesman. They quote in evidence a letter from Beaconsfield to Northcote of December 1, 1880: " I have had Gorst down here, and have confidence in his future conduct. I will assist you, as much as I possibly can, in looking after the Fourth Party." [38]

In view of the part they played in founding the Primrose League, the lives and personalities of the members of the Fourth Party group are of some significance.

If Randolph Churchill be admitted to the line of Tory Democratic leadership of Bolingbroke, Pitt, Peel, Disraeli and Chamberlain, it is rather for his promise than for his performance. His political activity extended over only six years before his break with Salisbury. After 1886 it was of a distinctly free-lance variety, and was curtailed on account of absence abroad and illness in the years immediately preceding his death in January, 1895.

Leadership, audacity in attack and magnetism for popular audiences as well as for individuals undoubtedly characterized Lord Randolph Churchill. One concludes that he fascinated or arrested the attention of his contemporaries to an unusual degree, but almost to that degree his personality today eludes analysis. His speeches are good polemics, often coarse and

36 Gorst, H., *The Fourth Party*, 148. Quoted by Wilkinson, W. J., in *Tory Democracy*, 91.

37 Gorst, H., *The Fourth Party*, 148.

38 Moneypenny, W. F. and Buckle, G. E., *The Life of Benjamin Disraeli, Earl of Beaconsfield*, VI, 589.

obvious in their composition and clearly designed for successful platform delivery. Probably for that reason they appear rather meaningless torn from their context of time and place.

Lord Randolph's personal appearance seems to have been one that lent itself to the pencil of the cartoonist; his small body and his pugnacious expression were caricatured continually in the press of the early eighties. As a small schoolboy he impudently lectures a dame school teacher, labelled " Northcote," crying, " Here, give us the book, old lady." [39] As Puck, he flits irritatingly over grave party councils, or as an excitable little pug dog he barks at large objects in his path. *Punch* shows him at a regatta, furiously paddling a small skiff, exclaiming delightedly as he places himself directly in the path of the racing sculls, " In the way again! Ooray!" [40]

The political atmosphere fairly bristled with personal abuse hurled at Lord Randolph Churchill. " Pug," " Toady," " Sycophant," " Quack," or " self-condemned and self-convicted as the coarsest lampooner and most nauseous, unprincipled and unmannerly humbug of our time " are only samples of the descriptions of Lord Randolph indulged in by contemporary pamphleteers.

When he entered Parliament in 1874 for Woodstock, the central Churchill stronghold, he gave no sign of any divergence from type. But by 1877 he showed sympathy with the obstructive tactics of the Irish Nationalists, and spoke outside of Parliament in their defense. His father, a former Lord Lieutenant of Ireland, wrote to Sir Michael Hicks-Beach, then Chief Secretary for Ireland: " The only excuse I can find for Randolph is that he must either be mad or have been singularly affected with local champagne or claret." [41]

Within a few years his reputation as a rebel and obstructionist was firmly established. He became a great friend of Joseph

39 *Punch*, June 13, 1885.

40 *Ibid.*, July 7, 1883.

41 Churchill, W. S., *op. cit.*, I, 92.

Chamberlain's, who at this time was fulfilling a similar role on the other side of the House as leader of a militant radical minority within the Liberal party. In matters of policy these two were often in agreement, and in matters of tactic they had both learned much from the Irish nationalists. The biographer of Lord Salisbury charges Churchill with raising difficulties for his Tory colleagues on account of his friendship with Chamberlain, " which made him insist that we should accept that statesman as our guide in internal politics." [42] Yet the Tories were destined to profit by this detested alliance, for it is probable that Churchill did more than any other Conservative to attract Chamberlain to the party.

Like Disraeli, the real father of Tory Democracy, Churchill represented his party as the true friend of the worker, and the Liberals as mere pretenders. " No; I quite admit that there is nothing democratic about the Whig," he said at Manchester in November, 1885. " He is essentially a cold and selfish aristocrat who believes that the British Empire was erected by Providence and exists for no other purpose than to keep in power a few Whig families, and who thinks that our toiling and struggling millions of labourers and artisans are struggling and toiling for no other purpose than to maintain in splendour, opulence and power the Cavendishes and the Russells." [43]

Lord Randolph's attitude toward British imperialism was in striking contrast to that of his party in his time, as well as to that of the League which he was to found. Although it is not possible to say that he ever favored Home Rule for Ireland in any true sense, yet he was consistently more friendly to the Irish Nationalists, more interested in genuine reform in Ireland, and more conciliatory to the Home Rule faction than was his party as a whole.[44] His friendship may well have played some part in

[42] Cecil, G., *The Life of Robert, Marquess of Salisbury*, III, 336-37.

[43] Churchill, W. S., *op. cit.*, I, 465.

[44] Blunt says Churchill told him it was only the words " Home Rule " to which he objected, as he felt that the public had not been educated up to the idea, and that it would be better to use a vaguer expression.—Blunt, W. S., " Lord Randolph Churchill," *Nineteenth Century*, 1906, LIX, 408.

inducing the Nationalists to throw their support to the Tories at the 1885 election, and may have borne fruit in Lord Salisbury's Land Purchase Act of 1888.

On other imperialist issues he often stood in direct opposition to his party. He differed from Beaconsfield on the Eastern question in his championship of the oppressed nationalities in the Balkans. He was sympathetic with Arabi Pasha in the Egyptian crisis of the early eighties, condemning, with his friend Wilfrid Scawen Blunt, what he called the meddling policy of the British Government. Clearly in such matters Lord Randolph was an insular Tory of the pre-Disraelian type, and like his colleague, Sir John Gorst, he showed an increased rather than decreased interest in domestic reform as he grew older.

Sir John Gorst contributed to the Fourth Party a vast wealth of experience in administration and in party organization. Born of a financially substantial family, he had gone out to New Zealand in his youth and there held important government positions. After his return to England, he entered Parliament in 1866, and after the Tory defeat of 1868, he was drafted by Disraeli to mend party fences.

Again after the defeat of 1880, W. H. Smith and Stafford Northcote sought to enlist Sir John Gorst's aid at the Conservative Central Office, but Gorst soon retired, feeling that he would never be permitted adequate freedom of action there. Soon afterwards he was openly allied with the Fourth Party on the floor of the House. In contrast to Wolff, Gorst combined an encyclopædic knowledge of public affairs with a dexterity in party tactics. As a contemporary put it, he was "a pointer to find game for Lord Randolph Churchill to run down."

Sir Henry Drummond Wolff's main interest was in international finance. His autobiography shows his concern for the advantageous export of British capital, especially where loans were followed by occupation. This is apparent in his accounts of diplomatic missions to the Near East, particularly in Egypt.

Wolff had taken part in the transfer of the Ionian Islands to Greece and had written an account of it for the *Morning Post.*[45] An M. P. for Christ Church from 1874 to 1880, he sat for Portsmouth from 1880 to 1885.

It is true that he signed with Sir John Gorst a manifesto which demanded a reorganization of the Conservative Party, and which appeared in the *Fortnightly Review* in November, 1882, over the signature " Two Conservatives." But his main interest was in the external affairs of the Empire rather than in the internal affairs of the party. Except for his general alliance with the Fourth Party, he does not seem to have shared Gorst's or Churchill's interest in social reform, and his later career was largely in the diplomatic field.[46]

Harold Gorst thought Balfour less of a Tory Democrat than the rest. Enough of one to cooperate during the earlier period with the Fourth Party group, he broke with them in 1883 when Lord Randolph directed his shafts at the personal leadership of Lord Salisbury. As the nephew of Lord Salisbury, he was torn between loyalty to his kinsman and his adherence to his insurgent colleagues, with whom his caustic wit gave him a certain kinship. It is evident that Churchill valued his support less than that of his colleagues. For instance, when Churchill heard that Gorst was thinking of leaving for India, he declared: " To the Fourth Party, it is ruin!" But the news that Arthur Balfour had become the Conservative leader in the House moved Churchill to write from Mafeking, " So Arthur Balfour is really leader, and Tory Democracy, the genuine article, is at an end."[47] Churchill's words were indeed prophetic. Arthur Bal-

45 Wolff, H. D., *Rambling Recollections.* See chapters XL, LIX, LX, LXI and the quotation, pp. 56-66.

46 After the founding of the Primrose League, Wolff was commissioner in Constantinople, and later British Envoy in Persia, Romania and Spain. He died in 1908. See Wolff, H. D., *Rambling Recollections,* and the article on H. D. Wolff in *Dictionary of National Biography, 2nd Supplement, Twentieth Century,* 1901-1911.

47 Gorst, Harold, *op. cit.,* 260-261.

four's career, most of which still lay before him when Lord Randolph Churchill's was over, was to travel the traditional road to the highest places in his party's councils. In any event, the showy, if not vulgar, truculence of Lord Randolph Churchill could not long have commanded the talents of the cultivated and skeptical Balfour.

The time came when these four, and especially Churchill, could no longer be content with the rhetorical glories of expounding Tory Democracy, nor with the role of mere carping opposition within the party ranks. Churchill wanted nothing less than control of the machinery of the party, and immediately after the death of Disraeli in 1881 he tried to get it. The National Union of Conservative and Constitutional Associations, as the only body at hand representative of the rank and file of party members, was the natural objective for him to seize upon to realize his ambition.

It will be remembered that the real power in the party was its Central Committee, representing the inner circle of leadership, and that the National Union, representing the rank and file, was completely subservient to the Central Committee. It was the custom, for instance, for the Central Committee to choose the leader of the party when the occasion arose. After the death of Disraeli, the Fourth Party opened its campaign by demanding publicly that the new leadership be chosen by the National Union, instead of by the Central Committee. To this claim the party peers and M. P.s turned a deaf ear. Lord Salisbury in the Lords and Sir Stafford Northcote in the Commons were to lead the Conservative Opposition. At the Conference of the National Union in 1882 one of Churchill's followers engineered a resolution, and got it carried, demanding that the National Union take steps to assert its " legitimate influence."

In 1883 Churchill was elected chairman of the Council of the National Union and his following was strengthened among the members of the Council. The Council thus became a lever at hand for the Fourth Party to use against the existing leadership, as embodied in the Central Committee of the party. However, Lord Percy, a member of the Old Guard, remained chairman of the Union itself. Under the Churchill influence the Council appointed a committee to consider the question of obtaining by negotiation with the party leaders a more important place in party councils for the Union. Churchill presided over this committee, but Lord Salisbury continued to address all his communications on the subject to Lord Percy.

At the same time Churchill launched a personal attack on the party leaders. At the annual dinner of the Central Committee at which Salisbury and Northcote were the speakers, the absence of Lord Randolph aroused some comment. A few days later a letter signed "A Tory," but really emanating from Churchill, appeared in the *Times* of March 29th, 1883, protesting against the announced plan to have the chief speech at the unveiling of Lord Beaconsfield's statue made by Sir Stafford Northcote. Another letter from the some source followed shortly, expressing doubt and misgivings as to Northcote's powers of leadership. A week later the moribund state of the Conservative Party itself came under attack by the same pen. These letters described leadership in the Commons as being in the hands of " third-class statesmen," " bourgeois placemen," or " honourable tadpoles and Irish lawyers." At once letters appeared in the press in defense of Sir Stafford Northcote. But when he unveiled the statue, the members of the Fourth Party were absent.

In the meantime Churchill continued his struggle within the Union in the name of democracy and popular control of party policies by the rank and file of party members. He pointed out that the Birmingham caucus had taught the public to expect a voice in the organization of parties. In October of 1883 the conference of the National Union passed a resolution reiterating its demand for a voice in party councils, and declaring : " The Central Committee (i. e. of the Conservative Party) is a self-elected and irresponsible body, while the Council is an elected and responsible body." [48]

48 National Union of Conservative and Constitutional Associations, *Minutes of the Conference* (Ms.), October 2, 1883.

" I look to the Associations to popularize the organization of our Party," Lord Randolph Churchill announced in addressing a Birmingham audience. " Our object is to obtain a representative executive who will hold itself responsible to the electors who appoint it. In fact my idea, and it is the idea of my friends, is that the Tory Party shall be like the English people—a self-governing party." [49]

On January 29, 1884, Lord Salisbury wrote Churchill a letter defining the functions of the National Union as he saw them. An exchange of bitter letters between Salisbury and Churchill ensued, culminating in a demand by the party agent that the Union vacate its offices at party headquarters. At this point, McClean, a Churchill supporter, drew up a compromise plan. Churchill, to test confidence in his leadership, resigned as chairman of the Council of the National Union. Thereupon a large group of local associations threatened secession, and Churchill found himself reëlected.

At the party conference at Sheffield in July, 1884, the battle was fought out to a drawn peace. In spite of the personal endorsement of Churchill by the rank and file, the vote for the members of the Council did not split on controversial lines. Perhaps for this reason, Churchill suddenly came to terms with the leadership, and the National Union's spell of vigorous life was at an end.[50] One of the terms of the compromise was the official recognition of his newly born child, the Primrose League, by the leadership of the Conservative Party.

By August Salisbury and Churchill were speaking from the same platform. The *Times,* making a virtue of necessity, was singing the praises of the " horrid young mutineer," as the *Spectator* had described Churchill. The breach with Salisbury was healed for the time. Two years later Churchill actually held the key position in Salisbury's cabinet, but he was destined to

49 See *Morning Post,* May 5, 1884.

50 For the details of the controversy, see Churchill, W., *op. cit.,* I, Chapters VI, VII, and VIII.

hold it for only a few months. A disagreement with Salisbury caused Churchill to hand in his resignation at the end of 1886, perhaps confident that popular opinion would endorse him, and sweep him back into office again, as it had done when he challenged Salisbury to a duel for control of the National Union. But the rank and file, like Salisbury, accepted his resignation.

After the outburst of 1883-84 the National Union lapsed again into a profound sleep so far as any control of party policy was concerned.[51] At the annual meeting of the Union in 1906, the resolutions begin: " Though the Russian Duma has been dissolved, the National Union will still be allowed to meet, possibly because it is even more impotent than the Duma." [52]

V

In the meantime, Churchill had not been confining his activities to the struggle for the control of the National Union. In 1883 two incidents brought to his attention the need for a popular organization to mobilize opinion and votes for the Conservative Party. The first was his unsuccessful contest in Birmingham, which he and Colonel Fred Burnaby fought together that year. They were impressed by the enormous and mounting expenses involved in such a campaign, and consequently the desirability of recruiting volunteer workers at once. They had seen the smooth working of the efficient Liberal local machinery in that stronghold, and realized their party's handicap.

---

51 See *Minutes of the Conference of the National Union*, 1886. Also Churchill, W., *op. cit.*, I, Appendix II, *Further Correspondence Relating to the National Union of Conservative Associations.*

52 The National Union continued to grow. In 1891 there were 1,241 affiliated bodies and ten provincial divisions.—*Minutes of Conference*, 1891. The agenda at a typical conference included such subjects as: Inequalities of parliamentary distribution; The unjust burden of local taxation borne by the clergy; The Workingman's Dwelling Act; The greater production of food in the country; Pauper aliens; A railroad in Uganda; The reform of the Lords; A preferential colonial tariff on the Canadian model.—*Minutes of Conference*, 1898.

The other incident was the passage of the first reasonably effective Electoral Corrupt Practices Act, in the same year, thanks to the efforts of Sir Henry James, Attorney General in Gladstone's Government.[53] One of its provisions called for a rigid restriction of the number of paid political helpers permitted to a candidate at election time, a situation which made it imperative to tap some source of unpaid political work.

It is probable that Churchill was thinking of the National Union of Conservative and Constitutional Associations as that source when he read his *Morning Post* on April 20th, 1883. It is also probable that he read the leading article commenting on the widespread wearing of primroses on the previous day, the second anniversary of Disraeli's death. It reported that business men had worn them in their buttonholes, that bouquets had appeared for sale in flower baskets, and that cabbies had stuck primroses in their caps and behind the ears of their horses. " The April primrose shall be a perpetual reminder of the statesman of Hughenden," the *Morning Post* editorial proclaimed, " and of a fame which will not perish from the page of history until the primrose, in such demand today, shall itself become extinct."

With more restraint, the *Times* remarked editorially: " We found no speculative theories upon the fact, except the simple one that the personality of Lord Beaconsfield has, beyond all doubt, made a deep impression on the popular imagination of his own time. The sentiment may prove to be evanescent, but while it lasts it is real and vivid. Lord Beaconsfield," the editorial continued, " is the object, we do not say of a cult, but at least of an admiring and affectionate curiosity, differing in kind rather than in degree from the cool political judgment which appraised the claims to remembrance of men like Peel and Palmerston a year or two after they had passed away." [54]

53 46 & 47. Victoria (C 51). For the text of the Act, see Edge, J. B. and Hardy, W., *On the Management of Parliamentary Elections*, 217-263. For discussions of other effects of this Act, see below, Chapter III, 96 ff.

54 *Times*, April 20, 1883.

In later years the *Morning Post* claimed that its editorial was responsible for the idea of a Primrose Day, and thus indirectly of a Primrose League. Several cab drivers (Primrose Day, apparently, continued to have an especial appeal for London cabbies) said, when interviewed, that it was the *Morning Post* which had suggested to them the idea of decorating themselves and their horses on the anniversary of Disraeli's death.[55]

Sir George Birdwood, an admirer of Lord Beaconsfield's literary works, and an official at the India Office, had suggested primrose decorations for St. Stephen's Club, one of the Tory headquarters. Although nothing in the way of organized effort had come of this suggestion, some of Sir George's friends agreed to wear primroses in their buttonholes on the day. An advertisement of these boutonnières appeared in the *Times,* and Sir George Birdwood on April 14th wrote a letter to that newspaper on the subject.[56] Sir Edwin Arnold of the *Daily Telegraph,* Mr. Frederick Greenwood of the *Pall Mall Gazette,* and Professor Chenery of the *Times* were active in forwarding the scheme, while the criticism of the Opposition press furnished the necessary additional publicity to make the first Primrose Day a success. The journalistic advocates went the rounds of the florists, holding out to them prospects of an annual festival, of another " oak apple day." [57]

On the morning of the second anniversary, a large number of members had appeared in the House of Commons with primroses in their buttonholes. Mr. Cove, the attendant at the House, is said to have given Sir Henry Drummond Wolff a primrose boutonnière, and as Wolff walked home with Lord Randolph Churchill, the story runs, he proposed a Primrose Society to perpetuate the political memory of Disraeli.[58]

55 Lucas, R., *Lord Glenesk and the Morning Post,* 296-7.

56 Pitman, J. H., *Lord Beaconsfield, K.G., His Writings and the Primrose League, With a History of Primrose Day.*

57 *Illustrated London News,* April 23, 1892.

58 Churchill, W., *op. cit.,* I, 256.

Lord Randolph Churchill and his Fourth Party colleagues were in the habit of meeting for Sunday lunch at the home of Lady Dorothy Nevill and there talking over and preparing future political strategy. At one of these luncheons, the idea of forming a new society, a sort of corps d'élite of younger, more democratic and more militant Conservatives, was conceived and plans discussed. It was felt that such a group might attract those Conservatives who now looked askance at the established party organizations as closed corporations of parsons and landlords.[59]

During October and November of 1883, the members of the Fourth Party, with the exception of Arthur Balfour and with the addition of Sir Alfred Slade, met frequently in the card room of the Carlton Club to perfect their plan. Sir Henry Drummond Wolff is credited with the original idea of such a League, and it is said that at first his colleagues, including Lord Randolph Churchill, had scoffed. It was Wolff, all agree, who suggested the original name, " The Primrose Tory League."

There appears to have been some discussion about the desirability of a secret form of organization. Lord Randolph Churchill had at first leaned toward a society formed along the lines of the Buffaloes, but he was over-ruled on this point by the others.[60] Wolff, impressed by the Masonic degrees of membership as a means of interesting and holding members, was also mindful of the successful use of quaint titles by such current benefit societies as the Foresters and Oddfellows and Druids.[61] Another type of organization which was said to have influenced the founders of the Primrose League was the Orange Loyal

59 Nevill, Ralph, *The Reminiscences of Lady Dorothy Nevill*, 284.

60 J. B. Stone of Birmingham wrote Lord Randolph Churchill on November 26, 1883, " I have given much consideration to the proposal to found a Primrose League. I am now more firmly convinced than ever that it would be a worthless effort to try to found a Patriotic *Secret* Society, having merely a general programme of principles without embracing a positive line of action." Wright, Thomas, *The Life of Colonel Fred Burnaby*, 209-10.

61 Wolff, H. D., *op. cit.*, II, 270.

Institution. A local Orange lodge in Lord Randolph Churchill's own constituency, Portsmouth, was supposed to have furnished the model.

Meanwhile Gorst had drawn up a declaration to which members were asked to subscribe.[62] In its original form the declaration ran, " I, A. B., declare on my honour and faith that I will devote my best ability to the maintenance of Religion, of the Estates of the Realm, and of the Imperial Ascendancy of Great Britain; that I will keep secret all matters that may come to my knowledge as a Member of the Primrose Tory League; and that consistently with my allegiance to the Sovereign of these Realms, I will obey all orders coming from the constituted authority of the League for the advancement of these objects." In a corner of the card room of the Carlton Club on November 17, 1883, the four conspirators against orthodox Conservatism swore to this declaration and then constituted themselves a Ruling Council.[63]

Between this inaugural meeting and the middle of December another meeting was held at which some others joined the original members. Statutes and ordinances for the new League were drawn up by Wolff, and secretly printed,[64] and a registrar, J. D. Thomas,[65] and an organizing secretary, the Hon. Claude Hay, were appointed. During this period of organizing activity behind the scenes, the *Morning Post* kept its readers advised that a new league was in process of formation.[66]

In its issue of December 18, 1936, the 53rd anniversary of its original appearance in the columns of that newspaper, the *Morning Post* reprinted the following advertisement: "·The

62 Initiation rites were never introduced.

63 Arbuthnot, G. A., *The Primrose League Election Guide*, 14.

64 For the original resolutions, see Appendix I.

65 A devoted adherent of Lord Randolph Churchill, who aided materially in the foundation of the League.

66 *Morning Post*, November 17, 1932. An article reviewing the origin of the Primrose League.

Primrose Tory League—Gentlemen wishing to be enrolled in the Primrose Tory League must apply in writing to the Registrar, Primrose League, care of Messrs. Lacy, Hartland and Co., Bankers, London, E.C. or Messrs. C. Hopkinson and Sons, 3 Regent Street, by whom all information will be supplied." This notice appeared on December 17, 1883 in the *Times, Standard, Telegraph, England* and in *Vanity Fair,* as well as in the *Post.* A speaker years later at a Primrose rally pointed to the " must " in the advertisement as unmistakable proof of Lord Randolph Churchill's authorship.

A meeting of the Ruling Council on December 22, 1883, disclosed that other members had been added. Among these were Sir Algernon Borthwick,[67] proprietor of the *Morning Post,* who had attended the lunches at Lady Dorothy Nevill's and had given generous space in his columns to the Fourth Party, as well as to the formation of the new League. Dixon Hartland, Colonel Burnaby, Sir Henry Hoare, Percy Mitford, Seager Hunt, and Sir William Hardman,[68] editor of the *Morning Post,* were other new members.

The next step was to win over the party leaders. Sir Stafford Northcote had always distrusted the Fourth Party, and the organization of the League only added to his distrust, according to Wolff.[69] Gathorne Hardy recorded in his diary on January

---

67 Algernon Borthwick (Lord Glenesk) was born in 1830. Editor of the *Morning Post* in 1853, he became its proprietor in 1876 and at his death in 1908 the paper was, in effect, inherited by his daughter, Lady Bathurst. Borthwick sat in Parliament for South Kensington from 1885 to 1895. The Duke of Marlborough, in proposing Lord Glenesk for Chancellor of the Primrose League for the third time, wrote to him: " No one has the knowledge and experience that you possess in the past workings of the League." Lucas, R., *op. cit.,* 374.

68 *A Short History of the Formation of the Primrose League,* corrected and revised by the founders (MS.) Sir William Hardman was born in 1828, and practiced at the Bar for many years. For over twenty years he was connected with the administration of justice in the county of Surrey and was chairman of its quarter sessions. He was editor of the *Morning Post* from 1872 until his death in 1890.

69 Wolff, Sir H. D., *op. cit.,* 270.

5, 1884, " Northcote wrote me a curious account of Randolph Churchill's Birmingham intrigues, and seems to suspect that he is secretly moving the Primrose League, whatever that society be or contemplate." Hardy commented on this: " Much I fear that disunion will destroy our chance of checking the revolutionary race which Gladstone has started, and Chamberlain will run." [70]

It will be remembered that one of the terms of Churchill's compromise with Salisbury in the summer of 1884 was the recognition of his new protégé, the Primrose League. Apparently Salisbury managed to override Sir Stafford's fears, for in November Salisbury wrote to Wolff, " Northcote and I agree that there is no objection to our becoming Patrons of the Primrose League if it should be thought desirable. But I suppose we shall have no such commonplace name. What do you say to Vavasours? " [71]

In December, 1884, an official delegation from the Primrose League waited on Lord Salisbury and Sir Stafford Northcote to ask for official recognition by them for the new organization.[72] Lord Salisbury thanked the League for its election work, mentioning conspicuously effective aid given to the party in Hackney, Brighton and South Warwickshire. The party leader admitted to the delegation, " I cannot say that I know exactly very much about the character of the Primrose League. I believe that it was set on foot by those who are familiar with the mysteries of another craft which, unhappily, I do not belong to."

Nevertheless, both Salisbury and Northcote, after receiving an address by Borthwick, signed declarations and were presented with their diplomas. " We may fairly regard the official connection now established with the leaders," the *Post* con-

70 Hardy, Sir H. E., *Gathorne Hardy, First Earl of Cranbrook. A Memoir*, II, 193.

71 Wolff, Sir H. D., *op. cit.*, 271.

72 *Morning Post*, December 22, 1884.

cludes, " as the final chapter in the history of the League's childhood."

Wolff puts it rather differently and more tersely in his article on the League in the Encyclopædia Britannica: [73] " When the League had become a success, it was joined by Lord Salisbury and Sir Stafford Northcote." On official recognition by the party, the League increased the membership of its Grand Council to include the party whip in each house, and the head of the Conservative Party. [74]

At the General Election in 1885, it was obvious that the most conspicuous successes of the Conservative Party were made in the very centers where the Primrose League was the strongest, and here large numbers of urban workers and young people, the voters to whom Churchill seemed to have the strongest appeal, were found to have voted for the Conservative candidates. Churchill and his political followers had been specially helped by the League and by the Primrose Dames in his contest against John Bright in Birmingham. Largely as a result of this, Churchill became Secretary of State for India in Lord Salisbury's cabinet. Among the conditions of his acceptance of this post again appeared the official recognition of the Primrose League. [75]

---

73 Thirteenth Edition.

74 On the foundation of the Primrose League, see: *A Short History of the Primrose League, Its Rise, Progress and Constitution*, by one of the staff; *The Primrose League Election Guide*; *The Primrose League, A Retrospect*, by Reginald Bennett; Wright, Thomas, *The Life of Colonel Fred Burnaby;* Churchill, W., *Life of Lord Randolph Churchill*; Wolff, Sir H. D., *Rambling Recollections*; Aspden, Thomas, *History of the Primrose League*; Lucas, R., *The Life of Lord Glenesk*; *The Reminiscences of Lady Dorothy Nevill*; Nevill, R., *Leaves from the Note Books of Lady Dorothy Nevill*; Encyclopaedia Britannica (13th Edition), Article on the Primrose League; "Links with the Morning Post", *Morning Post*, November 17, 1932; " The Jubilee of the Primrose League ", by Emery, R. G., *Primrose League Gazette*, Jubilee Number, November, 1932; Fox, George Lane, " The Primrose League," *The Paternoster Review*, October, 1890 (No. 1); Borthwick, A., " The Primrose League," *Nineteenth Century*, Vol. XX, 1886; *The Primrose League—Our 50th Birthday* (Jubilee Shilling Fund); *Primrose League Hand Book*, 1929.

75 Wilkinson, W. J., *Tory Democracy*, 102.

VI

Disraelian hagiography is especially rich in extended discussion of the exact relationship between the sophisticated statesman and the field flower, a matter which afforded Liberals much amusement and some concern.

Gladstone wrote Lady Dorothy Nevill, " Tell me, Lady Dorothy, upon your honour, have you ever heard Lord Beaconsfield express any particular fondness for the primrose? " When Lady Dorothy admitted that she had not, Gladstone commented, " The glorious lily, I think, was more to his taste."

Liberals delighted to declare on what they called " St. Beaconsfield's Day " that surely the peony, the hollyhock, the gardenia or the orchid would have been much more appropriate. One such writer declared triumphantly that no one could combine love for the peacock (several had strutted on the terrace at Hughenden in Disraeli's time) with a love for the primrose.

A search through the pages of Beaconsfield's novels disclosed the fact that the flower was mentioned but twice. In *Coningsby,* a dish of ham and eggs on the table at an inn is likened to a bouquet of primroses. Lord Jerome in *Lothair* exclaims, " Primroses, I believe, make a capital salad."

Even the testimony of the wreath of primroses sent by Queen Victoria for Disraeli's funeral with the well-known inscription, " His favourite flower," came under Liberal fire. It was said that " his " could refer only to the Prince Consort and not, as might have been thought, to the dead statesman. The *Westminster Gazette* quoted a letter from the Queen's secretary, Sir Henry Ponsonby, dated May 1, 1888, contradicting the statement in the *Times* at the time of the funeral about the wreath and the inscription on the Queen's card.

In their turn, the Tories pointed to the primroses that had been allowed to grow wild in the " German Forest " and in the Park at Hughenden during Disraeli's lifetime. Conversations with Disraeli about the flower were reported carefully, and Disraeli's notes to the Queen thanking her for her gifts of spring flowers from Osborne were cited.[76]

One historian traces the origin of the tradition to a wager made by the youthful Disraeli at a dance at Highbury as to whether the primroses fastened to the curls of one of his partners were real or artificial. Finally, the *Primrose League Gazette* often published on Primrose Day a woodcut of Mrs. Brydges Williams, an elderly admirer, offering Lord Beaconsfield a bouquet of primroses on his visit to her at Torquay.

In a lyrical editorial on the third anniversary of Disraeli's death, the *Morning Post* likened the simple primrose to the Victorian statesman: "As the primrose strives forth from its chill surroundings, looked down upon and overlooked by the dry stumps of plants that flourished luxuriantly in the prosperous blaze of the previous year, so the aspiring statesman, undeterred by the chill reception accorded him, unawed by the stiff looks of the worn out remnants of previous Conservative Ministries, ventured forth from his obscurity." [77]

By 1887 the annual celebration of Primrose Day had become such a fixture that it was no longer a matter of comment. Processions became common on that day and special concerts were well attended, it being necessary at Perth one year to have a second concert for the overflow.[78] Many clubs had formed the habit of decorating their club houses on the anniversary. One such club, at Windsor, is described as displaying on its façade masses of primroses against a scarlet background illuminated at night by thousands of colored lamps over a multitude of gas jets. It was reported that the leading hotel in far-away Cyprus had copied this decoration.

As the years went on, an increasing number of working men wore primroses in their buttonholes or on their caps, while

76 It will be remembered that one of the famous notes to Queen Victoria from Disraeli in his last illness reads, " some bright bands of primroses have visited him today, which he thinks shows that Your Majesty's sceptre has touched the enchanted isle."

77 April 19, 1884.

78 *The Scotsman*, April 20, 1894.

cabbies wound them around their whips. Young girls sold bunches of primroses to passengers on railway trains. W. De Lesseps and Louis Pasteur, setting out from London on April 19, 1884, for the Edinburgh University Tercentenary, were introduced on the platform to Sir Stafford Northcote, who was observed to be holding a bunch of primroses in his hand.[79]

On Primrose Day in 1885 the entire foot of the statue of Lord Beaconsfield in Parliament Square was a carpet of yellow flowers and many tradesmen of London and other English cities decorated their shop windows with statuettes of Disraeli. In Glasgow the statue of Beaconsfield was reported to be " besieged all day " and to be the scene of " manifestations of political adoration." [80] A workers' mass meeting at the foot of the statue was a regular feature of the celebration of the anniversary in Liverpool.[81] Banquets were held in many parts of the country. At Covent Garden, behind the speakers' platform was hung an oil painting entitled " Primrose Day," which showed a little girl putting a primrose in the buttonhole of a chimney sweep.

Up to the first World War, on each anniversary primroses were commonly worn in the streets of several of the provincial cities, as well as in London. Apparently the wearing of primroses on the Beaconsfield anniversary spread even to army barracks. In 1892 Colonel Nolan, a member from Galway in the House of Commons, rose to defend the wearing of shamrocks by Irish soldiers on St. Patrick's Day. His retort to critics was that " some people say that it is wrong to wear the primrose on Primrose Day in the army. Let them have their primroses, but I say it is a party badge." [82]

In 1885 over six thousand people made the pilgrimage to Hughenden on Primrose Day. These pilgrimages, sponsored by

79 *Morning Post*, April 21, 1884.

80 *North British Daily*, April 20, 1885.

81 *The Glasgow Herald*, April 20, 1887.

82 Great Britain. *Parliamentary Debates*, 4th Series, Vol. II, col. 1771.

the Primrose League to the grave of Disraeli at Hughenden, near High Wycombe, on April 19th, have continued throughout the years.[83]

Sir Wilfrid Blunt voiced a typical hostile reaction when he exclaimed of Primrose Day, " It seemed to me too entirely comical that the aristocracy of England should be allowing themselves to be persuaded . . . to worship, after his death, the old Jew statesman who had always laughed at them, and, of all things in the world, under the form of a primrose! " [84]

Truth pictured the apotheosis of Lord Beaconsfield by the League and by the party which had regarded him with so much suspicion through much of his political life. Beaconsfield's statue in Parliament Square, late at night, after the Primrose Day worshippers have left, plaintively addresses the surrounding statues:

> This hanging of damp, smelly wreaths round my neck,
> This hawking of blossoms in Parliament Square,
> This odour so earthly pervading the air,
> Though I own, none the less, that some pleasure is mine
> When I see all these Tories thus flock to my shrine.[85]

On the other hand, Sir Robert Peel on his pedestal in the same square complains:

> I gained my countrymen cheap bread,
> And gave the land free trade,
> And yet no votive wreath or crown
> Has at my feet been laid.

83 For years Major Coningsby Disraeli, the nephew and heir of Lord Beaconsfield, received and entertained the Primrose League on these pilgrimages, which included the decoration of the grave, a ceremony attended by a large local gathering, and a visit to the house where Beaconsfield relics were exhibited—the trophies and testimonials which his triumph at the Congress of Berlin had brought Lord Beaconsfield, as well as portraits of Lord and Lady Beaconsfield and many of their family and political friends.

84 Blunt, W. S., " Lord Randolph Churchill," *Nineteenth Century*, 1906, LIX, 409.

85 *Truth*, April 23, 1891. *Truth* was a witty radical weekly under the editorship of Henry Labouchere.

No Tory crowd has flocked to me
To floral tributes yield;
Though with the Spring's most treasured flower,
They've smothered Beaconsfield.[86]

VII

Lord Randolph liked to described the Primrose League as "a transformation into political energy of the emotions which were aroused by Lord Beaconsfield's death and the sentiments which were excited by the knowledge of his career." [87] *Punch,* which dubbed Churchill "The Grand Young Man," showed a pugnacious schoolboy staring up at the newly unveiled statue of Beaconsfield, and saying, "Ah, they'll give me a statue some day!" [88] Churchill often quoted Beaconsfield in his speeches, and his interest in social reform might give some validity to the idea of the leader of the Fourth Party and founder of the Primrose League as a Disraelian.

On the other hand, Churchill was an insular Tory. His stand on Ireland was less imperialistic than that of his party, and his attitude on overseas questions, such as the South African and the Egyptian, was not of the "spirited" variety of Disraeli's own, nor of that of his party in the late eighties and in the nineties. On the Near Eastern question, Lord Randolph's attention to the oppressed peoples was in striking contrast to that of his master.

It was imperialism that was the Primrose League's most conspicuous legacy from Lord Beaconsfield. In his Crystal Palace speech Beaconsfield had anticipated the coming boom in imperialistic sentiment. Although he had retained some of his "Young England" interests, his Sanitas Sanitatum, or public health and housing campaign, after all, was contemporaneous with his conversion to imperialism. The party itself as well as

86 *Ibid.,* April 23, 1891.

87 *Primrose League Gazette,* April, 1900.

88 *Punch,* April 28, 1883.

the Primrose League, during the eighties and nineties, found it increasingly difficult to yoke the two interests. In the League, as in the party, imperialism rather than social reform took the center of the stage.

" Rallying the people round the throne " through the agency of " a free aristocracy " might be said to have been achieved, if in somewhat crude form. In " habitation " activities, especially in rural areas, the local gentry mingled, it was boasted, with their farm laborers. Whether sheer opportunism be the explanation or not, both Disraeli and the League realized the necessity of enlisting the urban worker's support by offering him a satisfying rôle in the party organization as well as promises at election time.

The League was destined to be far more imperialistic than its founder, and far more dependable in its loyalty to the ruling powers in the party. As time went on, the League became orthodox and Churchill increasingly heterodox.[89] On the occasion of his final break with Salisbury, League meetings passed resolutions of regret that Churchill had left the Government, coupled with expressions of confidence in Lord Salisbury. Some Primrose League speakers also urged suspended judgment until Churchill could explain his stand more clearly.

Churchill continued to be identified with the League, though less closely than in its earliest years. We have the evidence of one of Phil May's charming sketches in St. Stephen's Review,[90] showing Lord Randolph as a small boy hawker impudently shoving a bunch of primroses under the austere nose of a gentleman in a high collar and hat (Mr. Gladstone), and bawling, " Buy a primrose, Sir."

But rumors of a serious breach leaked out. In 1890 the London Gazette said there had been considerable opposition to the reëlection of Lord Randolph Churchill as an official of the Constitutional Club habitation. In 1893 Truth accused the Duke

89 See Churchill, W. S., op. cit.

90 April 20, 1889.

of Norfolk and others prominent in the League of using their League positions to revile its founder. Churchill was nevertheless devoting some of his time to the League, speaking against Welsh Disestablishment before Primrose habitations throughout the year. His own explanation, given at about this time to a Primrose League meeting, was that pressure of work prevented him from maintaining a more intimate connection with the League, but he remained one of its Trustees nevertheless.[91]

After Churchill's death in January, 1895, the speaker of that year at Grand Habitation (the great annual meeting of the Primrose League) said of him, " Curiously enough, when we became a great power, he, while always approving and helping whenever he was called upon, did not take that vital interest in us in our later years when we had succeeded so well. Why? I want to mention this particularly. It was because, as you know, in these later years, the shadow of illness was upon him, and the shadow of a certain want of success. What is so greatly to his credit is this : that he, who had so much to do with building up this, the strongest organization in the Kingdom, never for one moment tried to use it for his own benefit or his own ambition."

Two years later, Lord Salisbury, as he rose at Grand Habitation to acknowledge the vote of thanks for his speech, said, " I could not help feeling when I was listening to the Duke of Marlborough that honour does not always fall where honour is due and that to his uncle, who has gone from us, the foundation of this Society was greatly due and that in celebrating its triumphs we ought to remember that they are largely due to his untiring action, and his energetic and powerful spirit." [92] On the occasion of Churchill's funeral, the *Primrose League Gazette* declared, " We have sent a wreath, but we ourselves are this wreath." [93]

91 *Primrose League Gazette*, December 1, 1893.

92 *Morning Post*, May, 1897.

93 Winston Churchill, the son of Lord Randolph Churchill, made his maiden political speech before the Bath Habitation of the Primrose League, in August, 1897. See Churchill, W. S., *A Roving Commission*, 204-207.

CHAPTER II
THE PRIMROSE LEAGUE AND THE PARTY

I

" To instruct working men and women how to answer the arguments of the Radicals and the Socialists and the Atheists in the workshops and in the public-houses, and at the street corners,—" such was the primary object of the League, according to one of its own pamphlets,[1] issued at the height of the social unrest at the end of the last century.

If this was indeed the purpose of its founders, they failed to make it explicit at the outset. Their avowed program maintained the splendid vagueness characteristic of League pronouncements throughout its history. To perpetuate the memory of the statesman of Hughenden they inscribed on their banners such slogans as " True Union of the Classes," and " Imperial Ascendancy of Great Britain." To be sure, the " Maintenance of the Estates of the Realm " might become a controversial issue in those debates in " workshops and public houses and street corners " to which the pamphleteer referred.

Lord Randolph Churchill's original conception of a corps d'élite of vigorous Tories did not survive long. At the very outset the League had only one class of membership, the Knights and Dames, and their dues were fixed at a guinea a year, a sum which in itself served to exclude proletarian membership. When they gathered for the first general meeting of the League in July 1884 (the first " Grand Habitation," as it was called), it was announced that 3,500 Knights and 370 Dames had already been enrolled.[2] Or, to quote from *The Primrose League, Its Rise, Progress and Constitution*, by one of the staff : " The unprovoked aggression of the proletariat found a

1 Primrose League Pamphlet No. 237.

2 *The Primrose League, Its Rise, Progress and Constitution*, by one of the staff, 12.

solid army of Knights and Dames confronting and frustrating their knavish tricks."

But during the first year of the League's existence a new class of membership was created, the associate members, who paid much lower dues than the Knights and Dames, and who were drawn largely from the working class. Apparently the corps d'élite deemed it more effective to enroll the proletariat in the advancing army than to march against it. This change in the type of membership was to have far-reaching results. Before the end of the decade the Primrose League was to become a popular organization whose membership topped the million mark. As such it provided a far more effective bulwark against the threat of revolution than a more select group of political aristocrats could have done.

Another important change was made during the first year, when the word "Tory" was struck from the name of the League. Assuming that the high ideals for which the League stood transcended party lines, its leaders welcomed people of all political faiths into the fold, and disavowed adherence to any political party. The original declaration of faith was modified to read: "I declare on my honour and faith that I will devote my best ability to the maintenance of Religion, of the Estates of the Realm, and of the Imperial Ascendancy of the British Empire; and that consistently with my allegiance to the Sovereign of these realms, I will promote with discretion and fidelity the above objects, being those of the Primrose League."

Thus the League became technically a non-partisan organization very early in its career, though it was destined to defend the policies of the Conservative Party on all occasions with a blind regularity which at times tried even the patience of the *Morning Post*.

Complexity of machinery, coupled with extreme simplicity in program, was an outstanding characteristic of the organization of the Primrose League. Ostrogorski speaks of its organization as composed of "much old-fashioned bric-à-brac." Mediaeval terms abound—dues are called "tribute," locals are "habitations," members who pay one guinea are known as "Knights" or "Dames"; the honorary President is a "Grand Master," and the official notices are "Precepts." [3]

Popular representation was achieved, if in somewhat diluted form. The central executive body, the Grand Council (originally known as the Ruling Council), was composed only in part of representatives elected directly and indirectly from the local associations or habitations. It consisted—with some changes from time to time—of forty-five elected or appointed members, and six *ex officio* ones.[4] Of the last, four were trustees who were responsible for the funds of the League, and another the Treasurer. Sixteen of the remaining forty-five were chosen by delegates from the various habitations at an annual meeting, which was called Grand Habitation. Nine members of the Grand Council were elected on nomination of habitations in nine divisions or provinces. Twenty of the Grand Council were nominees of Grand Council itself, twelve of these being nominated by the retiring Council and eight co-opted by the newly elected one.[5] It will be observed that, counting the *ex officio* members, the elected members of Grand Council were not in the majority.

3 Ostrogorski, M., *Democracy and the Organization of Political Parties,* I, 538.

4 As finally constituted, the original Ruling Council consisted of the following: Lord Randolph Churchill, J. B. Stone, Dixon Hartland, Sir Henry Hoare, J. S. Hopkins, H. H. Wainwright, F. S. Hunt, J. Bateman and a few others of Lord Randolph Churchill's Birmingham supporters,—Wright, T., *The Life of Colonel Fred Burnaby,* 212. The name of the Ruling Council was changed to Grand Council and on February 23, 1884, in addition to the original members, Lord Abergavanny became Grand Councillor. On July 1, 1884, the following were elected to the Grand Council: Sir M. Hicks Beach, M.P., W. T. Marriott, M.P., Robert Burke, M.P., Lord John Manners, M.P., Lord Elcho, M.P., J. Sclater Booth, M.P., Lord Charles Beresford, the Earl of Hopetoun, Capt. Fellowes, M.P., Sir Samuel Wilson, Maurice Mocatta, Esq.—*Minutes of the Grand Council of the Primrose League,* 28.

5 See Appendix I for original constitution.

Before the League was received into the party fold, its highest officer was known as the Ruling Councillor, elected at Grand Habitation. With the aid of three Executive Councillors, he presided over the Ruling Council and the League in general.[6] In 1885 the joint leaders of the Conservative Party, Lord Salisbury and Sir Stafford Northcote, were both given the title of Grand Master and became honorary heads of the Primrose League. A Chancellor, a paid executive official, was appointed and directed by Grand Council until 1890, when the office became an honorary one, filled by election at Grand Habitation, while Vice Chancellor became the title of the professional executive head of the League.[7]

There were two classes of membership, as we have observed: the Knights and Dames, who paid an initiation fee of half a crown and yearly dues, or " tribute," of a guinea,[8] and the associates, who paid much lower dues, fixed by the individual habitations. The tribute paid by Knights and Dames went directly into the coffers of Grand Council. They might be assessed for additional payments by the habitations to which they belonged. The dues paid by associates, and their initiation fees if any, varied in different habitations. Grand Council received nothing whatever from the dues or other fees paid by associates; all such monies were retained by the habitations.

A separate Grand Council for Scotland was set up in August, 1884, through the efforts of the Earl of Kinlore and W. H. Hadow. The Scottish Knights and Dames paid their tribute to the Scottish Grand Council, which administered its own funds,

6 The Marquis of Abergevanny was the first President of the Council and elected Grand Chancellor in 1884. See Appendix IV.

7 George Lane Fox was then made permanent Vice Chancellor, an office which he was to hold until his death.—*Minutes of the Grand Council of the Primrose League*, February 20, 1890.

8 One half of the initiation fee was returned to the habitation and various arrangements were offered by Grand Council for compounding for life payments, and for deductions for prompt payment by habitations. See " Statutes of the League," *Primrose League Gazette*, August 6, 1893.

and issued warrants for its own habitations. It was thus an autonomous body, though cooperating closely with the English Grand Council.[9]

Women were admitted to membership in the League almost from its beginning. In 1885 the Ladies' Grand Council was established, and two years later boasted a membership in the thousands. As a counterpart of the Ladies' Grand Council, Captain Phillip Green, a member of Grand Council in 1892, launched the first chapter of the Knights Imperial. Gentlemen subscribing a guinea yearly were eligible. In 1901 about one half the Knights Imperial were at the same time ordinary Knights of the League, and the membership elected its own President, a Prior, and held banquets at which prominent Conservative speakers spoke on national or party politics.[10]

The League actually admitted children to membership after some hesitation on the part of Grand Council.[11] In the nineties Croydon reported a membership of six hundred " buds," as juvenile members were called.[12] At the request of the Warden of the juvenile branch at Croydon, Grand Council drew up an explanatory leaflet for juvenile branches all over the country. Papers on Primrose League subjects were submitted by juvenile members in competitions; prizes were given for letters written in foreign languages, and special Primrose badges and pins were issued for children. Lectures on patriotism were delivered at various juvenile branches, and special leaflets were written

9 In 1892 there were 158 habitations in Scotland with a total membership of over sixty thousand, and in 1905 over ninety-four thousand members.— *Primrose League Gazette*, Dec. 17, 1892.

10 In 1904 there were 155 chapters and a membership of over a thousand,— *Primrose League Gazette*, June, 1904. The first Council of the Knights Imperial contained the following members: The Earl of Lathom, Duke of Abercorn, G. Shaw Fox, Lennox-Irvin, Borthwick, Capt. Phillip Green, W. De Eresby, Seager Hunt, M.P., Jos. Greer, G. Hulst, M.P., A. S. Barry, M.P., Col. Malleson.

11 *Minutes of the Grand Council of the Primrose League*, December 19, 1889.

12 *Primrose League Gazette*, November 12, 1892.

for children on the issues of the day.[13] Sometimes Primrose propaganda was offered to children in the form of fiction.[14]

From the Grand Council of the Primrose League emanated all expressions of policy, in the form of statements called " precepts." Grand Council was kept in constant communication with locals through lectures and agents. Habitations, however, enjoyed a large degree of self-determination on membership qualifications, on the expulsion of members and even in the relations between themselves and outside organizations.[15] Actually Grand Council worked through a series of appointive committees—General Purposes, Agency, Joint Consultative (with the Ladies' Grand Council), Literature (with joint representation for the Ladies' Grand Council) and a financial committee.

The financial support for the central body of the League came largely from tribute and initiation fees. In addition, new habitations paid a pound for their warrants. The Ladies' Grand Council allocated a sum annually for publications of the central body and occasionally made extra payments to Grand Council.[16]

13 *Ibid.*, March, 1900, February, 1901, November, 1904.

14 See Chapter V.

15 Grand Council occasionally interfered in such matters. For instance, at the height of the Home Rule excitement it closed a habitation in Ireland which had attracted criticism by opening its proceedings with a Church of England prayer. But on another occasion when a habitation appointed a chaplain to conduct prayers at its meetings, Grand Council decided to take no official notice of the matter until there should be complaints from local sources.—*Minutes of Grand Council of the Primrose League*, November 3, 1889. During the following year a council resolution was proposed to the effect that officials of a habitation might not at the same time be officials, agents or employees of local political bodies. But it was not passed, as it was felt wiser to let habitations control themselves, and for Grand Council to intervene according to the circumstances involved.—*Minutes of the Grand Council of the Primrose League*, June 5, 1890.

16 In an average year the receipts from tribute amounted to £5,663/3/9. Expenditure for the year amounted to £6,464/16/2, the deficiency being met by Grand Council " from other sources." An income of £1,226 and a total of £12,050 invested was reported in the financial statement to Grand Habita-

At first a Conservative paper, the *Primrose Record,* was allowed to state that it was published under the patronage of the Grand Council of the Primrose League and supplied regularly with accounts of Grand Council and habitation activities. It came in for criticism from members at one time for acrimonious attacks on Lord Randolph Churchill, and at another for not carrying material likely to appeal to the rank and file of the organization. One critic furnishes a list of incomprehensible terms from one number of the paper, citing " jeu d'ésprit," " coryphees " and " cum grano salis " to illustrate the point. When an article appeared in the *Record* in 1886 attacking the Liberal Unionist leader, Hartington, now a political ally, Grand Council decided to withdraw its permission to the paper to state that it was issued under its patronage.[17]

During the following year, the *Primrose League Gazette,* financed directly by the League, became the official organ. At first a weekly, with much space given to current affairs, the *Primrose League Gazette* became a monthly in September, 1893. One of the arguments advanced for embarking on the expense of a League newspaper was that it would save much expense in circulating notices, reports and financial statements to the habitations. In fact, the text of many of the League's pamphlets appears in the pages of the *Gazette*. Especially after 1893 the *Gazette* became more definitely a " house organ " than the *Record* had ever been.[18]

Weekly and monthly habitation news received, as a matter of fact, considerable publicity in the columns of the *Morning Post,* which carried almost as full reports as those to be found in the

tion, April 19, 1888,—*Morning Post.* In another year the financial sheet reveals: Tributes £4,486/11/4; Ladies' Grand Council £800; Donations £153/10/3; Interest on capital £396/3/2. The larger expenses are: Office Staff, £2,034/0/4; Speakers and Organizing Secretaries, £2,431/6/9; Literature, £84/1/7.—*Grand Habitation, Business Meeting,* May 6, 1897.

17 *Minutes of Grand Council,* May 5, 1886. A few numbers of the *Record* can be seen at the London headquarters of the Primrose League.

18 A complete file of the *Primrose League Gazette* is to be found at the British Museum as well as at the offices of the League.

Gazette. Another Conservative paper, *England*,[19] spent considerable energy in denouncing the *Gazette* as an unnecessary competitor in furnishing Primrose League news since it, too, carried many columns of local Primrose news. These items in *England* were somewhat curtailed in 1892 and in the following year came to an end.

Habitations elected their own chairmen, Ruling Councillors as they were called, while in habitations composed exclusively of women the chairmen were known as Dame Presidents. Some Ruling Councillors might belong to other habitations as well as the one over which they presided. An executive committee was appointed to help each Ruling Councillor and appoint the Warden and Subwardens of the habitation jointly with the Councillor.

To the Warden was allotted the actual planning and carrying out of the canvass and the preparation of the voting lists on which the canvass was based. The Warden was the successor to the local Tory solicitor of the mid-nineteenth century, who had served frequently as the only link between party headquarters and the constituency between elections. There is a certain amount of comment in the *Gazette* on the lack of appreciation shown by leading local Conservatives of the work of these volunteer League workers. Wardens are reported to complain of a sense of social inferiority in local Tory gatherings. One gathers that the life of the Warden was not altogether a happy one, politically or socially, outside of his own habitation.

Divisional Councils were set up, corresponding theoretically to parliamentary divisions, and containing a varying number of habitations. League County Councils were inaugurated as well, but seem to have been regarded by Grand Council as potential rivals, or at any rate as forces which threatened the highly centralized control of the League. These County Councils never achieved much importance. In fact, except for local con-

19 *England*, a conservative paper designed to interest working class readers, came to an end in 1898.

ferences, often held in connection with some Conservative Party gathering in a locality, League vitality found its outlet almost exclusively through habitation activities.

II

To mark the successful completion of the first year's work of the League, as well as the third anniversary of the death of Lord Beaconsfield, an inaugural banquet was held on April 19, 1884, at Freemason's Tavern in London. Some four hundred Knights and Dames were on hand for the occasion and Lord Egmont presided. A letter was read at the banquet from Lord Randolph Churchill at Birmingham, in which he regretted that illness prevented him from being present.

The campaign of Churchill at Birmingham was praised by the speakers at the dinner, including Lord Borthwick and Colonel Burnaby, who dubbed it a gallant attack on a hot-bed of radicalism. Toasts were drunk to the Royal Family, to Parliament, to the Primrose League, to " the Conservative candidates at the next election," and to " the local associations throughout the country," and the banqueters sang " The Song of the Primrose Knights," which had become popular in the Birmingham contest. Much applause greeted the announcement that twenty habitations were already in existence.[20]

The League won its spurs in the General Election of the following year (1885), when it was noted that the Tories scored conspicuous successes in those very areas where the Primrose League was most active. Immediately after the election Lord

20 They were the following: Birmingham, Bradford, Blackpool, Brighton, Portsmouth, Exeter, Taunton, Bristol, Southampton, Tenby, Wednesbury, South Devon, Northumberland, Yorkshire, the Strand, which were established in 1884; and also Crystal Palace, Westminster, Paisley and habitations at Cork and Dublin,—*The Primrose League, Its Rise, Progress and Constitution*, by one of the Staff, 10. Ten habitations formed in 1884 were reported to be in existence in 1937: South Kensington, Wednesbury, Ryde, Scarborough, St. George's Hanover Square, Derby, Bedford, Leamington, Ealing, North Islington.—Information obtained from Primrose League headquarters, June, 1937.

Salisbury wrote to the League that evidence from every section of the country pointed conclusively to the fact that it was hardly possible to exaggerate the value of the Primrose League in organizing Conservative opinion for electoral purposes.[21] Electoral successes were reflected in an ever-increasing growth in League membership. A glance at the membership figures reveals some plausibility in the defense frequently made for the League that its mushroom growth after 1886 had fairly swamped its central office. For from a total of a little over eleven thousand in 1885, the membership rose to slightly over a hundred thousand a year later, and in the course of the succeeding year, 1887, it jumped to well over five hundred thousand. By 1891 the membership had passed the one million mark.[22]

It should be noted that the League never subtracted or indeed made any public estimate of its yearly losses in membership. It frankly declared that it was not possible to investigate them and so contented itself with simply adding its new members each year to the total of the previous year. A gargantuan increase took place immediately after the injection of the Home Rule issue into the political picture, but a substantial yearly increase was maintained during the first twenty years of the League's history.

In the Liberal press it was estimated that the total net yearly increase in League membership in the early years was no more than 20,000 at the most,[23] while on the other hand the League

21 Ms. letter, January 18, 1886. On file at the Central Headquarters of the Primrose League in Victoria St., London.

22 See Appendix III.

23 "The Secrets of the Primrose League by an ex-Leaguer," *Pall Mall Gazette*, March 23, 1886. A Liberal paper accused the Primrose League of including "the dead, the dying, the decayed and the seceded" in its current membership, while *Truth*, on the announcement by the Primrose League of its membership figures for 1897, offers advice to the League on how to obtain further statistics on its membership:—

> Our prisons, too, must doubtless hold
> Some once-be-Primrosed batches.
> There must be numbers in the Wards
> Of local Colney Hatches.

claimed that it lost no more than 6% to 7% yearly. The *Morning Post* answered a Liberal charge that the actual membership of the League in 1890 was only 200,000, with the assertion that it was at that date in reality well over 900,000.[24] Again in 1894, a *Morning Post* editorial on Primrose Day says that an investigation of two years before showed some 800,000 Primrose League members.[25]

Some indication of the number of active Knights and Dames is furnished by the amount of tribute collected yearly by Grand Council. By 1890 this tribute had reached its peak, and after that date tapered slightly but regularly year by year.[26] Of course it is possible that in certain years tribute was harder to collect, and there is evidence that the practice of turning Knights and Dames into associates for purposes of paying tribute prevailed in certain places.

Habitations were organized throughout England, Scotland, Wales and Ireland, and multiplied rapidly in the latter eighties. By 1890 there were a number of them in each of forty-one English counties as well as in the Metropolitan Boroughs and in Ireland, Scotland and Wales.[27] But a decline became evident early in the nineties. Liberal organs such as the *Manchester Guardian* commented on the slump in the League's activity after its first flush of success; and the League's own Agency

> So let the Ruling Councillors
> Give out revised instructions,
> And tell us where the total is,
> Less the above deductions.
>
> *Truth*, August 9, 1897.

24 May, 1890.

25 April 19, 1894.

26 A total tribute of £5,663/3/9 was reported to Grand Habitation in 1888; £5,668/3 in 1889; £5,690/1/14 in 1890; £5,021 in 1893; £5,459 in 1894; £4,755 in 1895; £4,537 in 1896; £4,486/11/4 in 1897; £4,356, in 1898; £4,215 in 1899, and £3,604 in 1904. (See reports of Grand Habitation Business Meetings for these years.)

27 In 1890 there were 129 habitations in Wales grouped in eleven Divisional Councils,—*Roll of Habitations, 1890*.

Committee reported to Grand Council in 1891 that unless a special effort were made at the coming General Election the League would be in imminent danger of waning to extinction through a lack of new blood.[28] The Committee further reported that many habitations had been dormant since 1889, and that heroic efforts would be necessary if the organization were to be galvanized into any semblance of life.

The Committee's pessimism was hardly justified by the League's history in the following years, but the mushroom growth and phenomenal vitality of the first half dozen years were never quite matched after that. To some extent League activity was linked to the fortunes of the party, and its comparative lethargy in 1891 was one of several presages of the interlude of Liberal rule which was shortly to break the almost solid twenty years of power which the Home Rule issue had bestowed on the Conservative Party. But the most convincing explanation is to be found in the relation of League vitality to the public interest in Home Rule. It was the whirlwind of excitement over that issue which gave the League its tremendous fillip in the late eighties, and set a standard of feverish activity which its workers would never be able to realize when the political temperature dropped.[29] As the public grew bored with Home Rule, and no new issue arose to take its place, League activity inevitably slumped. In the nineties the solid social legislation of Lord Salisbury's government failed to capture the public imagination, and it was not until the outbreak of the Boer War that the League found an issue comparable to the Irish question in dramatic possibilities.

III

Primrose League habitations varied considerably in size, character, wealth, and the nature of their activities. The habita-

---

28 *Minutes of the Grand Council of the Primrose League*, May 14, 1891. Agency Committee Report.

29 See Chapter VI.

tion in a Welsh village which might contain a dozen houses and a church necessarily offered its members something quite different from the activities of a habitation in a London borough such as Bayswater, Kensington or Southwark. One rural habitation covered an area of one hundred square miles where 2,000 of the population of 7,000 were in the Primrose League organization, and its membership reflected the social pattern of landlord, farmer, tenant farmer and farm laborer. In contrast were the Brighton Dames with their comfortable incomes and socially uniform and middle-aged membership, or the rich Victoria habitation in London which raised money 'for poorer habitations. A habitation in West Lothian contained 1,000 miners; one in Derwent Valley was composed predominantly of coal miners; in Bolton, where an average of four thousand attended Primrose League gatherings, artisans and factory workers formed most of the membership.

Great glee was exhibited by the League over its habitation at Hawarden, the home of Gladstone. This Conservative outpost in the heart of enemy country moved the *Gazette* to jubilation in verse:

> Within the Hawarden premises
> A " Habitation " stands,
> Which, like the ancient Nemesis,
> Lays slow but certain hands
> On the Grand Old Mumble Gumble
> And his daily-dwindling bands.[30]

For many years it remained difficult for the League to gain a foothold in Birmingham, although a great effort was made to do so after the second Salisbury Government had been formed, and again when Joseph Chamberlain had taken office in the Unionist Cabinet. In 1903 it was admitted by headquarters that Primrose organization in the Midland city was still in an undeveloped state.

30 *Primrose League Gazette*, December 29, 1888.

Probably largely as a result of the mushroom growth of the League during the years 1886 and 1887, and the consequent swamping of headquarters with work (during 1886 fifteen extra employees were kept busy at headquarters making out new diplomas), there was considerable criticism of Grand Council's administration, within the ranks of the Conservative party, and within the League itself. As early as 1887 the Conservative newspaper *England,* whose owner, Ashmead-Bartlett,[31] was accused by some of personal pique in connection with the League, attacked the autocracy and inefficiency of the Primrose League Council and the clique who, it was claimed, controlled the *Gazette.*[32] Three reforms were demanded at that time by *England*: the publication of accounts by Grand Council, reduction in the proportion of funds from habitations allocated to the Council, and lastly " free and open elections for the Council." [33]

31 Sir Ellis Ashmead Bartlett (1849-1902) was born in Brooklyn, N. Y. and went to England in early boyhood. He was the brother of William Burdett Coutts (William L. Ashmead Bartlett, who assumed his wife's name). During the Russo-Turkish War he visited Turkey and treasured a lifelong distrust of Russia in consequence. In 1899 he visited the Turkish army in the field. An M.P. from a Suffolk division from 1880 to 1884, he sat for a division of Sheffield from 1885 until his death. He was chairman of the National Union of Conservative and Constitutional Associations from 1876 until 1898. In 1880 he started *England*, the first penny Conservative weekly. Ashmead Bartlett's speeches were noted for their grandiloquence and verve, and he was a great favorite on Conservative platforms. An ardent imperialist, he went to the front as a spectator at the beginning of the Boer War. See *Dictionary of National Biography*, 2nd Supplement, Twentieth Century, 1901-1911, and the cartoon by Spy, *Vanity Fair*, April 30, 1887. For an account of his attack on the Primrose League, see the *Daily Chronicle*, August 5, 1887.

32 *England*, June 5, 1886. A letter signed " Rural Knight " complains that headquarters are badly managed, that local habitations are too heavily drained financially for the support of the central body, and that Grand Council is not representative of the rural habitations. On February 5, 1887 the editor writes that he could fill the columns of *England* with letters he had received complaining of the management of the Primrose League.

33 *England*, May 1887.

England speaks too of the League's weakness for speakers with double-barrelled names to the exclusion of those more likely to interest audiences. There are dark references to a clique and " aristocratic hangers-on and needy relations." In this connection Cusack Smith, Vice Chancellor, appears personally to have come under heavy fire. This campaign continued during the year and finally, at Grand Habitation in 1889, some modifications in the elections for Grand Council were introduced.

Grand Council in 1891 appointed a special committee to look into a reorganization of its machinery, and at the same time revised its statutes. But in 1893 the *Standard* published an attack on the Grand Council of the Primrose League, calling the League the mere showy adjunct of the Conservative Party. It said that " activity in support of the Constitutional cause either in the House or in the country, seems no qualification for this Caucus," and that in order to be a living force its central body should descend from its pedestal. " Each year there is a mock election of these august personages," it continued, " who hold their elections in the heart of the most aristocratic part of London, and as if to prevent any mistake, even in this close borough, co-optate a large number of their body and this central body remains year by year an almost fixed quantity." [34]

Not long after another attempt at revolt against Grand Council was launched by a group in the Cheshire Council of the League. To the familiar charges were added accusations this time of steam rollering in the provincial elections, and there appears in addition to have been some friction concerning the League's resolution in connection with the death of Lord Randolph Churchill. It was reported to Grand Council that only a few members in Surrey, Suffolk and Cheshire were behind this movement.

A Dr. Garstang, the moving spirit of the opposition group, demanded the names of those who had passed the Churchill

34 *Standard*, May 12, 1893.

resolution.[35] Though he was said to have obtained the signatures of sixty-nine prominent members of the League to his
petition, this seems to have been an obvious exaggeration. The
only subsequent sign of life from the dissentient group occurred
in the summer of 1895, when the Knutsford habitation (apparently under the control of this group) refused to take part
in the provincial elections of that year, alleging that the elections were a farce, since official nominees alone were invariably
returned.

By way of counter-attack, Grand Council charged that the
habitation in question contained neither Knights nor Dames,
and therefore, strictly speaking, should not be participating in
general League affairs. It was an old complaint, cropping up at
regular intervals at League meetings, that habitations allowed
their Knights and Dames to enroll as associates, and so cut off
revenue to Grand Council. Not only might more members be
attracted by the lower affiliation fees charged associates; there
was the further inducement that the habitation retained all fees
paid by associates, whereas they had to hand over part of those
paid by Knights and Dames to Grand Council. Since the
privileges of both kinds of individual members were the same,
according to the League's constitution, this was a tempting
manoeuver against centralization, in the absence of a definite
ruling.

There was some truth in Knutsford habitation's charge. It
was quite true that only twenty-seven candidates were nominated
in 1890 for the fifteen seats then elective.[36] Yet there was no
conspicuously increased participation by the membership in the
elections for Grand Council or for Divisional Council membership after these periods of internal criticism.

35 Grand Council decided to withhold this information on the ground that
it might be invidious to those who had been absent when the resolution was
passed,—*Minutes of the Grand Council of the Primrose League*, February
7, 1895.

36 *Primrose League Gazette*, April 19, 1890.

IV

One service provided by the Primrose League for the Conservative Party was the use of an annual platform from which the leader of the party might address the country at large. As a Tory paper put it, " It is one of the compensations of a somewhat ridiculous anniversary that it brings us a speech by Lord Salisbury."

At the first Grand Habitation only the transept of the old Albert Palace in Battersea had been filled. The next year Westminster Town Hall was needed to hold the gathering, and then the old Opera House at the end of Haymarket. Still growing in size, Grand Habitation moved to Covent Garden, and by 1897 the Primrose League actually was meeting in the great Albert Hall.

Large rallies staged by the League at strategic moments and places vied in pageantry with Grand Habitation. At the Crystal Palace in 1889, before an audience of over fourteen thousand, Lady Salisbury and Mr. Balfour were preceded to the dais by ushers carrying primrose wands and wearing silken sashes with scarlet League monograms and a procession of banners. Later an Elizabethan page presented a bouquet of primroses to Lady Salisbury while a ballet and a hypnotic performance followed.[37]

From a platform elaborately decorated with primroses and other spring flowers and blazing with a host of bright banners, and before a galaxy of Tory Knights and Dames displaying their League brooches, badges and pendants, the party leader, after a few references to the League, usually seized the occasion to deliver a message of some significance to the party and to the country.

At the gathering in 1887, Lord Salisbury's speech was largely an answer to a speech made by Mr. Gladstone the previous night at the " 80 " Club. The Tory leader dubbed the Liberal outcry against coercion in Ireland as false, and called on Parnell

37 *Ibid.*, July 25, 1889.

to answer in an English court-room the accusations made against him.[38] In his annual speeches in 1898, 1900 and 1902, Lord Salisbury discussed the Government's policy on the prosecution of the Boer War.

Lord Salisbury always evoked much applause from Primrose audiences by stressing the role of the League in awakening imperialistic sentiment, as well as in its practical work for the party.[39] On the other hand, Balfour, who occasionally spoke in place of his uncle before he was Prime Minister, as well as later in his own right, apparently erred at times on the side of neglecting his immediate for his wider audience. His speech in 1895 to Grand Habitation apparently did not strike a particularly popular note for his audience. After touching on the difficulties of the pact with the Liberal Unionists, he took pains to point out that the pact was a permanent bond which should outlast the Home Rule issue,—a prediction hardly calculated to please a die-hard Tory audience.

Again in 1899, at Grand Habitation, Balfour dwelt at some length on the financial situation, on the extravagance of paying national debts too fast, and on the relation of British finances to the development of the Empire. " Not a very attractive subject for such an audience " the Morning Post exclaimed editorially the next day, and the paper commented on the fact that this part of the speech had fallen depressingly flat on the Albert Hall audience, but that when, in conclusion, he reminded his hearers " that to talk about our glorious Empire, and our historic Navy, and to shrink from the sacrifices these involved, was mere lip service,"—his audience, so long quiescent, responded with an enthusiastic shout of approval.[40] In 1904 when he was Prime Minister, Balfour concentrated his address al-

38 *Ibid.*, April 21, 1887.

39 The *Daily News* spoke of Lord Salisbury's address to Grand Habitation in 1900 as one in which the Government had announced that it proposed to abdicate in favor of the Primrose League.—May 10, 1900.

40 *Morning Post*, April 20, 1899.

most completely on the French treaty and on the Macedonian question,—probably to the disappointment of his hearers.[41]

A business meeting always preceded the rally but, according to reports, discussion from the floor, when not perfunctory, was scattered and desultory. An evening reception tendered the delegates by the wife of the Chancellor topped off the annual gathering.

Another form of service to the party was the literature which was issued in great volume by the League before general elections, while a steady barrage was sustained between elections. This literature was prepared especially for the League, which also acted as distributing agent for pamphlets prepared by the Central Conservative Office and the National Union. It was claimed that the League's yearly record compared favorably with that of the Anti-Corn-Law League during its entire existence, when its tracts were described as piled at its central depot " like the packets of muslin and calico, in the great warehouses of Manchester." [42]

A peak in the volume of leaflets was reached at the time of the first Home Rule Bill and in the period following.[43] Fifty-one different leaflets, prepared especially for the League, were in circulation in 1890. In 1891 a total of two million leaflets was reported, falling off in 1896 to one million. With a dangerous General Election to fight, the report to Grand Habitation in 1906 lists many more leaflets prepared and sent out under the League's auspices.

Leaflets on the League itself bore such titles as: " Why Should I Join the Primrose League? " " The Reason Why," " What are the Principles of the Primrose League? " " A Valuable Political Engine," " The Primrose League. How it Sprang into Existence," " Our Grand Master's Letter to the Primrose League." Among those on general political subjects

41 *Ibid.*, May 12, 1904.

42 Prentice, A., *History of the Anti-Corn Law League*, II, 27.

43 *Minutes of the Grand Council of the Primrose League*, June 5, 1890.

were: "A Plain Statement of the Eastern Question," and "Our Colonial Empire and its Responsibilities." Others were entitled: "England's Protest on the Separatist Movement," "Sir Edward Clarke on Lord Beaconsfield's Famous Speech to the People, 1872," and "The Powers and China." A large number of leaflets were inspired by the Boer War. After 1902 an increasing proportion of leaflets were published defending property rights and attacking the "socialism" of the Liberal Government.[44]

Lastly, at habitation meetings all over England, Scotland, Wales and Ireland, Conservative speakers presented their case, consolidating party opinion among the rank and file, and winning new adherents to their cause. They explained and defended the acts of the Conservative governments, and attacked the Liberal program. For instance, League audiences were told that the Tories between 1895 and 1900 had fulfilled eleven out of fourteen promises, while the Liberals had fulfilled but two of the fifteen pledges contained in the famous Newcastle program. Thus the League, though still officially a non-partisan body, discharged the functions which the party-sponsored National Union had failed, or partially failed, to discharge.

The technically extra-party character of the League gave it a certain value to the party as a device for creating the impression of popular support on current issues. Almost invariably the resolutions and the endless expressions of confidence synchronized completely with the Conservative Party line. A practice was made of passing resolutions after political speeches at habitations, and forwarding them to headquarters, where they were united into a general one from the League.

These resolutions might take the form of a general expression of confidence in the Government. There were resolutions

44 The text of many of these pamphlets can be found in the *Primrose League Gazette*. A few leaflets published before 1906 are in the London University Library, and there is an incomplete file at the League's headquarters. At the British Museum can be found leaflets issued after 1906. See Appendices V, VI, and VIII.

on concrete issues, such as one of thanks to the Lords for opposing the Home Rule Bill, and another of congratulation to Lord Salisbury on his success in dealing with the question of Venezuela. On larger issues, such as Home Rule or the Education Bill, Grand Council invariably sent forms to the habitations for the resolutions which it desired to have passed. At other times habitation resolutions seem to have followed spontaneously after a political speech.

The Primrose League always occupied itself with stressing general Conservative principles, insisting on these to the exclusion of various concrete issues. In this respect its work contrasts with that of the pressure organizations which concentrated on getting a special piece of legislation passed, such as the Anti-Corn-Law League, or the Chartist Movement, or the anti-slavery movement led by Wilberforce. Some of these movements died by reason of their victories, which automatically terminated their usefulness. Others, like the Chartists, failed because they had dissipated their energies on too many special issues. If the program of the Primrose League, in contrast, was incapable of immediate realization, at least there was no moment at which victory could destroy its *raison d'être*. This very limitation prevented the League from straying into political byways, or spending its power prematurely.

To keep its platform concentrated on Conservative principles, and free from what it felt were lesser issues, the League rebuked members, for example, who wrote that they wished to withdraw from the League because of the Education Bill·of 1891. The League pointed to its own lack of partisanship on such issues as woman's suffrage, or vaccination, and poked considerable fun at a member who wrote that he wished to withdraw from the League on account of the Government's Dog Muzzling Act.

Its blanket endorsement of Government policies, critics of the League charged, was at times tantamount to indifference to national issues of vital importance. In 1898, when rumblings from South Africa had grown ominous, even the *Morning Post* protested against the League's resolution of gratitude to the Government " for upholding the honour of Great Britain abroad, not only in the face of unexampled difficulties, but also at a time of great Imperial crisis." [45] It found it difficult to account for such action by a League, " whose foundations were inspired by the memory of Lord Beaconsfield, and whose inception was largely due to the exertions of Lord Randolph Churchill," and moreover by an organization which prided itself on being a non-party organization.

V

We have seen that the value of the Primrose League's election work was demonstrated very early in its existence. The following Precept of the League was issued in 1886: " In view of the immediate importance of prompt action in order to secure the return of members of Parliament pledged to support the unity of Empire, the Grand Council call all members of the Primrose League to use every effort consistent with the law to support such candidates in their respective districts, placing themselves at the disposal and acting under the instructions of the duly constituted agents of their candidate, and working in harmony with all other candidates having the same objects." [46]

The membership responded with gratifying zeal, and as we have seen, the League won its political spurs. Candidates were profuse in thanks to the Primrose League ladies in particular for their loyal work. It was announced that owing to the efforts of Grand Council ten thousand outvoters had recorded their votes for the Conservative Party in one election.[47]

The election work was entirely under the direction of Grand Council, and not under the individual habitations in the early years. In fact, it was thought necessary at this time to disband

45 *Morning Post*, May 17, 1898.

46 *Ibid.*, February 22, 1886.

47 *Ibid.*, June 16, 1886.

habitations whenever an election was called, so that the habitation as such could not be identified with electioneering activities. An early statute of the League had provided that between elections each member, unless engaged in other political duties, should be willing to place himself at the disposal of Grand Council for political work. Especially was he to canvass thoroughly any sub-district to which he was assigned. He was to report to headquarters the political topography of his own neighborhood—the local influence, and any specific political developments—and to keep watch continuously on the local opposing political forces. In addition, each member was enjoined to register all adherents in his area and to furnish a record of this register to his Ruling Councillor.[48]

A few habitations on their own initiative hazarded not disbanding when an election date was set, and in 1893 Grand Council came to the conclusion that disbanding its habitations was not necessary and was, moreover, harmful to their political continuity.[49] Accordingly, Grand Council in 1895 announced that although each habitation must continue to place itself for an election at the disposal of the local Unionist agent, it might do so as a unit, keeping its identity through the election.[50]

To what extent the Primrose League was active in the elections for the County Councils is somewhat difficult to determine. Even during the first County Council election, held in 1889, there is evidence that the League was a particularly effective auxiliary to the Conservative Party, exciting the usual taunt that caucuses were by no means peculiar to the Liberals in either national or local politics.[51] Yet when a League agent

48 Statute 14. See *The Primrose League, Its Rise, Progress and Constitution*, by one of the Staff, 36.

49 *Minutes of the Grand Council of the Primrose League*, October 19, 1893.

50 A League pamphlet (no. 237) reads: " The habitation shall work as an organized body and the Ruling Councillor shall place himself entirely at the disposal of the election agent of the party which the League supports."

51 *County Council Magazine*, I, 65.

asked permission to mobilize habitation officials in his jurisdiction for the County Council elections of that year, the General Purposes Committee of the Grand Council replied that
" Grand Council did not think the time has arrived for them
to recommend any official or corporate action of the Primrose
League with regard to the County Council elections." [52] At the
next elections, however, Grand Council specifically directed its
membership to participate along party lines.[53]

In spite of the democratic form of elections to the new
County Councils set up in 1889, the Councils themselves continued, almost unbroken, the tradition of local rule by the
privileged classes in rural areas. In fact, as the Webbs have
pointed out, many of the old town magistrates were elected to
the new Councils.[54] The prestige of a long tradition, the custom of cooperation by the two parties in local politics, the
expense involved in traveling to the county seat, often twenty
miles away ("government by horse and trap," as its critics
said), the fear of eviction by landlords, and a substantial
measure of satisfaction in the previous arrangement,—all
these contributed to keep the County Council elections far freer
of class issues than the parliamentary elections. Especially in
the Midlands, the Home Counties and the southwest counties
did the former local governing class continue to predominate.
It is impossible to determine the exact share of the Primrose
League in the perpetuation of the older regime under these
newer democratic forms, but its rural activities must have
played a considerable part, even if an indirect one, in the results.

During the interlude of Liberal government at Westminster,
the Parish Councils Act was passed in 1894. Severely limited
in spending power, and shorn of many important administrative

---

52 *Minutes of the Grand Council of the Primrose League*, October 4, 1889.

53 *Primrose League Gazette*, February 6, 1892.

54 Except in Wales, where in the first election a campaign against the old
magistracy's power in local government was successful. — *County Council
Magazine*, I, 217.

powers which were confided to other authorities, the parish as a unit of government was soon found to be too small and weak to be effective. Many students of government considered that the Parish Councils Act was like a new roof raised over a deserted house. Even more than in the case of the new County Councils, these new Parish Councils remained in Tory hands, and contests for Councillors were few and lacking in public interest.[55]

As far as the new Act affected the rural worker, it had left him in such a position, as one authority puts it, that he was " hardly . . . able to employ a single weapon out of the whole armoury of formal democracy which has been hung up by Parliament in his cottage." [56]

In municipal elections, as opposed to those for rural County Councils, the League was active only in London. Elections for London's new County Council presented problems sharply distinguished from those of other County Councils, as well as from those of other municipalities.[57] The first London County Council election was not fought frankly on party lines, but in the second election in 1892, party lines were clearly drawn for the first time, the Moderates attracting Conservative voters, and the Progressives attracting the Liberal.[58] This was due in

55 Parish Councils elections have continued to attract only listless attention from the public. Most seats are uncontested, and where there are elections, these are more often than not effected by a show of hands.—*Times*, March 15, 1937.

56 Redlich, J. and Hirst, F., *Local Government in England*, II, 46.

57 London has been technically a county since 1888, ruled by a County Council, as is Surrey or Buckinghamshire. But of course in many ways it is more convenient to compare it with municipalities, as its problems are those of urban areas. The County of London is subdivided into boroughs, but many of the functions of local government are vested in the County Council rather than in the Borough Councils.

58 The division along party lines in the new Council became apparent when it was evident that the majority of the elected members, although adopting the name of Progressives on the Council, were Liberals so far as national politics were concerned; while the minority, the Moderates, were nationally Conservatives.—Davies, A. E., *The London County Council 1889-1937. A Historical Sketch*, Fabian Tract No. 243, 5.

part to the imminence of a general election, which caused each party to view polling as a preliminary test of party strength for the approaching national election. From that time, local elections in London were fought along party lines, and it was unusual for a candidate not endorsed by either of the great parties to be successful.[59]

National and local party preferences were often in clear opposition. Many municipalities during the nineties and the first decade of the twentieth century continued to send Conservative representatives to Westminster while retaining substantial Liberal majorities on their own councils, or, in the case of London, on its County Council. Like the other great municipal councils, the London County Council, during its first twenty years, remained largely under Progressive or Liberal control, while the London delegation at Westminster was predominantly Conservative. Out of a total of fifty-nine members from London in 1895 there were fifty Unionists, and in 1900 London was responsible for sending fifty-one Conservative members to Parliament.[60]

In the London County Council election of 1892 the Primrose League advised its members to give all possible assistance to the Moderates, who not only were in direct opposition to the previous Progressive council, but actually stood for office under the title of " Unionist." [61] The Moderates were defeated. Their failure was ascribed to many causes: apathy on the part of the middle classes in London; the weakness of the Conservative candidates, and the late entrance of some of them into the field. There was non-partisan approval for many parts of the Progressive program on the one hand, and criticism by the diehards on the other, of Lord Salisbury's Government as being

59 Redlich, J. and Hirst, F., *op. cit.*, I, 273. This was also true in other urban elections, as is illustrated by the case of Bradford in Yorkshire, which was a stronghold of the I. L. P.

60 Munro, W. B., *The Government of European Cities*, 348.

61 *Minutes of the Grand Council of the Primrose League*, February 19, 1892.

too radical.[62] It was reported to Grand Council that the Moderates lost because the Conservative Party had no separate municipal organization in London for this election, and because the great body of Conservative voters appeared to think the issues non-political, and had therefore either abstained from voting, or had voted for the Progressives.

Actually, the Conservative defeat was simply another example of the failure of the party to deal with local issues, especially in an urban community, and to mobilize its adherents in such a community into an army of alert politically conscious soldiers on the Birmingham model. The vagueness and splendor of the Primrose League appeal, which constituted its strength in national elections, were its weakness in local elections, where the issues concerned concrete matters, familiar to the average voter.

Before the second London County Council election, many Primrose League habitations had been in existence in the metropolitan area.[63] Members of the League were especially active during the London election of 1895, when the Moderates obtained majorities in Belgravia, Holborn, Westminster, Dulwich, Paddington, St. George's in the East, Wandsworth, Peckham and Hammersmith. Primrose Leaguers were drafted for canvassing, addressing envelopes, and for general assistance to the Moderate forces.[64]

After the next election Bayswater became the seat of a conspicuously active habitation. Before the municipal elections of 1904 delegates from the London habitations pledged themselves

62 *Minutes of the Grand Council of the Primrose League*, April 1, 1892.

63 Clapham, Bethnal Green (2), Crystal Palace, Chelsea (5) City of London (3), Deptford, Finsbury (5), Fulham (4), Greenwich (6), South Kensington (7), North Kensington (1), Lambeth (4) Lewisham (5), Marylebone (3), Newington, Paddington (3), St. George's Hanover Square (5), St. Pancras (4), Shoreditch (2), Southwark, Strand (3), Tower Hamlets (3), Wandsworth (3), Westminster (4).—Roll of Habitations, 1890.

64 *Minutes of the Grand Council of the Primrose League*, March 7, 1895.

to work for the Moderate cause and, in particular, to emphasize the importance of the new Education Act as an issue.[65]

From 1900 on, Fabian influence on the Progressive platform was evident, inspired by the enthusiasm of the Webbs for using local government as the most likely field in which to begin socialist penetration, as well as to furnish an excellent laboratory for a public demonstration of the benefits of socialism. The introduction of the socialist issue at the turn of the century made the rival parties in local elections offer platforms whose contrasts more nearly resembled those in the twentieth century between Tory and Labour than those of the nineteenth between Conservative and Liberal.[66] For that reason the League, with its insistence on principles rather than on narrow party issues, as well as in its growing emphasis on the rights of property, realized its own philosophy more nearly in working for Moderate candidates in local elections than in working for Conservative candidates in parliamentary elections. That it did so with conspicuous lack of practical success was perhaps an omen for the future.

VI

" To stand before the Primrose League is to stand before the Pretorian Guard of the Conservative Party," Stanley Baldwin told the League on one of its anniversaries.[67] Yet a Primrose League pamphlet read: " By maintaining the Constitution the Primrose League does not mean that its members are

---

65 *Ibid.*, February 19, 1904.

66 Sir Henry Fowler, a prominent Liberal in national politics, never supported the London Progressives, and this was true of a number of other Liberals. On the other hand, a certain number of Liberal Unionists continued to vote for the Progressives. Henry Cust, Editor of the *Pall Mall Gazette*, a Conservative of independent views, supported the Progressives, as did John Burns and Ramsay Macdonald of the I. L. P. and socialists of other stripes. It was not until 1906 that the Labour Party obtained a real foothold on the London County Council.

67 *Morning Post*, November 18, 1932.

obliged to support any particular government or particular party policy, but simply that they must hold those principles which all loyal citizens of England have held for generations. It is not the hasty product of a day, but the well-ripened fruit of wise delay." [68]

Grand Council went even further in disowning any obligation to the party when it received a request that direct help should be given by the League to the Conservative Party. It replied: " to become a party Organization, and thereby subject itself to the will and behest of party leaders either partly or wholly out of sympathy with the objects the Primrose League has in view, would be to destroy the very purpose for which this gigantic power was brought into existence." [69]

The *Gazette* described the duty of the League to the party as follows: " We seek to convert the many political sinners into saints, and then hand them over to Conservative associations, whose duty it should be to see them placed on the register and brought to the polling booth." [70] It was no doubt true that the Primrose League groups, in spite of some difficulties, had succeeded in breathing new life into the often dry bones of Conservative organizations in the constituencies.

The League maintained practical contacts with other Conservative organizations. In its early years it used to sell leaflets published by the Central Conservative office and the National Union at less than cost. Later leaflets bearing on the League alone were issued directly by the League, and other Conservative literature was merely recommended and advertised for League members. Several delegates from habitations attended the conference of the National Union in 1884.[71] While it is true

68 *Primrose League Pamphlet*, No. 237.

69 *Minutes of the Grand Council of the Primrose League*, September 17, 1892.

70 *Primrose League Gazette*, October 1, 1894.

71 *National Union of Conservative and Constitutional Associations*, Minutes of Conference, 1884.

that Grand Council, in general, objected to the affiliation of habitations, as such, with the National Union, nevertheless, in 1903, representatives of habitations are recorded as present at National Union meetings.[72]

Some friction was inevitable between the habitations and the local Conservative associations or the agents of local candidates. Opposition to the Primrose League from local Conservatives seems to have been met chiefly in the larger towns.[73] Occasionally Grand Council found it necessary to iron out difficulties arising from overlapping of jurisdictions or from jealousy between the various local Conservative elements. An early editorial in the *Morning Post* described the League as " a second party line laid down to meet the increased traffic," and urged that the Primrose League might be of the greatest assistance in the " unravelling of the political threads through its informal type of work." [74]

Grand Council held that while members of Conservative Associations were eligible for Primrose League membership, they must join the League as individuals.[75] Ruling Councillors were also instructed not to turn over habitation funds for Conservative Party uses without the express authorization of their own membership.[76]

A habitation reported to be insisting that prospective members pledge themselves to vote only for a Conservative candidate was advised to desist, and warned that if it did not do so it might run afoul of the Corrupt Practices Act.[77] Registration for elections, headquarters decreed, was not to be undertaken

---

72 *Ibid.*, 1903.

73 *Minutes of the Grand Council of the Primrose League*, Conference of Provincial Secretary at Primrose League Offices, November 27, 1891.

74 *Morning Post*, June 9, 1885.

75 *Minutes of the Grand Council of the Primrose League*, July 4, 1889.

76 *Ibid.*, March 19, 1891.

77 *Ibid.*, 1888. For discussion of the Act, see Chapter III, 96 ff.

by habitations unless there was no local Conservative association available and then only when permission should have been
granted by the Central Conservative Association.[78] League
members were enjoined not to attend Orange lodge meetings,
wearing their Primrose badges.

The League, like the party, was cordial to the Liberal
Unionists, and frequently declared that there had never been
any reason why " a true Liberal " might not subscribe to the
declaration of the Primrose League. From time to time prominent Liberal Unionists addressed habitations. By 1889 a new
League scroll emblazoned " Hartington " [79] had taken its place
amongst such earlier ones as " Imperium et Libertas," " Peace
with honour," or " Salisbury." In the election of 1895 the
Liberal Unionist Women's Association combined in election
work with the Oxford habitations.

On the other hand, the *Spectator* testified that the Primrose
League as an ally was one of the bitterest pills that its Liberal
Unionist position forced it to swallow.[80] Earl Fortescue, a
Liberal Unionist who threw his park open for a Primrose
League fête, told his guests that " speaking as a Liberal from
early youth," it was not that he found separation from Mr.
Gladstone painful, nor even that he complained of the Govern-
ment's legislation, but that he could not join the Primrose
League, which was distinctively a Conservative organization.[81]

A caricature by F. Carruthers Gould in the *Westminster
Gazette* of September 25, 1902 shows Joseph Chamberlain

---

78 *Ibid.*, December 21, 1888.

79 It was a great triumph for the anti-Home Rule forces when Lord
Hartington, leader of the Liberal Whigs (and later Eighth Duke of Devonshire) broke with Gladstone on the Irish issue.

80 Admitting " nausea " at Lord Salisbury's praise of the League, and its
own steadfast dislike of the intimidation of tradesmen and of social climbers,
the *Spectator* consoled itself with the reflection that even these were to be
preferred to threatening men with social leprosy — (a reference presumably to the National Land League's use of the boycott). May 25, 1889, 701.

81 *Morning Post*, September 26, 1889.

gingerly sniffing a flower and murmuring, " Ah, yes, that *used* to be a primrose—twenty years ago." It was not until 1899 that Joseph Chamberlain consented to appear on a platform under the auspices of the Primrose League. He then spoke at Leicester at a meeting arranged by the Midland Division of the League and the local Liberal Unionist and Conservative organizations. Chamberlain's speech on that occasion was almost entirely concerned with foreign policy, and he did not once mention the Primrose League.[82]

In a moment of frankness a contributor to the *Gazette* confessed: " Of course, we do not admit here that the League is a party organization, but an Imperial and Constitutional one; but I am afraid appearances are against us, when viewed from afar by people who know that the League was founded by Lord Randolph Churchill and other leading Conservatives to perpetuate the memory of Lord Beaconsfield, one of our greatest Conservative statesmen; who see Lord Salisbury's name appearing in our books as Grand Master of the League, and all the great Conservative families in Great Britain represented on its Grand Council, and who remark that up to this time the whole of its influence and its efforts have been exercised on behalf of and in support of the Conservative Party." [83]

Lord Salisbury's famous charge to the League: " You are the general missionaries of the principles which you profess, and, if I may say so without irreverence, you are rather the preaching friars of the message that you have to convey than the regular clergy attached to each particular district," [84] undoubtedly explains truly the relationship of the League to the party. Though disowning a party label, the League followed

82 *Ibid.*, November 30, 1899, At a Primrose League meeting of the previous year Austen Chamberlain, eldest son of Joseph Chamberlain, had been amongst the speakers.

83 November, 1897.

84 *Grand Habitation*, April 19, 1886.

the Conservative Party line as assiduously as any speculator the quotations in the market.

Yet it was in 1913, for the first time, that the Primrose League declared formally its support of the Conservative Party. " It is only because the modern Radical has made it so impossible for us to maintain an attitude of independence," the Chancellor explained, " that we have definitely enrolled ourselves in the ranks of the party with whom, for so long, we have found ourselves, through force of circumstances, in sympathy." [85] He added that in the future the League might conceivably turn to the Liberal Party as the interpreter of its principles, " though in the present state of politics this would hardly seem to be possible."

VII

The party orthodoxy of the Primrose League on a specific and controversial issue is well illustrated by a discussion of its position and that of its party on such a question as that of protection. This issue, one of the most invariably controversial in political life, was responsible for sowing much party dissension and to some degree even the seeds of defeat in the Conservative Party.

After the trade collapse of the early seventies, there had been much discussion of " fair " trade—that is, protection—as a possible panacea. The Fair Trade League, formed in 1881, proposed a moderate import on foreign manufactured goods only, to be lifted in cases where a reciprocal free trade arrangement was in existence for the benefit of British manufacturers. The significance of the League lay less in its economics, for they were negligible, than in its sense of a changing world and in its appreciation of modern nationalism. The Chamberlain tariff program snuffed out the Fair Trade movement, but the Fair Trade League undoubtedly was not without influence in shaping the thinking of Joseph Chamberlain.

85 Arbuthnot, G. A., *The Primrose League Election Guide*, 9.

Disappointed in the failure of the fourth Colonial Conference to take any definite step toward imperial unity, Chamberlain was especially chagrined by its deafness to his plea for a Council of the Empire.[86] It was the trade resolutions of the Colonial Conference that had alone seemed promising from the viewpoint of imperial policy. On his return from work on the South African Union in March of 1903, and after some altercation over the Cabinet's repeal of the corn duty, which had come to have a kind of symbolic value, Chamberlain finally cast the die and came out for imperial preference.

As a result of Chamberlain's stand the Cabinet split three ways—for free trade, for imperial preference according to Chamberlain's program, and for a compromise such as was advocated by Balfour and Lansdowne. Rank and file Conservatives seem to have followed Chamberlain and imperial preference. As Chamberlain unleashed his forces in the autumn, Balfour dropped the extremists of both sides from the party leadership, and the Cabinet presented a united front for moderate imperial preference.

In the meanwhile the Liberal ranks, so lately split by the imperial issue involved in the Boer War, were able to reunite on firm tactical ground in upholding free trade. Asquith dogged Chamberlain's footsteps in the tariff campaign, giving him speech for speech; the slogan " the Big Loaf and the Little Loaf " provided an effective and popular answer to the Chamberlainite cry of " work for all." A revival of trade early in 1905 after a year of unemployment, together with the unconvincing Balfour compromise on the tariff, helped to give the *coup de grâce* to the long Tory reign.

The National Union became a battlefield during the tariff controversy. Its conference, as one Conservative put it, had been purposely designed by the party leadership to allow the Conservative rank and file to blow off steam. The burning question at the meeting of the Union in 1903 at Sheffield was,

86 For the conference, see Jebb, Richard, *The Imperial Conference*, I.

of course, the fiscal question, and the fiscal resolution, as passed, pleased neither the extreme protectionists led by Henry Chaplin in the Union, nor the pure free traders led by Gorst.

In 1905 Chaplin's protectionist resolution was carried overwhelmingly in the conference against one for the Balfour compromise.[87] In fact the National Union was merely reaffirming a host of earlier resolutions passed by large majorities.[88] In the light of the disparity between the views of the Conservative leadership and the Union on this point, speakers at the National Union as early as 1892 cited the protection question as an example of the deafness of the party leadership to an issue dear to the hearts of the Union.

As far as the local speakers and the reactions of its local audiences went, the Primrose League had shown an unmistakable predilection for some kind of protection. Many Conservatives in the protection ranks were prominent in the Primrose League as well.[89] As early as 1884 habitations had been in the habit of passing resolutions to " buy British." The strength of the League in rural districts and its close ties with landlords account for the strong enthusiasm for protection within its ranks. From early days Primrose League speakers drove home to rural audiences the advantages of Fair Trade for working people.[90]

Grand Council, asked to give a ruling on the question, declared the issue one of personal opinion rather than of principle,

87 National Union of Conservative and Constitutional Associations, Minutes of Conference, 1905.

88 Resolutions were passed favoring protection by unanimous vote or by large majorities at the conferences held in 1887, 1891, 1892, 1894, 1895, 1896, 1898, 1900, 1902, 1903 and 1904. See National Union of Conservative and Constitutional Associations. Minutes of Conference, 1905.

89 Dunraven, Earl of, The Labour Question. A Letter from the Earl of Dunraven, K. P. to the Chairman of the Workmen's Association for the Defense of British Industry, June 6, 1885.

90 See Morning Post, May, 1886, or Primrose League Gazette, March 31, 1886.

and so not one on which the League need take an official stand.[91] That Fair Trade or protection was not necessarily incompatible with League principles was pointed out, and debates and lectures continued throughout the eighties and nineties.[92]

In the end however the League followed Balfour's compromise with complete obedience, and no murmurings are on record against this decision. Though the banquet of the Knights Imperial in July of 1903 was told that Chamberlain was under attack unfairly, the Knights present were also told, pending the official inquiry, to preserve a judicial spirit on the subject.[93]

League meetings multiplied on the subject of protection, and at most of them the protection side was vehemently presented. But the League did not allow itself to be committed to any official resolution on the subject, nor were habitations allowed by Grand Council to affiliate with any of the fiscal associations. In 1904 Wardens were warned to stress the Education Bill and Home Rule in canvassing, as well as the fiscal question.

Balfour at Grand Habitation in 1903 announced that on the tariff " we are not divided." The Vice Chancellor of the League wrote officially on July 16, 1903 on the subject of the tariff : " I am directed by Grand Council to say that they are awaiting the results of the inquiry and of the further information promised by the Government before advising the habita-

91 *Minutes of the Grand Council of the Primrose League,* October 22, 1903.

92 Fair Trade speakers at habitations liked to illustrate their points by citing conditions in the United States, the land of the McKinley tariff. Pettifer, a " working man " speaker regularly employed by the League, and also connected with the Fair Trade League, visited Pawtucket when in the United States, and told League audiences when he returned, of Utopian working conditions there since the passage of the high tariff. See *National Review for Fair Trade League; Prospectus of the National Fair Trade League. Conference held at Westminster Palace Hotel,* May 31, 1881 ; and *Considerations of Opinion on the Federation of the Empire,* 1885, and also *Tracts on Trade, Finance and Statistics,* No. 2.

93 *Primrose League Gazette,* August, 1903.

tions on the fiscal policy of the country." [94] Habitations were told that they might invite speakers to express any point of view on the fiscal question, but might not, as habitations, join any fiscal associations.

With the General Election imminent, an official letter was sent out from headquarters on November 2, 1905, in answer to a member who had asked for the position of the League on Chamberlain's tariff. This letter from Grand Council reminded the correspondent that though members as individuals were entitled to vote as they pleased, no habitation might aid any candidate who opposed one officially endorsed by the Conservative Party. It was again explained that the League " cannot use any influence as a corporate body which might help a Liberal to gain a seat, inasmuch as the Liberal Party of today stands pledged to injure, as far as possible, all three of the principles which the Primrose League was formed to maintain."

At Grand Habitation in 1905, while Sir Edward Clarke was moving a resolution at an Albert Hall meeting " that the Government should not allow fiscal reform to disrupt its ranks," at the very door of the Hall yellow handbills (to suggest that they originated from Primrose League headquarters) issued by the Tariff Reform League were being distributed to all ticket holders.

On Primrose Day in 1905, at the foot of Lord Beaconsfield's statue in Parliament Square, there was deposited a great slab of primroses bearing these words picked out in forget-me-nots: " Protection is not only dead but damned." Later in the day the Office of Works discreetly removed another wreath bearing the legend: " The time has come when a Primrose Leaguer may not quote Lord Beaconsfield on Primrose Day." [95]

After the Conservative defeat of 1906, the activities of Lloyd George made the League stress such slogans as guardian-

94 *Minutes of the Grand Council of the Primrose League,* July 16, 1903.
95 *Truth,* April 27, 1905.

ship of the " Institutions of the Country " in its declaration
rather than the earlier " Imperial Ascendancy " and its corol-
lary, protection. Then, after the first World War, there appeared a sharper cleavage in social and political philosophy between the Labour and Conservative Parties than there had been
in the days when the Conservatives faced the Liberals. The
new cleavage gave new justification to the claim of the Primrose League that it supported enduring and underlying Conservative principles rather than particular party issues. Its
bitterest critics admitted that its acknowledged brilliant aid to
the party came largely from this extra-party appeal.

CHAPTER III

THE METHODS OF THE PRIMROSE LEAGUE

I

"I TRUST that we Radicals," Labouchere [1] once said, " will never teach the people to confound their politics with a donkey or a Negro entertainer," [2] and quoted from what he claimed was a Primrose handbill distributed in Windsor, reading, " Primrose Day, Primrose Day—Don't forget the Grand Negro Entertainment."

Lady Salisbury answered a committee of Grand Council who were demurring at a proposed Primrose League entertainment as too vulgar by retorting, " Vulgar? Of course, it is vulgar! But that is why we have got on so well." [3] *Clarion,* the socialist paper, quoted the Primrose League as having advocated officially that entertainments be " not so distinctly elevating as to be pronounced dull," and as suggesting to its habitations that " a few boards laid down and a loyal band " would be all that was necessary to produce Tory votes. [4]

W. H. Mallock, who was for many years the member from Torquay in Parliament and who owned himself much indebted to the local habitation for his electoral successes, described a Primrose League meeting he once attended in his constituency. A solid county politician sat in complacent dignity at the end of the platform, bowing graciously at the gusts of applause from the audience, whose gaze was riveted on a greased pole set up directly behind the platform and the politician. [5]

---

1 Henry Labouchere (1831-1912) was a leading radical Liberal M. P. from 1865 to 1906, as well as editor and proprietor of *Truth.*

2 *Primrose League Gazette,* August 2, 1890.

3 West, Mrs. George Cornwallis, *Reminiscences of Lady Randolph Churchill,* 100.

4 *Clarion,* June 12, 1897.

5 Mallock, W. H., *Memoirs,* 158-9.

The Liberals said that the advice issued by the League to promoters of their fêtes included a reminder to be careful that the merry-go-round was stationary during the political speech. They claiméd that the League also warned its speakers that " refined embellishments will fall flat with League audiences, while selections from the ' Man's Joker ' will be preferred to Pinero's Epigrams! " The *Gazette,* it must be admitted, found it necessary to admonish its habitations constantly not to forget to inject a political speech into their entertainments and also to be sure to give the Conservative speaker, when he was permitted to appear, adequate time on the program.

Even a movement as dignified in its aim and membership as the Anti-Corn-Law League had felt the necessity for a popular appeal. Lord Sydenham once said of the unsuccessful work of the predecessor of the Anti-Corn-Law League, " We hammered away with facts and figures and some arguments; but we could not elevate the subject and excite the feelings of the people." [6] Later, during the course of the Anti-Corn-Law campaign, Cobden wrote of his audiences, " If they are simply lectured, they may sit out the lesson for once, but they will not come again; and as I have required them again and again, I have been obliged to amuse them, not by standing on my head or eating fire, but by kindred acts of jugglery, such as appeals to their self esteem, their combativeness, or their humour." [1]

The long pull between general elections, the laborious and continuous nursing of constituencies in the Conservative interest was the peculiar charge of the Primrose League. This took the form, not only of a constant distribution of leaflets, but above all of a constant barrage of small meetings where prospective voters were provided with visual political education in the form of posters, tableaux vivants, magic lantern displays, or with aural instruction through lectures, phonograph auditions, dramatics and community singing.

6 Morley, J., *Life of Richard Cobden,* I, 143.

7 *Ibid.,* I, 207-8 (Letter to George Combe, December 29, 1845).

Much of the political propaganda of the League was cleverly disguised with a coating of popular entertainment, or was so surreptitiously introduced into the evening's gaiety as to be almost unnoticed. At times the aim was merely to produce good will through entertainment innocent of all political message, in the hope of subsequent enlightenment.

Gladstone once told a Liberal gathering that the Conservative spirit might be likened to the spirit of Egyptian art, " a spirit of repose and static," in contrast to the Liberal spirit, which he said resembled that of Greek art, " one of motion and life."[8] Yet the mere catalogue of the activities of the Primrose League habitations leaves the reader with anything but a spirit of repose.

A rich profusion of punchinellos, pierrots, jugglers and ventriloquists vied for favor on habitation programs with oriental illusions, equilibrisms, wax works, conjuring tricks, marionettes, and exhibitions of microscopic objects or of Egyptian antiquities. Dances with very low admission charges attracted many young working people, especially in the northern districts of England. Critics charged that young men and women would have joined any kind of organization for the chance of enjoying inexpensive dances.[9]

A report of a typical habitation entertainment of the period ran, "A monster demonstration of Primrose Leaguers took place on Tuesday at Southend. The proceedings were held in the new pavilion on the pier, the stage of which was elegantly fitted up and adorned with choice flowers and potted plants. Shortly after two o'clock the brass band of Upminster Habitation under Mr. Kingsworth marched in procession from the station of the London, Tilbury and Southend Company, followed by their colours and a colours-guard of six stalwart Prim-

8 *Proceedings attending the Formation of the National Liberal Federation with a Report of the Conference,* Birmingham, May 31, 1877.

9 Grand Council was forced to rebuke a habitation for burning the local vicar in effigy because he objected to their dances' continuing until 2 A. M. *Minutes of the Grand Council of the Primrose League,* Aug. 1, 1889.

rose Leaguers, armed with long staves. This was a signal for the hundreds of excursionists who were disporting themselves on the beach to flock to the pier, and the pavilion gradually filled. The programme included an entertainment by Professor Golding, a ventriloquist, an illusionist, and a mimic, who was assisted by Madame Stevenson, pianist and vocalist from the London Concerts. The professor's sketches, sleight of hand tricks, and mimicry were fairly good; and Madame Stevenson's songs and solos evoked warm applause." [10]

Much of this entertainment, belonging as it does to a less democratic age and antedating cheap mechanized popular entertainment, seems an echo from another world. Yet its success over a period of twenty years proves that it must have answered a real need, dissipating, as it did, some of the bleakness of late Victorian social life in the provinces.

A tenet of the League, it will be remembered, was the formation of a true union of classes. Construed in a coarse sense, the entertainments offered by habitations no doubt did provide a sort of social amalgam, especially in the smaller and the more isolated habitations. People of different social backgrounds, the Knights and Dames and the associates, mingled in Primrose League gatherings, not only at election time but at regular intervals during the entire year.

One habitation offered the following program of entertainment for its members: first a political speech by the titled M. P., followed by a song by a local baker, next a violin solo offered by the librarian, and finally animal interpretations presented by the valet from the big house.[11] A presentation to a retiring habitation official of a massive black marble clock, followed by a Negro minstrel entertainment, not only provided a break during the dull winter months in many a small village, but probably helped as well to cement the local Conservative community.

At times one class seemed to provide all the entertainment for the others. A report from the Edgcumbe habitation described

10 *Primrose League Gazette,* October 25, 1890.

11 *Ibid.,* February, 1900.

the evening's entertainment as follows: The Ladies Albertha and Edith Mt. Edgcumbe play a duet on the pianoforte, followed by the Earl of Mt. Edgcumbe, who speaks " at considerable length " ; again some music, and finally, the Earl again in a poetical recitation.

Fêtes were substituted for political rallies during the summer months, and invariably crowded the calendar, and became quite a specialty of the Primrose League. All classes in the neighborhood mingled in the preparations for these fêtes as well as during the course of the afternoon's entertainment. An article entitled " How to Organize an Outdoor Fête " concluded, " In these happy open-air festivals, provided with so much tact and energy by the Primrose League, all classes mingle. The lower middle class of the country towns is attracted by that social ambition which actuates every class to cooperate with the smaller and the greater gentry. The rank, the beauty, the kindliness of the ladies are enlisted to brighten the brutal and monotonous lives of the country poor." [12]

The fêtes supplied Liberal members of Parliament with light ammunition. The *Manchester Guardian* included the following tilt in its Report of Today's Proceedings in the House of Commons :—" Public Business : In reply to a statement by Mr. Balfour for date of reading of bill on a Thursday, Mr. MacNeil suggested a sitting on Saturday. Mr. Balfour thought the honourable members would prefer to sit later on Wednesday next.

" Mr. MacNeil :—A Saturday sitting would perhaps interfere with the political garden party at Blenheim.

" Mr. Balfour :—Very likely (Laughter).

" Mr. Balfour's answer to Mr. MacNeil will recall some other occasions on which the Tory Party in the House of Commons have found party social distractions conflicting with their Parliamentary duties. In July, 1890, the Government of Lord Salisbury narrowly escaped defeat by a majority of four, owing to a garden party given by Lord Salisbury at Hatfield. Again in

12 *Ibid.,* July 1, 1896.

1897, the Government was defeated no fewer than three times in Committee of Supply by the absence at a Jubilee garden party at Marlborough House of the bulk of its supporters." [13]

A fête held at Howbery Park in Dorchester was described by the *Gazette* in considerable detail: " The most prominent feature of the fête was contributed by eight young ladies in pretty Primrose costumes, who danced the Singing Lancers charmingly and were called upon three times to repeat the dance." At six o'clock came the finale: " The members being gathered in front of the terrace, which forms a natural platform, the silk banner of the habitation was displayed behind the chair of the Ruling Councillor, and Mrs. Williams Wynn in a few gracious and pleasant words bade the habitation welcome." And then " the various decorations being handed to her by the Hon. Secretary, she pinned each of them on with some happily expressed words of compliment." [14]

The golden age of the magic lantern coincided with the rise of the Primrose League in the eighties, and its share in moulding the political thinking of the period should by no means be overlooked. [15] Especially is this true in the development of popular interest in the British Empire. On the retina of the British public, the magic lantern stamped scenes of the flag flying at some outpost of Empire, of the fleet in battle formation off

13 August 10, 1901.

14 *Primrose League Gazette*, August 27, 1892. (See Appendix IX).

15 With the substitution of the powerful camera lens for the opaque mirror and of the " oxy-hydrogen light " for the oil lit lamp (the sciopticon bridged this gap), the " camera obscura " ceased to be a mere plaything of flickering candle light. In 1833 the introduction of the safety jet and the popularity of the device of dissolving views—first used with conspicuous success by Henry Langdon Childs in a series of lectures on the Holy Land at Manchester during 1837—contributed further to the growing popularity of the magic lantern. A distinct boom was observable in the decade·after 1876, and the magic lantern became an integral part of British social life until displaced by the moving picture in the second decade of the twentieth century. See Bolton, H. C., *Notes on the History of the Magic Lantern;* Chadwick, W. I., *The Magic Lantern Manual;* Parker, E. J., *The Lantern. Being a Treatise on the Magic Lantern and Stereoptican.*

Spithead, of the death of Nelson on the deck of the Victory, or of the Queen enthroned as Empress of India. In that pre-moving-picture, pre-colored-supplement, pre-radio age, the magic lantern achieved what these more highly mechanized agencies do for us today. Lectures with slides thrown on a screen were the mainstay of habitation entertainment during the eighties and nineties of the last century, penetrating isolated crannies and neglected backwaters of British rural and town life.

Rousing choruses often punctuated lantern lectures, serving to deepen, through emotional association, the imprint of the screen picture on the consciousness of the audience. Recitations of a patriotic order were at times substituted for the singing, and were overwhelmingly popular. In 1888, a bugler who had been at Balaklava recited " The Charge of the Light Brigade," to warm applause. During the Boer War " The Absent Minded Beggar " became an inevitable item on habitation programs. Lectures or selected readings (John Bright's article on Home Rule was an early favorite) were prepared by Grand Council and often read aloud to habitations by the vicar or some other locally prominent figure.

During the nineties, exhibitions of the phonograph frequently were reported as habitation entertainment,[16] though Primrose bands in gay uniforms continued to be in demand. A description of entertainment at habitations during a winter month reads : Views of the Jubilee; a lecture on " How the Concert of Powers had saved Greece from annihilation and Europe from War " ; French conjuring; a tour in Switzerland; a lecture on Toynbee Hall; a lecture on " Sociable Socialism " ; and an exhibition of the gramaphone.[17]

However, the League did not neglect the more orthodox political methods. Leaflets poured forth from headquarters to be distributed at Primrose League meetings, and in public places, by canvassers. A fairly substantial part of the annual

16 One habitation in 1898 reported its members as "much amused by the exhibition of a gramaphone "—*Primrose League Gazette*, October, 1898.

17 *Ibid.*, December, 1897.

budget of the League was devoted to the purpose.[18] Leaflets
were in the usual British form of political handbills—hardly
ever running over one page. They were written simply and expressed simplified ideas, but were not couched in especially popular language.[19] Wardens and lady canvassers were constantly
admonished to explain these leaflets, to use them to engage
the prospective convert in conversation rather than merely to
deposit them on his doorstep.

The efforts in this field were conventional enough in type
and bulk for an organization of the period concerning itself
with politics. It was the personal and more informal approach of the Primrose League which not only distinguished
it from its contemporaries, but also constituted its more significant contribution to political life. An Opposition paper exclaimed: " Just as Ulsteria is not so much an argument as a
disease, so Primrosery is not so much a reasoned faith as a
social cult." [20]

II

Undeniably some practices of the League involved sailing
close to the wind so far as the provisions of the Electoral Law
were concerned. As compared with the Liberals, the League
not only had a local monopoly of social prestige, but also commanded the services of many active women workers, constitut-
ing a large number of influential local consumers. Liberals
sometimes charged that the League practiced downright intimidation, ranging from delicate hints to friends, or individual
withdrawal of custom, to the actual circulation of blacklists of
local tradesmen.

18 For an average non-election year, out of a total expenditure of over
eight thousand pounds, the League spent over five hundred pounds for literature, and another two hundred fifty or so on circulars and precepts.—*Statement of Receipts and Expenditures by Grand Council*, April 1, 1890-March
31, 1891.

19 See Appendices V, VI, VIII.

20 *Westminster Gazette*, April 20, 1897.

The Primrose League women workers were especially vulnerable to charges of boycotting and bribery. Their ignorance of the law, their rôle as housewives in direct contact with tradesmen, their activities in district visiting and church work in country districts, all put them under suspicion of using undue influence. In the minds of the villagers there was an inescapable connection between the good works of the Primrose Dame and her political canvassing. The League itself warned habitations against appointing Wardens who were also district visitors.[21]

It was not the first time that the activities of the fair sex had come under suspicion of political corruption. In the notoriously corrupt seventeen eighties the famous cartoonist Rowlandson portrayed the political activities of the Duchess of Devonshire in a vein not quite worthy of Caesar's wife. One of these cartoons shows the Duchess calling at the cobbler's shop in the course of her electioneering rounds.[22] While presenting the virtues of her cause, she ostentatiously offers the cobbler her patently new shoe for repair, while the cobbler's wife leans out of a window behind them to receive a heavy shower of coins from the Duchess. It should be said in defense of the peeress that she was no worse than her times.

But new times brought little real improvement. Neither the extension of the franchise nor the elimination of the rotten borough in 1832 really reduced the corruption which attended parliamentary elections. As late as the eighteen sixties a witness before the Commission on Parliamentary Elections testified that electoral morale had improved so far as Public House treating and money bribes went, but that this was offset by the influencing of tradesmen's votes through the threat of boycotting.[23]

21 *Primrose League Gazette,* December 12, 1891.

22 *Wit's Last Stake,* April 22, 1784, by Rowlandson. See Grego, Joseph, *Rowlandson the Caricaturist.* I, 131.

23 Great Britain. *Report of the Select Committee on Parliamentary and Municipal Elections (Parliamentary Papers) 1868-69,* Vol. VIII, p. 210.— Testimony of E. West, Mayor of Bradford. Another witness, A. Russell, when asked about the effect of introducing the secret ballot, cited the case of a lady

Again after the General Election of 1880 the public indignation about the corruption in certain boroughs during the campaign produced petitions for an inquiry, and the Commission set up to inquire into the conduct of the election found innumerable examples of grossly corrupt practices.[24]

As the result of the growing agitation about political corruption Parliament passed the Corrupt Electoral Practices Act of 1883.[25] This was the first act to deal with the problem in a really effective way. The most outstanding of its provisions were those reducing the expenses a candidate might legally incur in his campaign, and limiting the number of paid workers he might employ. We have already seen how this last provision had the effect of practically eliminating paid canvassing,[26] thus acting as an indirect stimulus to the birth and growth of the Primrose League.[27]

canvasser who spent half a day pleading with the keeper of a grade crossing for his vote. The secret ballot, the witness pointed out, might not only make such excessive tenacity by a worker unnecessary, but might also insure a greater degree of public safety.—*Ibid.*, 228.

24 *Great Britain, Accounts and Papers. Corrupt Practices.* (*Parliamentary Papers*) 1884-85, Vol. LXII, 259.

25 46 and 47 (Vic). Chapter 51. An Act for the Better Prevention of Corrupt and Illegal Practices at Parliamentary Elections. [August 25, 1883.] (For the text of the Act see Edge and Hardy, *On the Management of a Parliamentary Election*, 217-263). It is true that as early as 1698 an act had defined bribery for electoral purposes, and provided for a number of penalties, and new regulations had been added to this in 1728 and 1809. It was not until 1854, however, that the first comprehensive attempt was made to legislate on corrupt practices in parliamentary elections. (17-18, Vic., Chapter 102). Later the corrupt practices clauses in the Secret Ballot Act of 1872 had served to strengthen the Act of 1854.

26 One practice outlawed was the hiring by political organizations of carriages to convey voters to the polls. Primrose Knights and Dames hastened to evade this prohibition by providing private carriages. A complaint frequently voiced by both the Liberal and Labour Parties was that this part of the electoral law, they felt, favored the Tory Party.

27 See Chapter I, 35.

Among the practices defined as corrupt by the Act were brib-ing, treating, and using undue influence in connection with an election. Treating as distinguished from bribery involved a con-tract depending on a general sense of gratitude on the part of the guest to the treating party, rather than one based on a con-crete promise.

Some of the apparently harmless entertainments of the League came dangerously near to the legal definition of " treat-ing." At Wittington Habitation, for instance, a concert was held in connection with a children's sick fund. It was reported that most of the parents of the children were present at the party, and that the majority of them were of the Liberal per-suasion, while the hostess, the leader of the Wittington Habita-tion, " just happened " to be the wife of the Conservative candidate for the district.[28]

Critics of the League never tired of saying that its inveterate antagonist, the Irish Land League, had no monopoly in the use of the boycott. They claimed that a coffee woman at Northamp-ton had been boycotted on the instructions of the headmaster of a local school, a Primrose League member.[29] The *Spectator* warned the League that until it ceased meddling with the use of the vote, and boycotting tradesmen, it would hardly be a popular society amongst Liberal Unionists.[30]

John Morley and a group of fellow Liberals, aroused by what they claimed was widespread bribery and effective intimidation on the part of the Primrose League in rural districts, organized a County Voters' Protective Association. Apparently this asso-ciation achieved very little of concrete value, but it served as a gesture against the perpetuation of the Tory hold over the voter in the shires.[31]

28 *England*, January 15, 1897.

29 *Ibid.*, June, 1887.

30 May 25, 1889.

31 Direct corruption and bribery in the counties apparently never were as rampant as in the boroughs. See Porritt, E., " Political Corruption in Eng-land," *North American Review*, 1906, CLXXXIII, 1000.

Mr. Justice Williams in the Hexham case of 1892 mentioned " the Primrose League and other associations which unhappily seem to make a practice of giving entertainments, picnics, dances, suppers, teas, sports and what not." He observed, " Something will have been gained if collective bribery by treating—collective corruption I would rather say—has been made more difficult now, when, as Mr. Justice Cave has already observed, the size of the constituency makes individual bribery or corruption practically impossible." [32]

The Corrupt Practices Act also prohibited intimidation and the exercise of undue influence on the electors—a clause which proved to be of special concern to the Primrose League. Under the heading of undue influence were included the use or threat of using force, violence, emotional or spiritual injury, restraint so designed as to influence a vote, or fraud or duress impeding a man's free use of his vote. [33]

In 1889 Lord Spencer wrote Lord Harris, then Chancellor of the League, of the practice of intimidation, referring to " what is very generally believed in this county, namely that members of the Primrose League have used exclusive dealing and social isolation against political opponents." [34] Social ostracism was an extremely effective weapon in a small community of the period, and yet it was a peculiarly difficult ground on which to base a concrete charge.

To bring home a violation of the Act to a candidate, and thus unseat him, it was necessary to prove intent, since the courts held that corruption and illegality in treating hinged on intent. Thus each case tended to be decided on its own merits, and to

32 Seager, J. L., *Corrupt and Illegal Practices at Parliamentary Elections as defined in the Judgments in Election Petitions from 1886 to 1906*, 40-41.

33 46-47 Vic. Section 2. Threats of discharge by employers and of spiritual penalties by priests were held to come under this heading also. See Lowell, A. L., *The Government of England*, I, 223.

34 *Primrose League Gazette*, March 2, 1889.

offer small guidance for future situations.[35] In the case of a political association such as the Primrose League, it was necessary to prove agency as well. This left still more doubt as to whether the individual case could be established, and the various interpretations of the law on this point were confusing as guides to future decisions.[36] Thus a legitimate sphere of action for the political association was still not clearly defined.

Mr. Baron Pollock in the course of trying a case which involved the providing of free drinks to prospective Tory voters by the Lodges of the National Conservative League, said, " I, for one, would wish it to be distinctly understood that, if there be a political association upon one side or the other whose character is permanent, who from month to month and from year to year are industrious in watching the register, correct it, influencing people to get their names put upon the register, and are holding meetings and gatherings for that purpose, it is not to be too hastily assumed that because an election takes place at some particular period, every act which is done by the association, although it may be, perhaps, necessary in the furtherance of the election, makes that association, or the different members of it, necessarily agents for the candidate. It is not because an election takes place," he concluded, " that a political association should hold its hand from going on in its steady courses with regard to the register and other matters." [37]

In connection with another case, Mr. Baron Pollock remarked, " It has always been said that a mere registration agency is not an agency in connection with an association, and

35 For various cases involving an interpretation of the Act see Seager, J. F., *op. cit.* For a general discussion of the weaknesses of the Corrupt Practices Act and suggestions for amending it, see Buxton, C. R., *Electioneering Up-to-Date.*

36 Buxton, C. R., *Op. cit.,* 37-38.

37 Seager, J. L., *Op. cit.,* p. 42, Worcester case (1892). According to the Act the candidate and his election agent declared that to the best of their knowledge and belief no person, club, society or association had made any payment in respect to the conduct of the election.

is not a thing that is harmful, or from which the candidate, until the election actually takes place, need keep himself clear; and yet I should like to ask which is most effective? Which is the real thing that wins an election—a future election—it may be years afterwards—an industrial careful keeping up of the registration, or the holding of meetings—and meetings even combined with pleasure—where music may be heard, and drinks go round at the commencement? " [38]

The verdict in regard to the Brewers' activities in 1902 and 1906 provided a particularly startling construction of the Corrupt Practices Act.[39] The Courts held that the Brewers and Licensed Victuallers Associations had no direct stake in the elections, and therefore the free drinks offered by them did not fall under the provisions of the Act. Yet it was a well known fact that the evangelical and non-conformist temperance movements were of a definitely Liberal complexion, while on the other hand the propertied classes were heavily involved as stockholders in the brewing and distilling companies, and could count on the Conservative Party to protect their interests. This decision made it clear that the definition of political interests was open to very wide interpretation, and left considerable latitude for the activities of such an organization as the Primrose League.

Long before these decisions, however, League officials were well aware of the problems created for them by the Corrupt Practices Act, as so much of the League's work took the form of entertainment. On the delicate question of " treating," they soon discovered that, provided the candidate himself did not actually appear at the tea or fête, it was safe to provide food below cost in the candidate's interest.[40]

38 Lancaster petition (1896). See Seager, J. L., *Op.' cit.*, 47.

39 See Stepney case (1892). *Ibid.*, 54.

40 Grand Council found it necessary to issue instructions on treating to the habitations in the form of a question and answer: " Is it legal for habitations to pay 4d for a tea which costs 8d—the 4d coming from a private individual? Yes. If meeting for Primrose League principles and not for the

At Grand Habitation in 1893 the Chancellor in his report urged habitations to continue their entertainments, advising that the cost be met by the habitation and not by individual members. He counselled the League not to be too timid and not to stress overmuch the danger of running afoul of the Corrupt Practices Act. He cited the Hexham case as involving a special set of circumstances, for in that case the candidate actually had paid a large proportion of the expense of the entertainment in question.[41]

The League prepared a pamphlet for use in the General Election of 1892, specifically cautioning its members on the following points:[42]

1. That charitable gifts which in their private capacity they may have been accustomed to bestow, should not be given in the course of their political work, or in any way as an incentive to voting.

2. The use of undue influence upon any tradesman by any suggestion, direct or indirect, that custom may be granted or withdrawn according to the way in which he may vote.

3. The expenditure of money upon any matter connected with the conduct or management of the election, unless it be some personal trifling expense legally incurred out of their own money, and not repaid to them (e. g. cab hire in canvassing, telegrams or postage).

claims of candidate." It added that under the same conditions Wardens might give away free concert tickets and might after a party give free tea to the children, even if the candidate or M. P. were present on the occasions. Habitations might also provide free tea (donated by individual Knights) if the tea party was confined to members. Deficits from teas might be met later by habitations but never by the candidate, and at a meeting where the deficit was to be so met, the candidate might not address the meeting, nor might resolutions in his favor be passed. Between election periods M. P.'s or candidates might provide "political entertainment" but never offer food.— *Minutes of Grand Council of Primrose League,* May 22, 1893.

41 *Morning Post,* April 19, 1893.

42 "Election Hints for Habitations," *Primrose League Gazette,* June 18, 1892.

4. The hiring, borrowing, lending or using, for the purpose of conveying electors to or from the poll, of any animal or vehicle ordinarily let out for hire.

5. The payment for bands of music, torches, flags, banners, cockades, ribbons or marks of distinction, for the purpose of promoting the election of a candidate.

III

Yet the League had at its disposal perfectly legal forms of persuasion, more subtle than the questionable methods described, and equally effective. In its lavish use of a hierarchy of mediaeval titles, and in the pageantry of its awards, the famous advice of its patron saint on the necessity for flattery was by no means unheeded by the League. It may be said truly of the Primrose League that it applied its flattery with a trowel.

A variety of honors in the form of badges, jewels, clasps, stars and titles lent effective, if tinselled, glamor to membership in the League. From the beginning the Primrose League had imitated the secrecy associated with the ritual of the Masonic Lodges. As the League grew, an elaborate symbolism was developed, as well as a hierarchy in membership, and an ascending and carefully graded scale of honors and decorations.

Habitations recommended members for honors or promotions and these were issued by Grand Council, which had a right of veto over the award. Knight Harbingers might be recommended to be Knight Companions, Dames might become Dames of the Order of Merit (the title of Dame Companions being avoided!). An early title, soon abolished, was Knight Almoner, or Clerical Knight. Appropriate decorations were designed for each grade and any associate who had obtained at least one special clasp might become an honorary Knight or Dame.[43]

The Jubilee Grand Star, instituted in 1887, proved by far the most popular Primrose decoration. It had five points, representing the Empire in the five continents of the world and con-

43 *Primrose League Gazette,* March 31, 1888.

sisted of five grades, available to different types of membership, at various prices and with different ribbons. Lady Borthwick, the wife of the proprietor of the *Morning Post* and the founder of the Ladies' Grand Council, was presented by the League with a Grand Star of diamonds reputed to cost £100.

At the inaugural banquet of the League, many Knights had appeared wearing silver lozenged badges, suspended by striped violet and primrose silk ribbons. Other original badges were primrose buttons, like French Legion of Honor decorations, and a full dress badge with a silver background. Associates had their own pins and full dress badges, and indeed special decorations were provided for wardens, sub-wardens, honorary lady secretaries, the Executive Committee of the Ladies' Grand Council, and so on through all grades and types of membership.[44]

Members were urged to wear badges on all possible occasions, and particularly at election times, and according to the *Pall Mall Gazette,* some Knights even attended church in full regalia. Grand Council devised a pendant watch chain " to meet a want which used, in the early days of the League, to be so frequently expressed by business men." It was impossible, Grand Council explained, for them to wear continually any of the ordinary badges " without attracting an amount of attention which might, in some cases, be incompatible with success."[45] Wellington School boys, it was charged, were forbidden to wear primrose buttons because their headmaster was the son-in-law of Mr. Gladstone.

Special service clasps were obtainable for unusually conscientious work as a habitation official, or for offering parks for fêtes

44 The distinctive enamel badge for Knights, Dames and Honorary Knights and Dames in 1888 is described as having " an enamelled primrose in the center surrounded by a gilt scroll bearing the motto of the League, surmounted by a gilt crown and having the PL monogram at the foot of the primrose. The badge is made either as a stud or as a brooch, and costs in either case 2/." *Ibid.,* July 21, 1888.

45 *Ibid.,* July 21, 1888.

or providing ball rooms for dances grâtis, for decorating meeting places, for conducting especially assiduous canvassing before general elections, or for enrolling a conspicuously large number of habitation members.[46] Habitations received banners for special activity at general and bye elections, inscribed with the year of the election. Many banners were awarded even after the disastrous General Election of 1906.

The Primrose motif was much exploited by the League. Primrose stationery, Primrose register books, and even Primrose tea tables, and Primrose parasols were on sale at headquarters or were advertised in the *Gazette* by private shops.

As early as 1888, the *Gazette* declared that " Grand Council would, in 1884 and 1885, have been appalled had anyone prophesied that in three years time they would have been exercising an amount of patronage which is not enjoyed by even the Lord Chancellor, and which extends not only over almost every village and hamlet in the United Kingdom, but far away to Australia and Singapore, India and Mauritius, and nearer home, to Cyprus and Malta." [47] In fact, the secretary of a Berkshire habitation warned Grand Council that League members in the country districts had come to think of Grand Council as merely a huge shop for badges, ribbons or register books.

Photographs of Tory statesmen thrown on a screen, tableaux vivants of historic or contemporary Conservative figures, as well as the annual pilgrimage to the country seats of famous Conservative noblemen, no doubt were as effective in the party interest as a more seriously political education. The annual Primrose Day program invariably included an excursion such as the trip to Hatfield House, the historic home of the Cecils, where Arthur Balfour or Lord Robert Cecil would speak from a balcony after tea, or a trip to Belvoir Castle at the invitation of the Duke of Rutland, or a visit to the underground gallery of Welbeck Abbey on the invitation of the Duke of Portland.

46 *Ibid.*, March 31, 1888.

47 March 24, 1888.

A spluttering account by a local landlord of the " outrages " inflicted on his own tenantry by the Irish Land League, the halting reminiscences of a veteran fresh from Mafeking or Ladysmith, or the informal and amateurish description by some great lady of the neighborhood of her recent trip to India, all undeniably provided an effective defense against reasoned Liberal attacks on the Irish Coercion Bill, the exposure of the shocking statistics of mortality in the British concentration camps in South Africa, and the arguments advanced of the danger of Mr. Chamberlain's budget to the working man's budget. And when the home-made curtains of a village school-room parted to reveal a local Britannia weeping over the fate of General Gordon, the tableau was worth far more as general party propaganda than a two-hour tirade by a paid lecturer on some weighty pronouncement of Mr. Gladstone's.

CHAPTER IV

THE PRIMROSE DAME

I

Under the title " Mollitics," Labouchere's journal spluttered : " Every Parliamentary candidate must now have his Moll, to simper while he asks for a vote, to grin and wave her handkerchief at the telling points of his speech, and to be assaulted by the police, if the exigencies of the case render a little female battery expedient." [1]

Mrs. Gladstone once told the Liberal women's organization that " the efforts of women, as of men, should be open and clear, avoiding the method and manners of Primrose Dames."

The participation of women in practical political work antedated the work of the Primrose League by at least a century. Rowlandson's caricatures of the famous Westminster election of 1784 show the boisterous Duchess of Devonshire angling with the Duchess of Portland for the butcher's apprentice's vote, or portray the famous climax of the Duchess kissing the butcher himself.[2] " The Duchess of Devonshire is indefatigable in her canvass for Fox," Walpole quotes. " She was in the most blackguard houses in Longacre by eight o'clock this morning ! " [3] Since this poll ran for forty days, a high standard was set for future lady canvassers. However, duchesses were not to emerge again as active canvassers until a century later.

On the other side of the picture, women worked with men in the revolutionary clubs and secret societies which sprang up in England under the influence of the revolutionary Jacobin Clubs of France.[4] The philosophic radicalism of Godwin and his fol-

1 *Truth*, November 24, 1887.

2 *The Devonshire or Most Approved Manner of Securing Votes*, 1784. See Grego, J., *Rowlandson, the Caricaturist*. I, 126.

3 Grego, Joseph, *History of Parliamentary Elections*, 272.

4 Ostrogorski, M., *Democracy and the Organization of Political Parties*, I, 531.

lowers, which dominated and guided these movements in England, endorsed a feminism of a high spiritual type, which Mary Wollstonecraft voiced explicitly for the first time in her *Vindication of the Rights of Women*.

In the next period it was the women of the people who were active politically. During the agitation for franchise reform from 1815 to 1820 women again made themselves heard. Samuel Bamford, the famous radical, tells how he insisted at a reform meeting at Lydgate that the women present be allowed to vote by a show of hands.[5] " This was a new idea," he observes, " and the women who attended numerously on that bleak ridge were mightily pleased with it." From that time, not only did women vote at Reform meetings, but proceeded to form political unions of their own. One of these societies, the Female Reform Society of Blackburn, presented a Cap of Liberty to a Reform mass meeting there.[6]

Two women's clubs marched on the field before Peterloo behind their white silk flag. A picture of the Peterloo Massacre, now in the Reform Club in Manchester, is dedicated to " Henry Hunt, Esq., the chairman of the meeting and *to the Female Reformers of Manchester* and the adjacent towns who were exposed to and suffered from the wanton and furious attack made on them by that brutal armed force, the Manchester and Cheshire Yeomanry Cavalry." [7]

Although the Reform Bill of 1832 thus owed its passage, in some degree, to agitation by women, neither Radical nor Tory women appeared in appreciable numbers as regular party workers. It is true that the Tory ladies of Bristol were discovered to be distributing " blue beef " to the freemen of Bristol, but

5 Bamford, Samuel, *Passages in the Life of a Radical*, I, 165.

6 Ostrogorski, M., *Op. cit.*, I, 531.

7 Fawcett M. G., *Women's Suffrage. A Short History of a Great Movement*, 7.

there was no real organization of women for these party services.[8]

The Chartists, like the members of the Trades Union Movement and of the Labour Party in their early years, allowed their fear of women's economic competition, as well as the necessity of concentrating on practical demands, to prevent them from including women in their demand for equal franchise. To be sure, a few of the Chartist leaders (William Lovett conspicuously), believed in including votes for women in their demands, and women, of course, were caught up in this movement as wives, daughters, and mothers. It has been estimated that out of every 100,000 signatures to the 1848 petition, 8,200 were those of women.[9]

T. C. Salt of the Birmingham Political Union organized a franchise reform meeting in 1838 for women only. He wrote about this to Ebenezer Eliot: " I *alone* of Birmingham reformers dared either to convene it or to attend it," and explained that he made this appeal to women, for " We cannot afford their neutrality or hostility. They must be our enthusiastic friends."

Salt addressed a strong appeal to the women at this meeting. " The men in 1832 made a sad bungling job of the Reform Bills," he said. ". . . The men of England took the lead then. Now the women of Birmingham would obtain the immortal honour of setting an example to the women of England, which would be of the utmost consequence to all." [10]

Bastiat, the French economist, felt it necessary to defend the women who were involved in the Anti-Corn-Law agitation. He felt afraid that they might be accused of losing their grace in a " scientific melée," bristling with " such barbarous " words as " tariffs, salaries, profits, monopolies." In reality, women's ac-

8 Great Britain. *Report of the Select Committee on Bribery at Elections* (*Parliamentary Papers*) 1835, 415. Testimony of John Sircom, member of the Operatives Conservative Association at Bristol.

9 Slosson, P. W., *The Decline of the Chartist Movement*, 207.

10 Jephson, H., *The Platform, Its Rise and Progress*, II, 220-221.

tivities in the Anti-Corn-Law agitation were largely centered on such tasks as transforming Covent Garden Theatre into a Norman Cathedral for a bazaar that was declared at the time to rank with the Paris Exposition of 1849 or the Crystal Palace of 1851, and which brought in over eight thousand pounds for the cause. Teas and soirées, arranged by committees of ladies, were, in fact, quite a feature of a campaign usually associated with a graver technique.[11]

II

The founders of the Primrose League had originally planned that it should be a small select group of male Conservative workers. However, when the League was but a few weeks old an addition was made to the rules admitting women as honorary members under the title of Dames.[12] As early as 1884 women were joining habitations with the same status as men—the Primrose Dames corresponding to the Primrose Squires and Knights, and the women associates to the original men associates.

A central organization, composed only of women, the Ladies' Grand Council, was organized early in the following year.[13] On March 2, 1885, at a drawing room meeting called by Lady Glenesk, the wife of the proprietor of the *Morning Post,* the Ladies' Grand Council of the Primrose League was formed and fourteen members enrolled.[14] By 1887 the Ladies' Grand Council of the Primrose League was reported to have some thousand

11 Prentice, A., *History of the Anti-Corn-Law Association,* I, 142-143.

12 *A Short History of the Formation of the Primrose League. Corrected and Revised by the Founders. Minutes,* December 22, 1883.

13 See Appendix II.

14 Arbuthnot, G. A., *The Primrose League Election Guide,* 20. The original fourteen members of the Ladies' Grand Council were: The Duchess of Marlborough, Lady Randolph Churchill, Lady Charles Beresford, the Dowager Marchioness of Waterford, Julia, Marchioness of Waterford, Julia, Countess of Jersey, Lady Hardman, Lady Dorothy Nevill, Miss Meresia Nevill, Lady Blythswood, the Hon. Mrs. Armytage, Mrs. Bischoffsheim, Lady Wimborne and Lady Glenesk.

members, its sudden growth reflecting the increasingly important role of women throughout the League.[15] In 1892 a Council
membership of 1,370 had been attained;[16] and in 1896, from a
platform "tastefully decorated with double tulips, iris, calceo-
laria, and African marigolds," a membership of 1,605 ladies
was proudly announced.[17]

In the early years the Presidents and Vice Presidents of habitations composed exclusively of Dames were *ex officio* members
of the Council, but later the Ladies' Grand Council was in no
sense a representative organization and rested on no system of
local representation. A fee of one guinea for membership on the
Council suggests also that only Dames were likely to belong.

An Executive Committee of fifteen members rotating every
third year was elected by vote of the Council, but all candidates
for this Executive Committee had to be nominated or seconded
by a member of the Council. One *ex officio* member was on the
Executive Committee, the Dame President of the habitation
winning the champion banner for the current year. A Secretary
and a Treasurer were appointed for life by the Executive Committee.[18] The original officers of the Ladies' Grand Council were
appointed by Grand Council, who had also drawn up the constitution for the auxiliary organization. Grand Council also ap-

15 The Executive Committee in 1887 was composed of the following: The
Duchess of Norfolk, the Marchioness of Londonderry, the Countess of Jersey,
the Countess of Romney, Lady Gwendolyn Cecil, Treasurer; Viscountess
Folkestone, Dorothy Neville, Lady Charles Beresford, Lady Stanley (of
Preston), Hon. Lady Campbell of Blythswood, Hon. Mary Henniker, Hon.
Mrs. Armytage, Lady Knightly, Lady Hardman, Secretary, Mrs. Akers
Douglas, Mrs. Bischoffsheim, Miss M. Nevill.

16 *Morning Post*, May 14, 1892.

17 *Ibid.*, May 16, 1896.

18 See "Ordinances of the Ladies' Grand Council of the Primrose League,"
Primrose League Gazette, January 2, 1899. Grand Council did not permit
graded badges for members of the Ladies' Grand Council, but recommended
that "members of the Ladies' Grand Council wear a handsome, exclusive
badge of their own, especially designed."—*The Primrose League, its Rise,
Progress and Constitution*, 55.

pointed its own men's consultative committee as liaison officers between itself and the Ladies' Grand Council.

The Ladies' Grand Council was no mere drawing-room ornament. It paid over from £500 to £800 a year to the Literature Committee of the League; in the course of one year over three million leaflets financed by the Ladies' Grand Council were turned out by the Literature Committee.[19] From time to time the Ladies' Grand Council made contributions for special activities. In 1891 it sent out vans equipped with magic lanterns through Bedfordshire and Buckinghamshire, from which seventy-five speeches on the Irish question were delivered, and 1,000 anti-Home Rule leaflets distributed.[20] In 1893 the Ladies' Grand Council provided free concerts in the poorer districts of London, and financed a lecture by a Primrose speaker.[21] The last proved to be effective propaganda, according to the *Morning Post,* since the speaker, who concentrated on the Home Rule issue, supplemented his remarks with " life-like representations of Irish outrages."

Some uncertainty as to the powers and jurisdiction of the Ladies' Grand Council, and consequent friction with Grand Council, led to the appointment of a joint committee of both organizations to consider the proper sphere of action for the Ladies' Grand Council.[22] This Committee defined (if not confined) the powers of the Ladies' Grand Council as (1) the appointment of its own executive officer; (2) the collection of its own subscriptions; (3) a right of consultation on the Joint Literature Committee (whose funds came from the Ladies' Grand Council and which usually consisted of five Knights and four Dames); and finally (4) no power to interfere between habita-

19 *Morning Post,* May 30, 1890.

20 *Ibid.,* October 5, 1891.

21 *Ibid.,* September 30, 1893.

22 *Minutes of the Grand Council of the Primrose League,* April 28, 1887. A Ladies' Grand Council for Scotland was formed in 1888, and its funds were cleared through the original Ladies' Grand Council.

tions and the Grand Council of the League on the part of the Ladies' Grand Council..

Fun was sometimes poked at the Ladies' Grand Council for its decorative impotence, in contrast to its financial usefulness, and to the enormous and constantly growing numbers of women members in the League.[23]

An oil portrait of the Executive Committee of the Ladies' Grand Council of this period hangs today in the Council Room of the League's headquarters in Victoria Street, London. In bonnets and bustles, posed in stiff clusters, Duchesses and Countesses gravely hand papers to each other. In the foreground, two solemn King Charles spaniels squat on the thickly flowered carpet at their feet, forming a kind of pediment to the portrait. In these members of the Ladies' Grand Council, who sat on the platform at Albert Hall beside Lord Salisbury, one might see in apotheosis, the innumerable Dames who sat on draughty village school platforms, presiding over home-made entertainments at local habitation meetings.

In contrast to the Ladies' Grand Council, women members of habitations were to play a highly important rôle in Primrose League affairs. Even in the first years of the League, women were recognized as having valuable " information " to offer and were eligible for honorary membership in habitations.[24] Later they flocked into habitations with men and soon began to form habitations of their own, many of which were to be among the

23 The total enrolment of the Primrose League in the early years grew by gargantuan strides; from 957 in 1884 and 11,366 in 1885, to 273,283 in 1886, and 565,861 in 1887. A large proportion of this increase was undoubtedly due to new women members. From 57 Dames in 1884, the number grew to be 23,381 in 1886, and 39,215 in the following year. There were 50,258 enrolled Knights. Even if one were to put the number of women associates (which is not given separately) as lower proportionately than that of Dames, the growth of women members would be phenomenal.

24 *Morning Post*, March 6, 1884.

most powerful in the League and to survive to the present day.[25]

A Dame President, a title first used officially in 1888, some-times presided jointly with a Ruling Councillor over a mixed habitation as well as over a Dames' habitation. Many of these exclusively feminine habitations were formed from older mixed habitations, and inevitably questions of jurisdiction and of precedence appeared. Lord Randolph Churchill once warned these new habitations of women that they were to consider themselves subsidiary to the established mixed or male habita-tion in the locality.[26]

A veteran worker for the League once enumerated the oppor-tunities for women in the League—they might become Dame Presidents, arrange entertainments, supervise registration, do individual canvassing (while the habitation itself was virtually disbanded during an election), help the local Conservative asso-ciation, and address campaign literature.[27] An article of 1900 lists a number of habitations where women are the principal workers, such as " The Drummond Wolff " at Bournemouth, of 374 Knights and Dames and 3,587 Associates, run by Miss Scott Murray, or the Kent habitations, which were the special charge of Lady Logan. Miss Goring Thomas was the moving spirit in Enfield, Middlesex, one of the most important habita-tions in the Home Counties, which had fifty wardens, and a membership of nearly 1,100. Also prominent in habitation work were the Duchess of Buckingham and Chandos at Knutsford,

25 Grantham habitation, Victoria habitation and Croydon habitation, important in their day, were of this type.

26 A real union of sexes, as well as of classes, was boasted of by the League. The marriage of Cusack-Smith, at the time executive secretary of the League, is described in some detail in a contemporary newspaper account. A spray of primroses in her hair, the bride was preceded up the aisle by nine bridesmaids dressed in primrose nun's veiling, with hats to match and carrying gilt fans on which were spread their League diplomas. The bridegroom and many of the guests wore their Primrose League badges at the church and reception.—*England*, April 24, 1886.

27 Nevill, Meresia, " The Work of the Primrose League," by an Old Primrose, *Life*, September 13, 1888.

and Mrs. Hudson, who was President of a Dames' habitation at Brighton from 1884 to 1893.[28]

Many women headed habitations jointly with their husbands. Sometimes the wife of the local member of Parliament was the Dame President of the habitation in his district, as was Mrs. Mallock of Torquay. A Mrs. Sims founded the largest habitation in London, that in Poplar, while a Mrs. Shadwell started another flourishing one in the thickly populated district of East Finsbury.[29]

Croydon, always a Conservative stronghold, provided one of the oldest and most continuously successful fields for women. Lady Randolph Churchill officially opened the Grantham Habitation there on the first of August, 1885.[30] A membership of over one thousand women was reached by this habitation in 1894, and an article in the *Gazette* two years later reported a membership of 1,899.[31] An efficient local organization had been established in each municipal ward of Croydon, presided over by a Warden of the Grantham Habitation. Mrs. Peard, Dame President of the habitation, held office from 1885 until 1901, when she was succeeded by Mrs. Crowley, signer of the original warrant for the habitation.[32]

28 "Woman in Politics. Distinguished Workers in the Primrose League," *The Gentlewoman*, April 28, 1900, Home Counties, and May 12, Lancashire, Cheshire and Yorkshire.

29 *Primrose League Gazette*, April 2, 1892.

30 *England*, August 1, 1885.

31 *Morning Post*, April 30, 1894, and *Primrose League Gazette*, October, 1896.

32 According to its minute book, Grantham Habitation in 1891 boasted that the attention of its Dames to the Lodge Lists and the Parliamentary Revision Lists had resulted in a net Conservative gain of 580 voters on the register. There is an interesting account of canvassing in a bye-election in 1886 by a member of the habitation who went up and down the streets of Bethnal Green, which in that period were considered somewhat rough and rowdy for a lady. Today there are two flourishing Dames' habitations in Croydon —the Enfield and the Grantham. (Information copied from the minute book for the author by Mrs. H. Gray, Dame President of the Grantham Dames, June, 1937.)

Women were probably the greatest organizers of habitations. Lady Mary Henniker alone, for instance, was credited with founding nineteen habitations in Suffolk.[33] Lady Lathom was especially active in League affairs in Lancashire in the late nineties as well as on the Executive and Literature Committees of the Ladies' Grand Council. Miss Milner from Yorkshire, where a habitation was named after her, concentrated on fiery speeches against Home Rule, which she delivered for the League in various parts of England, and she also undertook an Irish tour.

The Countess of Brandon in the early nineties worked hard to build up sentiment in Cork for the League and the Unionist cause.[34] Lady Cynthia Graham was proposed by the Vice-Chancellor of the Primrose League for Tory work in the Cumberland district to counteract the influence of Lady Carlisle, an ardent champion of temperance, and a great Liberal personage of her day in the North of England.[35] Lady Jersey, Lady Gwendolyn Cecil (the daughter and biographer of Lord Salisbury) and Lady Montague were active in preparing League pamphlets.[36]

The Duchess of Marlborough (the mother of Lord Randolph Churchill) presided over the Ladies' Grand Council and spoke at Grand Habitation meetings in the eighties. Miss Meresia Nevill was for many years a Treasurer of the Ladies' Grand Council, and an active canvasser and popularizer of the League in articles and in speeches. She was the daughter of Lady Dorothy Nevill and had been described as the favorite " child friend " of Lord Beaconsfield.

33 *Primrose League Gazette,* March 26, 1892.

34 *St. Stephen's Review,* February 6, 1892.

35 *Minutes of the Grand Council of the Primrose League,* January 9, 1890.

36 Lady Gwendolyn Cecil. " To Fathers and Mothers." (On school board elections), 1897. Lady Jersey had revised a much used League lantern slide " Our Glorious Empire " and her address to the Ladies' Grand Council of May 24, 1887 was published as a League pamphlet. Lady Montague prepared a pamphlet entitled " The Reason Why," in 1888.

Women were employed by the League as speakers and as organizers. Two of the Metropolitan provincial secretaries during the election year of 1895 were women. Perhaps the most spectacular service rendered to the Unionist cause by a Primrose League Dame was that of a lady holding a diploma of the Grand Star, who, it was claimed, actually dispersed a crowd in Birmingham which had gathered to hear the socialist Hyndman speak, by suddenly singing the national anthem from another side of the square.[37]

By 1886 the report of the Ladies' Grand Council showed that out of some four hundred habitations, fifty-seven were composed exclusively of women.[38] In a later report there were said to be 300 women Ruling Councillors and 450 Honorary secretaries in England, 33 Ruling Councillors and 47 Honorary secretaries in Wales, 13 Ruling Councillors in Scotland, and 6 Ruling Councillors in Ireland.[39]

Although women were prominent in executive positions in habitations, they continued to be ineligible for membership on Grand Council. In the early years, a resolution was entered in the minutes of the Executive Committee of the Grand Council excluding women from membership on that body. But it was withdrawn at the following meeting, with the assurance that women members themselves were not in favor of pressing for such a right.[40]

A ripple of surprise ran through Grand Habitation of 1903 when a Mrs. Seale of Southend habitation suddenly injected the question—" Is the League willing to consider and to press for the right of women to places on Grand Council? " The chairman replied that the question was outside the province of

37 *Primrose League Gazette,* February, 1888.

38 *Morning Post,* February 22, 1886.

39 *Ibid.,* May 24, 1889.

40 *Minutes of the Grand Council of the Primrose League,* April 28, 1887 and May 5, 1887.

the meeting, since it was not dealt with in the report, and so apparently closed the matter.[41]

The work of the Primrose Dames inspired an attempt by a group of French monarchist ladies to organize a " *Ligue de la Rose.*" The Countess of Paris, organizer of the *Ligue,* asked Lady Randolph Churchill for advice, and an article on the French League appeared in the *Primrose League Gazette* of October 13, 1888.[42] The Countess of Paris proposed to nominate Madame Felix Fournier and the Marquise de Coriolis as " lady superintendents " of the *Ligue,* and gilt rose badges were to be issued to the members.[43]

In taking the startling step of asking French women to engage actively in elections, the French organization felt that it was justified by the unusual state of the country and the special danger it saw at the moment of atheism and radicalism in France. Lady Dorothy Nevill says that " France, however, manifested little enthusiasm at this attempt to breathe new life into Royalist circles," and after a short time nothing more was heard of the *Ligue,* " which soon relapsed into an obscurity from which indeed it can hardly be said to have ever really emerged." [44]

III

An article in the middle of the century in the *Quarterly Review,* in commenting on electioneering, says that " it illustrates our constitutional history, but it illustrates also our private life. It has one relation to Blackstone and Delorme, and one to Hogarth, light literature and brewing." [45] The Corrupt Practices Act of 1883 by making volunteer electioneers necessary had resurrected on a large scale the spectacular tactics of the

41 *Morning Post,* May 1, 1903.

42 *The Reminiscences of Lady Randolph Churchill,* 149.

43 *Primrose League Gazette,* January 26, 1889.

44 Nevill, R., *Leaves from the Note Books of Lady Dorothy Nevill,* 19.

45 " Electioneering," *Quarterly Review,* July, 1857, CII, 32.

Duchess of Devonshire and a knot of other ladies in the Westminster election of exactly a century before.[46]

As we have seen, canvassing was one of the most important services which the League rendered to the party, and the most zealous Primrose canvassers were the women. The League urged women canvassers to canvass in and out of season. Liberals enjoyed quoting a Tory M. P. who, they claimed, had urged Primrose Dames to argue with painters, paperers, and chimney sweeps; and the Liberals assured the Dames that this would be easy, as such workers were often paid by the hour!

Violent attacks on the Dame canvassers from the opposing ranks were, naturally, not slow in appearing. " Filthy witches," Sir Robert Peel had cried in the heat of electioneering.[47] To a volley fired at the Primrose League women by *Reynolds'* newspaper in 1894, the *Gazette* responded with: " Primrose Dames! Show your contempt for ' Reynolds ' and add to the services you have already rendered your country by putting into the hands of the masses such papers as ' The People ' or ' England,' to counteract the pernicious influence of such Radical organs." [48]

Outvoters were the peculiar charge of Primrose women workers. The *Morning Post* ascribed the Tory success in London in 1885 largely to the indefatigable efforts· of Primrose canvassers to reach outvoters.[49] Conveying outvoters to the polls within the letter of the Corrupt Practices Act was a problem faced by both parties, and met successfully by the Primrose Dames.

Lord Salisbury was careful to include women in acknowledging his debt to the Primrose League for its work in the 1885 election. He emphasized the service which the League had

46 See Grego, Joseph, *The History of Parliamentary Elections*, and Grego, Joseph, *Rowlandson, the Caricaturist*, I, 123-142.

47 In *St. Stephen's Review* of November 2, 1889, the Presentation Cartoon, shows Sir Robert Peel wielding a large tar brush in front of a bill board. It is entitled, " Sir Robert, the Ripper of Primrose Dames."

48 *The Primrose League Gazette*, July 2, 1894.

49 *Morning Post*, July 26, 1885.

rendered in bringing to bear the influence of the more highly educated class—both men and women.[50]

During the election of 1887 in South Kensington, a radical candidate appeared at the last minute, and within twenty-four hours the Tory candidate was provided with from eighty to one hundred lady canvassers by the Primrose League.[51] In London the West End Dames worked vigorously in East End districts, where the Liberal strength was felt to be especially menacing. A great success was recorded in Bethnal Green in the General Election of 1895.[52]

Truth describes a descent by West End Dames on Stepney in the interests of the Conservative candidate, Major Gordon, as follows: [53]

> The Belgravians drove down on the Radical fold,
> And their landaus were gleaming with purple and gold,
> And ' Jeames ' on the box was a picture to see,
> As he sniffed in his pride through the streets of Step-Nee.
> Like the leaves of the forest where Epping is green,
> These Dames, ere the day of the polling, were seen,
> Like the leaves of the forest when autumn has come,
> Their leaflets be-littered each alley and slum.

After the poll has been declared and the Liberals found to have won, the poem goes on:

> And the Dames of the Primrose were loud in their wail,
> And the sobs of the *Standard* were borne on the gale,
> To think that the East against the West would have
>   scored,
> And have thus put to rout the Belgravian horde.

---

50 See *Minutes of the Grand Council of the Primrose League.* Manuscript Letter to Sir William Hardman, January 18, 1886. Even as early as 1884 the Primrose League Dames of Plymouth had been conspicuous for their successful electioneering tactics.—*St. Stephen's Review,* July 5, 1884.

51 *Primrose League Gazette,* October 15, 1887.

52 *Minutes of the Grand Council of the Primrose League,* July 25, 1895.

53 *Truth,* March 17, 1893, 652.

A Rowlandson cartoon shows the rotund and inflated figure of Madame Blubber, political antagonist of the Duchess of Devonshire, in despair of covering her electoral area, finally taking to the air as a balloon and triumphantly floating over the scene.[54] It was no accident that the period which saw the success of the Primrose Dames as canvassers should have coincided with the successful marketing of the " safety " bicycle, which was to reach boom proportions by the middle of the nineties. Primrose Dames, as they took to the bicycle, doubled their value as political allies. Mounted on " Royal Sunbeams " and " Sea Breezes," they became mobile skirmishers.

The bicycling fever had set in about 1867, but the old " ordinary," with its large front wheel, high seat, and trailing small wheel, was heavy and difficult for women in their long skirts to mount and straddle.[55] The " safety " bicycle, perfected in the eighties, eliminated the high bar connecting the two wheels, and made it possible for women to mount decorously for the first time, their long skirts now falling clear to the pedals.[56]

" Rational " costume no longer being necessary, the feminine and conventional woman as well as the " emancipated " might take up the sport, and England of the nineties teemed with women on wheels. Bank holidays during the nineties found the highways crowded with these cyclists ; railroad vans and station

---

54 *Madame Blubber's Last Shift, or the Aerostatic Dilly,* 1784. Grego, J., *Rowlandson, the Caricaturist,* I, 134.

55 Duncan, H. O., *The World on Wheels* and Pemberton, A. C., *The Complete Cyclist* describe the ancestors as well as the mechanical details of both the " ordinary " and the " safety " bicycle.

56 Many contemporary trade pamphlets advise women on appropriate costumes for bicycling. Almost all urge prospective bicyclists to provide themselves with pure woolen underwear, straw sailor hats, skirts " no longer than 3 or 4 inches from the ground."—Davison, L. C., *Handbook for Lady Cyclists,* 1896. Mrs. Amelia Bloomer, an American feminist, who edited a paper called " The Lily ", herself abandoned the costume she had invented in 1857. She feared posterity might remember her in this connection rather than for her work for feminism!—Strachey, Ray., *The Cause,* Footnote, p. 387.

platforms were stacked high with women's bicycles; and even in 1896 the demand for bicycles for women was swamping home factories.

During the eighties and nineties a flock of pamphlets appeared, urging women to take to the bicycle. Tempting vistas of wider fields for sketching and botanizing were held out. "A New World of enjoyment is open to the woman who finds herself on the wheel," one circular proclaimed.

A speaker at Grand Habitation in 1898 gave a glowing account of "the recalcitrant voter being tracked to his lair by bands of enthusiastic and athletic Primrose Dames mounted on bicycles."

Grand Council drew up a set of rules for Primrose Cycling Corps and designs for special badges and for uniforms of "blue with yellow facings and blue and yellow ribbons on their hats and caps, if they like." [57] Miss Edith Munsey cycled over 1,000 miles in four months on a League mission, and two League delegates toured Southern Ireland, covering sixty miles a day. At headquarters a cycle corps was formed, with Arthur Balfour as leader. Soon week-end and early-closing-day runs organized by habitations followed by outdoor picnic meals became common. Imposing parades of bicyclists in massed formation, or intricate and elaborate bicycle drills frequently opened League fêtes.

A contemporary political pamphlet pictures the ghost of Lord Beaconsfield as warning his political descendants, "You are preparing for your Revolution, and you commence with unsexing your women. The Primrose Baggages . . . The craze won't outlast his (Gladstone's) time. It's taken up by servant girls and shop boys. Remember," Lord Beaconsfield's ghost ends, "the political women of the French Revolution. They brought their knitting . . ." [58]

---

57 *Minutes of the Grand Council of the Primrose League,* July 2, 1896.

58 Norma, G. W., *Lord Beaconsfield's Ghost* (1886), 13.

IV

An early official history of the Primrose League had re-minded its readers that the last of the Beaconsfield novels had held out special encouragement to women and to their efforts in politics and that, in fact, " all his good women understood political questions and devoted their lives and energies to the causes espoused by their husbands and brothers without fee or reward other than the satisfaction of having succeeded." [59] At an early meeting of the Ladies' Grand Council, Lord John Man-ners recalled that Lord Beaconsfield had always supported the enfranchisement of women.

Lydia Becker's " Women's Suffrage Journal" salutes the first meeting of the Ladies' Grand Council of the Primrose League with, " It is, we believe, a unique and unparalleled cir-cumstance that a meeting of ladies only should be convened for such an object, and addressed by so many statesmen in the first rank of politics, and the fact is, no doubt, to be regarded as a significant sign of the advance of public opinion as to the polit-ical influence and duties of women." [60]

On the one hand, Mrs. Fawcett, the great suffrage worker, declared that the opportunity for political work by unenfran-chised women in political parties, short of the vote itself, was " one of the most important political weapons which can pos-sibly have been put into our hands." [61]

On the other hand, Mrs. Pankhurst, on hearing that Amer-ican suffragists contemplated working for the existing political parties, protested with bitterness, " I can assure the American women," she declared, " that our long alliance with the great parties, our devotion to party programmes, our faithful work at elections, never advanced the suffrage cause one step. The

59 *The Primrose League, Its Rise, Progress and Constitution,* 5.

60 *Women's Suffrage Journal,* July 1, 1885, 109.

61 Fawcett, M. G., *op. cit.,* 33.

men accepted the services of the women, but they never offered any kind of payment." [62]

Gladstone had said of the Franchise Act of 1884 and its lack of provision for women that " the cargo which the vessel carries is, in our opinion, a cargo as large as she can safely carry," and the small but ardent group of suffragists felt that the Liberals had cast them overboard indeed. They had only the resolution in favor of women's suffrage passed by the Trades Union Congress of that year and the publicity which even failure gives a weak cause to comfort them.

Although parliamentary franchise for women, after 1884, seemed to be receding into the future, gains had been made in legal protection for women and in the provision for them in the local franchise.[63] In 1882 the Married Woman's Property Bill, the result of thirty years of agitation, and the Criminal Amendment Law,[64] the result of forty years' work, were real landmarks in the general progress of women toward equality.

Women slowly but steadily were taking part in municipal elections, were sitting on school boards, and becoming Poor Law Guardians. It was, however, only a handful of women who participated in these local government activities and later in those concerned with Parish Councils, and they were for the most part women already active in women's causes. The admission of women to these local franchises made very little mark on local government. Apparently an indirect contact with national politics was more attractive to most women than a direct one with local politics.[65]

62 Pankhurst, E., *My Own Story*, 15. Mrs. Pankhurst herself left the Liberal Party in 1883 and later the Independent Labour Party. After the first World War, she ended her party career as a Conservative parliamentary candidate. Mrs. Pankhurst liked to find in the formation of the Women's Liberal Federation a deliberate plot to sidetrack the suffrage movement of that time and one of Mr. Gladstone's shrewdest political maneuvers.

63 Women were not eligible for membership on County Councils until 1907.

64 A law for the protection of young girls against moral crimes.

65 Lowell, A. L., *The Government of England*, II, 15.

As far as parliamentary suffrage went, " the Cause " found itself in the curious position of being confronted with a Liberal Party, amongst whose rank and file were some of the most passionate believers in women's suffrage, but whose party leadership was opposed to the movement, and, on the other hand, a Conservative Party whose members were hostile or indifferent, but whose leaders were friendly to granting the suffrage to women.

Lord Salisbury, following Disraeli's policy, had publicly declared women " to be fit for the franchise." " I earnestly hope," he told an audience at Edinburgh in 1888, " that the day is not far distant when women will also bear their share in voting for members in the political world and in determining the policy of the country. I can conceive no argument by which they are excluded." [66]

In Covent Garden in 1896 Lord Salisbury told Grand Habitation, " No question divides politics more than women," but added, " There can be no doubt that their action through the machinery of the Primrose League has largely altered the development of both parties."

Both of the party organizations passed resolutions in favor of woman suffrage during the eighties, the National Union of Conservative and Constitutional Associations at its Oxford Conference in 1887. The previous year the Union had postponed voting on the subject on the ground that it was too great and lengthy for the Conference. The Women's Liberal Federation endorsed the cause of suffrage in 1890.

When a suffrage resolution was proposed at the Conference of the National Union of Conservative Associations in 1894, a speaker cited the Primrose League as an example of women's political work.[67] Speaking to the same resolution, George Renwick, Ruling Councillor of a large habitation in Tyneside, and

---

66 *Primrose League Gazette,* December 15, 1888.

67 *National Union of Conservative and Constitutional Associations,* Minutes of Conference, 1894.

the husband of the Ruling Councillor of an even larger one in Newcastle, described how women electioneers drove to the polls voters not nearly so well educated as themselves, and had to wait outside the booth for them, often to be a target for the jeers of loungers or political opponents. The resolution was carried with only one dissenting vote.

At Primrose meetings on suffrage, however, many a speaker would begin by telling women that they should have the vote, only to inject a note of " realism " by reminding his audience in the next breath that it might be difficult to recruit women for the army, and of other dilemmas likely to arise. One speaker, received with much applause by an audience of women, reminded them that, with the exception of nursing the young, there was nothing men could not do much better than women. In usual vein were remarks on belonging to a party or a League not only as Disraeli had boasted " on the side of the angels," but one which had " the angels by its side."

In the early days Primrose League meetings were addressed by lecturers sent by the central committee of the National Society for Women's Suffrage, and habitations frequently passed resolutions in favor of women's suffrage. Playlets entitled " Women's Rights and Men's Wrongs " and the like were given by habitations.[68] In Cumberland children staged a debate on the issue, assuming the names of famous Conservative statesmen to entertain the members of the habitation.

Miss Milner, an apparently tireless Primrose League speaker, as well as an ardent anti-suffragist, found herself routed at a habitation meeting at Bath after a speech containing some anti-suffrage allusions. The chairman, in her vote of thanks actually moved a resolution for women's suffrage; the speaker seconding the motion of thanks to Miss Milner took occasion to second the suffrage motion as well; while the audience voted both the thanks and the suffrage resolution, apparently simultaneously ! [69]

68 *Primrose League Gazette,* February and December, 1888.

69 *Women's Suffrage Journal,* August 19, 1889.

But the Primrose League early foresaw the danger that the issue might divide its ranks as disastrously as it had those of the Liberal women. Grand Council issued a precept in 1889 forbidding habitations to take part in suffrage meetings or to pass resolutions in support of the franchise for women, though speakers pro and con might continue to air their views on the subject from Primrose League platforms. There seems to have been some difficulty in enforcing this ruling, since Grand Council from time to time found it necessary to remind the members of the regulation.[70] Later an official pronouncement was made that the Primrose League as an organization held no opinion on the question of women's suffrage.[71]

As a matter of fact, the interest of members in the issue seems to have died down quite naturally in the nineties. Though reports show that habitations were debating the suffrage question frequently in 1888, we find it listed only occasionally after 1890 among the topics discussed at meetings. Primrose leaders congratulated themselves on having concentrated on their three fundamental beliefs, and not having frittered away valuable energy on a subsidiary question.

The reluctance of Liberal leaders to press the women's suffrage issue was due in part to the new activities of women as political partisans. *St. Stephen's Review* declared that Gladstone's distrust of women in political life had been confirmed by the success of the Primrose League. On the other hand a Liberal speaker, in pressing for the right of women to sit on the newly elected County Councils, reminded his opponents in the House of Commons that " women form a very active section of the Primrose League, a powerful and excellent organization in the interest of honourable members on the other side of the House." [72] Leonard Courtney, in moving a suffrage bill, tried to

---

70 *Primrose League Gazette*, October 19, 1889.

71 *Ibid.*, September, 1896.

72 *Ibid.*, June 13, 1889.

reassure his Conservative adversaries by reminding them that the principle of this bill had been objected to by many Liberals on the ground that it might strengthen the hands of the Primrose League.[73]

Primrose League women, as distinct from their Liberal contemporaries, were very rarely appealed to through their interest in purely women's questions, such as women's wages, the Contagious Diseases Act, or women's higher education. Sometimes speakers at habitations struck a vaguely feministic note as when Mrs. Lucas Shadwell opened her address before a habitation with, " Dames of the Primrose League, women of England, look back through the dim pages of our history, back to the time when Boadicea, the British Warrior Queen, sought vengeance of her country's Gods, for the insults and injuries of the Roman Conquerors." [74]

Some attempts were made within the Tory Party to found other organizations of women but none of these appear to have offered any real rivalry to the Primrose League.[75] One of the more important feminine organizations was that of the Liberal Unionist women. In 1888 the Liberal Unionist Women's Association was formed and branches of it occasionally cooperated with local habitations.[76] Mrs. Henry Fawcett, who worked hard in the organization and who helped to bring over a group of 800 Irish anti-Home Rule speakers, received most useful training for her suffrage work, according to her biographer, through this contact with " real " politics.[77]

Mrs. Fawcett had refused earlier to join the Executive Committee of the Women's Liberal Federation on the ground that

73 *Morning Post,* February 22, 1886.

74 *Ibid.,* May 18, 1895.

75 *Minutes of the Grand Council of the Primrose League,* March 17, 1898. Three organizations of women are described as started by the Conservative Party in one district, but all had failed during the course of the year.

76 *Primrose League Gazette,* July 28, 1888.

77 Strachey, R., *Millicent Garrett Fawcett,* 130.

Mrs. Gladstone's organization was " party—nothing but party."
Of the Women's Liberal Unionist Association, Mrs. Fawcett
characteristically wrote, " I have been getting very indignant
with the aristocrats who are patronizing the Women's Liberal
Unionist Association for saying that it is a very undesirable
thing for women to take part in politics, but because the other
side have done it we must too!"

Not only were the Liberal Unionist women active politically,
but many of them were also concerned with other social causes
and were later prominently identified with these movements.[78]
The Liberal Unionist women copied the Liberal women's form
of separate organization, and their political work was concentrated almost entirely on arousing sentiment against Home
Rule.[79]

Liberal politicians were not, of course, unaware of the
dazzling success which had attended the initial attempt of the
rival party to mobilize its new party auxiliaries. Several organizations of Liberal women were in existence before 1887, when
the Women's Liberal Federation held its inaugural meeting " to
promote a Women's Liberal Association in every constituency
and also the admission of women into any existing Liberal
Associations." [80] The earlier London Confederation Central
Union with Mrs. Theodore Fry as honorary secretary had been
merged with the new Federation.[81]

Punch pictures Gladstone and Chamberlain as rival chanti-
cleers crowing before the Women's Liberal Federation.[82] There
were some men members in the Women's Liberal Federation,

78 Strachey, R., *op. cit.*, 129.

79 Hill, G., *Women in English Life,* II, 305. The Executive Council of the
Liberal Unionist Women's Association in 1896 included: Lady Frances
Balfour, Miss Ainstruther, Mrs. Fawcett, Lady Arthur Russell, and a repre-
sentative from Leinster and Connaught and another from Munster.

80 Rules of the Women's Liberal Federation, 1888.

81 See *Women's Liberal Federation.* Annual Reports and Council Meetings.
1886. (Reprinted 1900.)

82 November 10, 1888.

however, since there were some mixed constituent associations, but in contrast to the Primrose League, the Liberal women functioned politically in a women's organization with women officers.[83] Perhaps for this reason the rôle of the Women's Liberal Federation was rather that of handmaiden to the Liberal men's organization.[84]

The programs offered at local meetings of the Women's Liberal Federation were also in contrast to those of the Primrose League. Such entertainment as " a talk on health, followed by a fruit supper " enjoyed by the members of the Bradford Women's Liberal Association, would probably have been rarely duplicated at a Primrose League gathering.[85] Occasionally what might be called a Primrose note was struck, as at a rally attended by Gladstone, and addressed by Parnell to thundering applause.[86] Here Mrs. Fry presented to Mrs. Gladstone, in the name of the Federation, " a bracelet containing a miniature of Mr. Gladstone set in diamonds and emeralds forming a shamrock." [87]

83 In 1890 there were 51,300 members (of whom 3,950 were men); in 1891 there were 66,721 members (of whom 14,987 were men); in 1892 " some 75,000 members " and 360 associations; in 1893 " some 76,000 members " and 397 associations. By 1898 the membership was 69,933 with 489 constituent associations and a budget of £998 11/6. (See *Women's Liberal Federation Annual Reports* for the years mentioned.)

84 In *Punch* of May 28, 1892, the Women's Liberal Federation dressed as Cricketers demand of Gladstone, " If we're good enough to scout for you, why shouldn't we take our turn at the bat? "

85 See *Women's Liberal Federation, Summary of Federation News. 1893-1905.*

86 *Morning Post,* May 23, 1889.

87 The Ladies' Liberal Social Council, formed apparently in imitation of the Primrose League, endeavored to strengthen Liberal sentiment through social activity rather than through political education. In 1902 the Council held four entertainments in London at which such Liberal women as Mrs. Spender, Lady Crewe and Lady Aberdeen officiated.—*Primrose League Gazette,* April, 1902. Although these names suggest an interest in the organization on the part of the leading Liberal families, the Council seems never to have attained strength or importance. See Lowell, A. L., *op. cit.,* II. Footnote p. 15.

Separate organizations of women laborers at this time were rare, and the voices of women in the few trade unions which admitted them were seldom to be heard. Only in the north, in the textile unions, were women a factor in the trade union world. They were making a beginning too in the cooperative movement. But it was chiefly to women of the upper working class that the trade union and cooperative movements appealed, and at this stage they were thwarted by men, and by their own inhibitions, when they attempted to take part in these two movements which so directly and vitally affected their lives.[88] The workingman's fear of the economic competition of women reinforced the fear which he held in common with the Conservatives and Liberals of collaboration by well-meaning but untrained amateurs.

V

It is obvious that the converging in the last quarter of the nineteenth century of such movements as that for higher education for women, the Contagious Diseases campaign, organized church and philanthropic work, the suffrage crusade, as well as the increasingly rapid rate at which women were entering business and industry, explains the emergence and success of women in the political field. There remains to explain the admittedly greater effectiveness of the political work of Conservative as compared with Liberal women,—a fact which cannot be entirely attributed to the disruption of the Liberal women's organizations by the suffrage issue.

88 In 1884 the Women's Co-operative League became the Women's Co-operative Guild. Mrs. Acland, a founder of the League, admonished the original group, "above all things, our influence must be quiet, our motto 'Study to be quiet, and do your own business,'" and added, "We must have no platform speaking, no advertising; no going out of women's place."— Djang, S. M., *Women's Part in the English Co-operative Movement and Related Problems*, 31. On the Women's Cooperative movement see Davies, Margaret Llewelyn, *Life As We Have Known It*, by Cooperative Working Women.

A larger proportion of Conservative leisured women free for party hack work and the day to day social contacts so valuable to local party organization; the unique position of women in rural community life where the Conservative party had its deepest roots; and lastly the more vivid appeal to women of the very issues, slogans and general propaganda of the Conservative Party during these years—all these factors together may account for the greater success of the Conservatives in mobilizing their women.

Bryce reminded a Schools Inquiry Commission that in all mercantile communities the women had an unprecedented amount of leisure time, " if indeed it should not rather be said that it is possessed by them alone." [89] The Conservative Party, especially after the Home Rule schism of the Liberals, undoubtedly had a far larger supply of women of leisure as well as of socially prominent wives. The wives and daughters of prominent Liberals, if interested in any work outside of their homes, were more likely to be already active in such fields as education, suffrage or social reform than were those in the rival party. At the same time the average Liberal wife or daughter was less likely to be economically independent enough for sustained volunteer work for her party.

As the bulwark against attacks on private property, and as traditionally the party of social prestige, the Conservatives could the more easily enlist the interest and efforts of women of the new rentier class. In the villas of the new suburbs which were beginning to dot the outskirts of many cities, as well as at resorts like Brighton or Bath, life for many women was not only often very narrow, but lonely as well, while household duties had become slight.[90] Today the Townswomen's Guilds fill a somewhat similar need in providing normal social life for

89 Great Britain. *Report of the Schools Inquiry Commissions* (*Parliamentary Papers*), 1867-68, I, 548.

90 Wingfield-Stratford, E., *The Victorian Sunset* enlarges on the preoccupations of this group.

women in the new garden suburbs and building developments which have multiplied since the first World War.

The character of girls' education in mid-Victorian days suggests that a simple and unintellectual approach to political subjects would have made the strongest appeal to the wives and daughters of voters. The great Secondary Schools Inquiry Commission of 1867 had been persuaded to hear some evidence on the state of middle class secondary education for girls. The Commission's findings were: a generally inferior tone in girls' preparatory schools usually taking the form of undue prominence given to acomplishments, especially music, and great indifference on the part of parents to any serious education for their daughters. The report of the same Commission demonstrated that everywhere the fact that the pupil was to become a woman, not a man, operated upon her course of study negatively and not positively.[91]

Since women usually entered the teaching field only as a result of financial or domestic misfortune, their lack of training was matched only by their lack of temperamental fitness. The private governess of the period, except in a few instances, probably was no better qualified than the school teacher.[92] Dorothea Beale, the organizer of Cheltenham Ladies' College, tells how her mother weeded out the most shockingly misspelled of the applications for the post of governess to her daughter. The usual wages offered to a governess may be judged by contemporary advertisements in the press: "A lady recommends a nursery governess, age 26. Resident or Daily, family or School. Very lady-like, willing to be useful. English thoroughly, Music, French, drawing, needlework. £20 to £25. Miss Robertshaw, 144 Paddington Green, West." [93]

91 Great Britain. *Report of the Schools Inquiry Commission* (*Parliamentary Papers*) 1867-68, I, 546-70.

92 See Neff, W. F., *Victorian Working Women,* Chapter V, *The Governess,* for a discussion of the Victorian governess.

93 *Times,* April 4, 1885. The salaries in such advertisements are stated on an annual basis.

Parents were even more apprehensive for their daughters than for their sons of any mingling of social classes at school. Wholesale traders, for instance, refused to have their daughters educated beside those of retail traders, and all feared any hint of solid study as a sure drawback to successful marriage.[94]

The inspectors for the Commission visited the small private schools in which so many British women of the last part of the nineteenth century must have received their education. Instead of an adequate curriculum or a qualified teaching staff, the principals of these schools would display many notebooks (the number out of all proportion to their contents) kept by each student in which " with ruled lines and many flourishes " had been recorded fragments from textbooks on such a variety of topics as " lightning conductors, the teak-tree, the Sicilian Vespers, mobility, the properties of the atmosphere, and the Pelagian heresy." Female pupils, moreover, in most of these schools were found to be " perpetually hovering between work and play, embroidering while they memorized their spelling; reciting their history lesson while on their daily walk." [95]

It is true that opportunities for higher education were opening up for women at the universities and professional schools, but their significance for the vast majority of women, who would receive only elementary, and possibly secondary education, was largely in their promise for the future,—in short for their daughters and granddaughters. The majority of middle class girls, especially in the country, continued to receive little or no practice in discussing questions of the day as they appeared in the daily press or even at the family dinner table; much less did they receive any training in independent thinking along these lines. It is not hard to understand their lack of interest in direct participation in municipal or school board affairs, or their preference for canvassing in behalf of their men relations and friends rather than studying the town budget.

94 Great Britain. *Report of the Schools Inquiry Commission* (*Parliamentary Papers*) 1867-68, IX, 282, 350.

95 *Ibid.*, IX, 279 ff.

Women living in the rural areas were especially cut off from interests outside of their immediate circles, and the problem of too much leisure, and too few resources, was even more acute for them than for the middle class women of the resorts and suburbs. A tea in the autumn given by the Church Society (attended only by those whose dues were paid), where the vicar would read "John Gilpin" or sentimental selections from Tennyson, and the oldest Church mother present would move a vote of thanks. And then no more entertainment all winter long, except a possible concert organized by the parson's family, if there should be enough moonlight for the villagers to find their way home.[96]

Even the wives and daughters of the agricultural laborers, who had household duties and the care of children, found time hanging heavy on their hands. Agricultural machinery, which came into use during the seventies and eighties, was eliminating the type of work done in the fields by women and children (though gangs of women still pulled roots for farmers in Norfolk and Cambridgeshire). Yet there was nothing pleasant or interesting which the women could do with their enforced leisure. In the seventies the National Agricultural Union had offered women as well as men a source of interest and a center of community life. Wives of members took part in union functions, and when the husbands had migrated north for work, sometimes attended union meetings in their places.[97] But by the eighties the Agricultural Union had collapsed, leaving behind it a real void in village social life.

It is easy to see that the sort of entertainment provided by Primrose habitations [98] was a magnet to these women, and to understand why 57% of their membership should have consisted of agricultural laborers' families, or persons living in small towns.[99]

96 See Courtney, J., *Countrywomen in Council*, 23.

97 Selley, E., *Village Trade Unions in Two Centuries*, 82.

98 See Chapter III.

99 See Appendix III for total membership figures.

Rural society in England preserved the pattern of an earlier period well into the twentieth century, and even the Women's Institute Movement, an outgrowth of the first World War, had to adapt itself to many vestiges of this earlier period, such as the influence of the local " gentry " and of the clergyman's family in politics and public life, and the prestige of the local " great lady " of the district. Few of the working class village folk were proof against the ancient reverence for the great families—and that fact had always been a factor in Conservative successes in rural areas. The Primrose Dame knew well how to use this situation for political ends.

Moreover, she was thoroughly at home in this background, and experienced in the kind of activity which the League demanded of her here. Political work, and especially house to house canvassing, came naturally to many middle class women accustomed to church visiting and volunteer charity work, which by the end of the seventies had become almost a fashionable necessity. To be sure, church membership was not always predominantly Conservative, but it was in the rural districts, where the relationship between visitor and visited was most personal, that church visiting provided the most valuable education and experience for the feminine propagandist. And it was in the rural districts that the Primrose Dames became most active and successful.[100]

To many a Primrose Dame in the country, her political work must have been essentially an outgrowth of her normal social

100 Many Primrose workers probably gleaned valuable training and experience in the Girls' Friendly Society, which had a membership of 3,000 in 1876, and was growing by leaps and bounds. Though its members were frankly anti-feminist, and many may have had an aversion to any kind of political work, yet the organization furnished practical training in organized work as well as in executive experience. Its work in country districts must have trained many prospective Primrose League workers. The membership of the G. F. S. grew steadily: 1886, 168,423; 1896, 229,458, and in 1904, 260,062. The division of classes of membership in the G. F. S. suggests the two types of membership, Dames and associates, of the Primrose League. See Money, Agnes L., *History of the Girls' Friendly Society* (1911).

life in the village. She canvassed voters primarily as the wife, mother, or sister of a neighbor, customer, or employer, and her methods necessarily reflected that relationship. An intimate knowledge of the families of a rural district, often gained through years of church visiting and household shopping and the like, was of inestimable value to the wives and daughters of the local Conservatives, or to single women of property, who were likely to be Conservative. That the Conservative Party was able to reap the benefits of the Franchise Act of 1884—for the Liberals made little headway with the agricultural laborer's vote during the first decade after its passage—was largely the result of this kind of feminine party work.

Finally, it is tempting to speculate on the possibility that the election issues of the Tory Party in themselves were especially attractive to the late Victorian woman. In contrast to the reasoned Liberal case for moderate self government for Ireland, the reforms in the Newcastle program, a critical appraisal of British arms, a tempered enthusiasm for the war in South Africa and a somewhat tepid imperialism, the Tory pleas for a far-flung Empire, the rights of Englishmen to be defended in the Transvaal, revenge for General Gordon deserted and trapped at Khartoum, a mother's right to have her children given religious training, a fear of terror loosed on respectable Protestant homes in Ireland,—may well have had an appeal to the untrained feminine mind, not only through their drama, but also because they were more closely intertwined with the roots of women's emotions.

The romantic symbolism of imperialism must have had an especial attraction for women. The charm of faraway places for those so circumscribed by their homes, the plea for the guardianship of the native peoples to those already interested in foreign church missions, and the stirring accounts of frontier warfare calling for individual bravery by the British hero, the " strong man " so dear to the readers of late Victorian fiction, must have entered into the success of the Primrose League.

" The Hallelujah Lass and the Primrose Dame march in the van of the Woman's Movement of the World," declared the *Pall Mall Gazette* in a leading article.[101] Startling as this juxtaposition is, it is true that both movements did yeoman work in the political emancipation of late Victorian women.[102] Certainly the Primrose Dames provide a curious footnote to the story of the struggle for the rights of women. Yet the League brought to life, politically, half a nation.

101 April 18, 1889.

102 The feminism of Catherine Booth was to continue to characterize the policy of the Salvation Army. Mrs. Booth had asked indignantly in a debate on women in the ministry, " Why should the swaddling-bands of blind custom, which in Wesley's day were so triumphantly broken, and with such glorious results thrown to the moles and bats, be again wrapped round the female disciples of the Lord Jesus? " Salvation Army regulations ran, " As the Army refuses to make any difference between men and women as to rank, authority and duties, but opens the highest positions to women as well as to men, the words ' woman, she, and her ' are scarcely ever used in orders, ' man, he, his ' being always understood to mean a person of either sex unless it is obviously impossible." There were 5,000 women officers in the Salvation Army at the time of Mrs. Booth's death in 1890. See Booth-Tucker, F. de L., *The Life of Catherine Booth*, also Strachey, R., *The Cause*, 214-216.

CHAPTER V

CLASSES AND MASSES

I

IN his autobiography, Joseph Arch, the leader of the rural trade union movement of the seventies, recalls an incident of his childhood in a rural parish, when he peered through a window of the village church to watch the celebration of Holy Communion. First he saw the squire, with his retriever at his heels, march up to the communion rail to take the sacrament alone. And only after he had risen did the farmers and their wives bustle up the aisle. Finally, the small boy saw the farm laborers, amongst whom were his own parents, shuffle diffidently to the altar.

That England, at least down to the outbreak of the first World War in 1914, was distinctly a country of class divisions, hardly needs argument. But that those class divisions constituted a problem was an idea which was spreading in the course of the nineteenth century. By the end of the Victorian era there was not a Tory die-hard in the country who did not have some sort of solution for it, even though it was nothing more than the dream of returning to the good old times.

> Gone are the days and gone the ties that then
> Bound peers and gentry to their fellow men.[1]

lamented Lord John Manners.

As early as the forties Disraeli was awakening the public to the dangers of spreading misery and growing discontent, and was breathing new life into the decaying ideal of noblesse oblige.

" I was told," says Egremont, the hero of the novel *Sybil,* " that an impassable gulf divided the rich from the poor; I was told that the privileged and the people formed two nations,

1 Manners, Lord John, *England's Trust, England's Trust and Other Poems.*

138

governed by different laws, influenced by different manners, with no thoughts or sympathies in common; with an innate inability of mutual comprehension."

Disraeli believed that the two classes should fulfill their respective functions in the community, but that class distinctions did not imply superiority on the one hand or inferiority on the other. " In the Church and at the polling booth all are equal," he once said. But their different social functions were to serve the same end of the common good, and toward that end the aristocracy and the people were to unite in a common cause. " The aristocracy are the leaders of the people," he once said in Parliament, " for the aristocracy and the labouring population form the nation, and it is only when gross misconception and factional misrepresentation prevail, that a miserable minority under the specious designations of popular advocates is able to prevent the nation's order." [2]

His novels are full of social criticism.

" If any fellow were to ask me what the Conservative cause was, I am sure I should not know what to say," says one of the characters in *Coningsby*.

" Why, it's the cause of our glorious institutions," Coningsby answers. " A Crown robbed of its prerogatives; a Church controlled by a Commission; and an Aristocracy that does not lead."

" Under whose genial influence," rejoins the other, " the order of the Peasantry, a country's pride, has vanished from the face of the land, and is succeeded by a race of serfs, who are called labourers and who burn ricks." [3]

---

2 Great Britain, *Parliamentary Debates*, 3rd series, Vol. 58, Col. 638 ff., July 10, 1840.

3 Kingsley's Lancelot " could not help thinking of that amusingly inconsistent, however well-meant scene in *Coningsby*, in which Mr. Lyle is represented as trying to restore 'the independent order of peasantry' by making them the receivers of public alms at his own gate, as if they had been middle-age serfs or vagabonds, and not citizens of modern England."—Kingsley, Charles, *Yeast*.

Speaking of Disraeli's novel *Sybil*, Earl Baldwin said at a Primrose League banquet: " When England was being industrialized with appalling speed, when the politicians, business men and professional economists were telling our people that all was well with the world, and that the wealth of the ages would be poured into our laps,—Disraeli wrote of the Two Nations. He spoke of class divisions, and he stood for the unity of the nation, and the policy of a party which would be national, and never lead any particular class, rich or poor." [4]

Lord Randolph Churchill also liked to describe the Tory Party as a national party of " a free aristocracy in historical and natural alliance with the masses," in contrast to its opponent, " a party," he charged, " of and for the new middle class whose interests are diametrically opposed to those of the workers, and which, in addition, could boast of no tradition of popular service."

Yet by the time that the Primrose League was trying to realize the " true union of the classes " as a practical program, the concept of a party of landed aristocracy versus a party of middle class industrialists had ceased to be very convincing. It was clear that the Conservative Party was closely allied with industrial capitalism, and at least as closely identified in its membership, and as sensitive to the needs and demands of industrial capitalism as the Liberal Party. A writer of the period warned the Conservatives that they could never actually " dish " the radicals, since they themselves were the party neither of individualism, nor of state control, but rather the custodians of the borderland between the two.[5]

In fact the idea most commonly expressed by the Tories was that of a community of interest among all classes. As the nineteenth century drew to its close, this idea was constantly invoked by the Tories against what they charged was the socialist

4 *Morning Post*, November 12, 1932.

5 Curzon, George N., " Conservatives on Themselves," *Fortnightly Review*, 1885, XLIII, 631.

division advocated by their adversaries in the Liberal and Labour camps. Needless to say, the identification of interest between capitalist and worker was often construed as depending primarily on the welfare of the former.

The position of the Liberals was hardly less equivocal. They had of course become identified as the party of laissez-faire during the Corn Law agitation, but a laissez-faire policy was hardly consistent with their chosen rôle as reformers and champions of the working class. Yet it was hard to reconcile their rôle as champions of the workers with that of representatives of the interests of the new capitalist class. And they numbered among their leaders, as the Conservatives were at pains to point out, a number of the largest landholders in the country. In short, the Liberals as well as the Conservatives found themselves in an increasingly confused position, shuttling between economic individualism and state control.

In the eighties a number of trade union officials were elected to Parliament as Liberals. By 1886 there were ten of these so-called " Lib Lab " representatives at Westminster, and at one time in the nineties the number reached fifteen. Arthur Henderson, later one of the greatest organizers of the Labour Party, and Foreign Secretary in the Labour Cabinet, contested the constituency of Barnard Castle as a Liberal, though unsuccessfully. The movement declined, however, by the end of the century, when the militant labor group, under the leadership of Keir Hardie, adopted a policy of independent labor action in the political field. From that time on the more class-conscious element of the labor movement grew increasingly skeptical of the promises which the two great traditional parties held out to the working class.

As a matter of fact, both Tories and Liberals emphasized the common interest of employer and employee in the safeguarding of private property and the maintenance of the status quo. Yet each party found it necessary to compete with the other in dangling special inducements with a definite class appeal before the various elements in the electorate. In the case of the working class, this inducement had to be of a more or less concrete character, offering redress or reform through new social legislation.

The Tory Party could boast of as great a tradition of social reform as its rival, and could point to a long record of social legislation, much of it passed in the teeth of Liberal opposition. A long line of Factory Acts stretching from the work of the elder Peel at the beginning of the century to Disraeli's last government; the work of Fielden and Sadler for shorter hours, —all seemed to justify the claim of the Conservative politicians that they were merely following a characteristically Tory tradition in their program of social legislation.[6] It was often acknowledged that the achievements of Chamberlain, even as a Conservative, were far more in the tradition of such Tories as Fielden, Northcote and Cross than of such Liberals as Forster or Harcourt.

The career of Sir John Gorst[7] provides a kind of Tory democratic thread through the full and lean years of Tory social legislation, and forms a link between the earlier Tory tradition of Peel, Huskisson, and Shaftesbury, and that of the modern

6 A standard history of factory legislation published in 1903 comments, "What proportion of the factory code is due to either of the great parties, which for so many years succeeded one another in the government of the country would not be very easy to determine.... It does, however, appear that, on the whole, the persons really interested in the reform of industrial conditions could get more help from the Tory party in the old days, while in more recent times the Liberals have been the more favourable of the two." And it adds, "The early Factory Acts were wrongly supposed by many to be of a retrograde tendency, harking back to the mediaeval standpoint, while the whole series is now, rightly enough, seen to be latently socialistic." — Hutchins, B. L. and Harrison, A., *A History of Factory Legislation*, 196.

7 For the career of Sir John Gorst see the *Times* obituary notice (April 5, 1916); the *Dictionary of National Biography*; Gorst, H. E., *The Fourth Party*; Wilkinson, W. J., *Tory Democracy*; and Gorst, Sir John E., *The Children of the Nation: How Their Health and Vigour Should be Promoted by the State*.

Conservative. Gorst organized the local workingmen's Tory associations in the seventies; and throughout his long career, in Parliament, and before the general public, he emphasized social legislation. He was often a rebel within the party ranks, as we have seen at the time of his association with Churchill just before and during the days of the founding of the Primrose League. His efforts spanned a period from 1866, when he first entered Parliament, to well into the first decade of the twentieth century, when he warned his party that its neglect of working class interests would lead to its downfall.

In the nineteenth century the Tory record on trade union legislation compared favorably with the Liberal. Tory speakers often made the claim that, with the exception of the Trades Union Act of 1871, it was not Liberal, but Tory legislation which had created the modern British trade union movement. It was the Tories who had originally legalized trade unions in 1824-25; they had to their credit the Tory Trades Union Act of 1859, the Commission of 1867, and the work of the ministries of Lord Salisbury.

Even the labor movement, after dissolving its alliance with the Liberals, acknowledged that the Tory record on reform was at least as good as the Liberal. " Tories are open enemies—but Liberals are treacherous friends," said *Justice,* organ of the Social Democratic Federation in 1885. In its next editorial it went so far as to say that a gain for the Conservatives (provided it did not give them a working majority) at the expense of the Liberals was probably the best thing that could happen for British socialists.[8] Hyndman, the disciple of Marx and the founder of the Social Democratic Federation, seems to have entertained hopes of Tory cooperation.[9] The local Conservatives

8 *Justice*, November 14, and November 28, 1885.

9 Hyndman's historic visit to the aged Lord Beaconsfield to ask for his cooperation in bringing to England his program of " Peace with Comfort " illustrates the faith on the part of some early British socialists in Tory help for the worker. It will be remembered that Lord Beaconsfield, impassive in his red gabardine dressing gown, merely remarked of the scheme, " The

did actually finance two Social Democratic candidates for Parliament in Kensington and Hampstead in 1885. The results were pitiable—thirty-seven votes in one constituency, and thirty-two in the other, but Conservative funds nevertheless had been given for independent labor representation.[10]

By the nineties labor was completely committed to the policy of fighting for its program through its own party. Labor had settled down to the attitude toward the old parties expressed by the *Clarion,* organ of the Independent Labour Party: " Telling the workingman that he must vote either Liberal or Conservative," it said, " is like offering a coal heaver demanding his pint of beer a strawberry ice or a lemon squash. For the worker the everlasting no of Toryism and the everlasting yea of Liberalism have but one sound." [11]

II

Sought after by both party organizations after the extension of the franchise in 1867, the Conservative workingman was not without previous training for participation in political organization. Membership in Friendly Societies, Building Benefit Societies, Workingmen's Clubs and Orders, as well as the experience offered by trade unions and later by cooperatives, had provided experience in organization for the educated working-

moment you tried to realize it on one side you would find yourself surrounded by a phalanx of great families who would thwart you at every turn: they and their women. And you would be no better off on the other side."— Hyndman, H. M., *Record of an Adventurous Life,* 224, 375.

10 This type of socialist or labor opportunism may be illustrated by the efforts at joint candidacy in New York City in 1938, between the New York Republicans, in eclipse at the time, and the apparently growing New York American Labor Party.

11 *Clarion,* July, 1892.

12 Two great benefit orders for workingmen, the Oddfellows and the Manchester Unity, dated from the first half of the eighteenth century and the first quarter of the nineteenth century respectively. Other important orders of the same kind were the Druids and the Foresters. Though probably the Liberal artisan predominated in the membership of these societies, the

man.[12] A Friendly Society Act of 1875 had so stimulated the growth of local Friendly Societies that by the end of the eighties the Manchester Unity and the Foresters each boasted a membership of over six hundred thousand, drawn from Britain and the colonies.

From the early part of the nineteenth century the Conservatives had endeavored to include working class membership in their party organization. After the Reform Bill of 1832 the party made efforts not only to form registration societies to meet the new requirements created by the Bill, but also to enlist active working class support. Conservative societies of mill operatives were formed during the thirties in a number of northern and Midland industrial centers. A contemporary account of these societies is prefaced by the remark: " The circumstance of an ' operative ' boldly and openly advocating Conservative principles is one, I know, rather novel in its nature." [13]

These societies declared their aim to be to rally round British institutions " and guard them from falling into the destructive hands of a Popish intolerance on the one hand, or a democratic ascendancy on the other." [14] Such societies usually had honorary members recruited from the gentry of the neighborhood. Reading rooms where newspapers, such as the *Church of England Gazette,* the *Conservative Journal, John Bull,* the *Times,* or the *Leeds Intelligencer,* were available, were a feature of these early Conservative artisan clubs.

training given many prospective Tory voters must have been considerable. See Baernreither, J. M., *English Associations of Workingmen.* The Workingmen's Club and Institute Union was founded in 1862, designed to offset the appeal of the Public House. Tories charged that the membership of the Union was almost entirely Liberal. Though the bulk of the working class voters remained in their " Pubs," the Union in 1883 had a membership of 560,000. See *Club and Institute Journal,* July 6, 1883, and *Minutes of the National Union of Conservative and Constitutional Associations, 1886.*

13 Quoted by Paul, W., *A History of the Origin and Progress of Operative Conservative Societies,* Introduction.

14 *Ibid.,* 13.

Peel's registration societies, which flourished in the forties and fifties, were formed on class lines in many districts. In Lancashire, the most fertile ground for these political associations, the working class Conservatives were organized into associations distinct from those of the middle and upper classes. Many of these north of England workingmen's associations had large and active memberships.[15]

Perhaps the organization of working class Conservatives into separate units was not in complete harmony with the idea of the true union of classes. Disraeli himself was highly inconsistent on this question, as Ostrogorski delights to point out.[16] On the one hand he told a delegation in Glasgow in 1873 that he had never consented to address a separate body styled " Conservative Workers," nor to induce Conservatives who were workingmen to form special societies confined to their own class.[17] But on another occasion he said to a deputation of 350 associations: " I wish to say one word upon workingmen's associations. I favoured them from the beginning and always had confidence in their future." [18]

It is probable that considerations of expediency rather than of principle determined the policy of the Conservative organizers in the long run. When Sir John Gorst set out on his campaign of organizing local Conservative associations, he formed some groups of purely working class membership, and others of mixed social elements. He found many workingmen's social clubs already in existence, some of which superseded or dominated the local associations.

15 The Liverpool Workingmen's Association testified before the Election Commission of 1868-69 that it had over fifteen hundred paying members and had canvassed over one thousand Conservative votes at the previous election.—Great Britain. *Report of the Select Committee on Parliamentary and Municipal Elections (Parliamentary Papers)* 1868-69, VIII, 135.

16 Ostrogorski, M., *Democracy and the Organization of Political Parties,* I, 256-260.

17 *Times*, November 24, 1873.

18 *Ibid.*, August 7, 1878.

The Conservative club was an important pillar of party strength before the rise of the Primrose League and even afterwards. Conservatives seem to have been more successful with their clubs than their rivals, partly through their closer tie in many places with the liquor interests, partly through their greater flair for staging entertainments. A workingman's club, a Conservative club, a Conservative association, and a Primrose habitation frequently existed side by side in the same locality, and all might touch at some point the local Tory workingman.[19] Probably the strongest working class Tory organization of its time was the Liverpool Workingmen's Conservative Association, with its 6,000 active members. During the eighties many large clubs of this type appeared.[20] Some of them were represented on the Council of the National Union of Conservative and Constitutional Associations, and thus some working class Conservatives achieved an indirect voice in guiding party policy.

The National Conservative League, founded in 1884, was designed, like the Primrose League, to furnish a meeting point for Tory gentlemen and Tory workers. It came into existence at about the same time as the Primrose League, but was more definitely a party-sponsored body. Its lodges, corresponding to the habitations of the Primrose League, were formed in Gloucestershire, Herefordshire, Kent, Middlesex, Northamptonshire and Worcestershire. The successful candidacy of Hart Dyke (a prime mover in the organization) in Kent was ascribed to the League.[21]

19 See *England*, January, 1886, or *Croydon Express*, January, 1886.

20 *Minutes of the National Union of Conservative and Constitutional Associations*, 1894.

21 *England*, February 22, 1890. The executive officers, a Grand Master, a Grand Secretary, and a Librarian, were elected, the Grand Master holding a seat on the Council of the National Union. Successful largely in Herefordshire, Worcester, Gloucester and Kent, the League was open only to men and appears to have appealed to a less educated type of working class membership than the Primrose League, while its meetings seem to have attracted

III

A social setting where class lines remained rigidly marked raised considerable barriers to the Tory program of a " true union of the classes." The popular organizations had not yet achieved a practical application of Disraeli's famous description of his party as neither a confederation of the aristocracy nor a popular multitude, but " a party formed from all the numerous classes in the realm." [22]

The founders of the Primrose League prefaced their account of its early days: " Having in view the failure of Conservative and Constitutional Associations to suit the popular taste or to succeed in joining all classes together for political objects, it was desirable to form a new political society which should embrace all classes and all creeds except atheists and enemies of the British Empire." [23]

The social mingling of the classes was a prime tenet of the League's philosophy and strategy. It will be remembered that very early in its history it created a class of associate membership with lower dues than Knights and Dames, but with equal rights in habitation government. By 1886 it was reported that nine out of every ten members of the Primrose League belonged to the working class category of membership.[24] In 1901 out of a League enrollment of slightly over one million and

little publicity. Friendly and benefit features, as well as the use of an elaborate society ritual, distinguished it from the Primrose League. In February of 1936, twenty to thirty lodges were reported in existence, largely in Northumberland, Cumberland and Durham. (Information obtained from the Secretary of the Association of Conservative Clubs.)

22 In 1885 the *Bedfordshire Standard* commended a local Tory candidate for holding a political gathering "in which all classes of society should be represented." It was thought to be rather venturesome on the part of Mr. De Ricci, who originated the idea.—De Ricci, J. H., *The Welfare of the People*, 1.

23 *A Short History of the Formation of the Primrose League. Corrected and Revised by the Founders.*

24 *Morning Post*, February 22, 1886. See App. III.

a half, the associates numbered over one million, four hundred thousand members.[25]

The League competed successfully with the Conservative workingmen's clubs, partly because women with their children were allowed to attend with their husbands. The list of volunteer entertainers or speakers at a meeting usually included many social types—a deliberate Primrose League policy.[26] Reports of habitation meetings state carefully that a resolution was proposed or seconded by " Mr. Egby, a workingman," or by " Mr. Harrison, a workingman." Grand Council urged habitations to put associate members on their governing councils, but there were never many in executive positions, perhaps because they had not enough leisure for the volunteer work required.[27]

Pettifer, always advertised as " a British workingman," and as representing that point of view, was a popular speaker at Primrose League meetings from 1890 to 1907. From his own account, originally a Birmingham Radical, he was a silversmith by trade, and during some of the years of his employment by the League he was also a speaker for the Fair Trade League.

Lord Salisbury paid the League a tribute in his speech to Grand Habitation in 1889. Despite the fact that industrial life had destroyed many of the earlier contacts between different social levels, he pointed out, the Primrose League had revived

25 Originally the title of " Esquire " had been provided as the name for the second step into Primrose membership for the associate, but in 1885 habitations were permitted to substitute " Companion." Eventually these distinctions in titles and honors between the classes of membership seem to have disappeared.

26 Occasionally the classes were separated at League social affairs, as at a Bournemouth habitation, where Lady Shelley provided tea in the Manor House for the Knights and Dames and refreshments in a large tent for the associates. In describing the presentation of decorations at a habitation, the *Primrose League Gazette* added, "Amongst those who were summoned to receive promotion was a working man, the subwarden of Benson, who had the good fortune to be decorated with the Hon. Knight's Badge and Diploma." —*Primrose League Gazette*, August 27, 1892.

27 See *Morning Post*, May, 1897, and *Minutes of Grand Council of the Primrose League*, July 12, 1906, and also Appendix VII.

the old union of the classes even in industrial areas where the new voters had previously followed Gladstone and the Liberals, and since the extension of the suffrage the Home Counties had become the bulwark of Conservatism.[28]

At the Oxford Union in 1890 a resolution was debated and carried: "That in the opinion of this House, the Primrose League has had a beneficial effect in bringing various classes together." [29]

It might be charged, perhaps, that the League interpreted the "true union of the classes" in terms of social opportunities rather than economic reform. One cannot escape the conviction that it did not stress a special labor appeal to its laboring class audiences.[30] A glance at the topics discussed at habitation meetings reveals that a very small proportion of them dealt with social legislation, and that a large number dealt with the more picturesque aspects of foreign or overseas policy.[31]

28 *Morning Post*, May 22, 1889.

29 *Primrose League Gazette*, May 17, 1890.

30 See Appendix VII for a sample of a Primrose League leaflet designed to appeal to the working class voter.

31 For instance, during January, 1890 immediately after the great Dockers' Strike had been settled, a list of the subjects taken up at habitations reads as follows: Better Defenses; Coaling Stations; Eastern views with the Magic Lantern; Home Rule; Home Rule Agitation dying down; Sir George Baden-Powell on Imperial Federation; a Lecture on Political Organizations; Lord Beaconsfield and Loyalists and Home Rule; Better Trade—"Distress in Bygone Days—"; Fallacies of the Radical Programme; a Lecture on Architecture; the Government and Portugal; Limelight Views of Ireland; the Work of the New County Council; Labouchere and Bradlaugh; Free Education and Housing; Housing and Foreign Labor; "Russia leaves India alone under a Tory Government;" a speech by a Blinded Veteran from the Transvaal against further Boer Encroachments; An exhibition of Stanley's medicine case, photograph and autograph; the Local Government Act; Allotments; King John and Magna Charta; Twenty-five Years' Residence in Ireland; Lord Salisbury on the Portuguese question as opposed to Gladstone and the African question; Taxes saved and Debts less; Home Rule and the Union of Scotland and England; Goschen and the Surplus; How Unions affect the Labour problem.—*Primrose League Gazette*, February, 1890.

The fight against Home Rule, the maintenance of the Empire in general, and the revision of the tariff, were proposed by League speakers as essentially questions affecting wages and hours, and as far more effective ways of remedying bad labor conditions than social legislation or trade union activity. Pettifer, the " workingman speaker " of the League, in his speech before the National Union, reminded workingmen that in addition to the social legislation passed for their benefit by the Unionist Party, there were " 500,000 fresh miles of territory for the social benefit of workers—to buy and sell our goods." An increase in wages would necessarily accompany, he said, any increase in the amount of national exports.[32] The tariff reformers attempted to associate their program with the cause of social reform, coining the slogan: " Tariff reform means social reform." Chamberlain had originally proposed that part of the proceeds of the tariff be devoted to setting up old age pensions.[33]

Early Primrose League speakers naturally reminded working class audiences of Tory legislation which had benefited the worker. They pointed to factory acts, housing and trade union legislation, and contrasted the achievements of the Conservatives with the laissez-faire attitude of the Liberals. In the late eighties the record of Lord Salisbury's Government was added to the list. Speakers emphasized especially the Miners' Acts of 1886 and 1887,[34] the Merchandise Mark Act, the Scotch Technical Education Act, and the Trucking Act,[35] The agricultural

32 *Minutes of the National Union of Conservative and Constitutional Associations,* 1890. This speech was adopted by the Primrose League as its labor program, and printed as a leaflet.

33 A Liberal leaflet of 1903 shows Chamberlain as Mother Hubbard telling her dog, " Want an Old Age Pension, do you? Bite off your own tail."— *Liberal Leaflets and Pamphlets,* 1903, No. 1922.

34 The Miners' Acts consolidated all previous laws passed for the protection of miners, and enacted new safety measures, and improved legal machinery for the prosecution of companies for negligence.

35 *Primrose League Gazette,* October 29, 1887. Trucking was the practice of paying workmen in goods instead of money, or in money on the under-

worker was reminded of the Allotments Act of 1887, the Glebe Land Act, the Tithes Act, as well as of the legislation affecting crofters in Scotland.[36] A League leaflet summarizing the accomplishments in social legislation in the three years of Tory rule from 1886 to 1889 listed thirty acts, and gave prominence to legislation concerning miners, crofters, Friendly Societies, superannuation, allotments and technical education.[37]

By the nineties, however, the paternalistic spirit which had inspired most of the Tory social legislation had ceased to meet the demands of labor. The working class demanded something better than the protecting arm of a benevolent upper class. Trade unionism represented labor's interest on the industrial front, and the Labour Party was soon to appear on the political scene. Proposed legislation now dealt with the eight-hour day, with the land tax, with the rights of labor as opposed to the rights of capital. On these issues the Tories could not claim to represent the working class point of view. The Conservative Party could no longer regard the industrial front from the safe distance of a landholding class. Tories were as heavily involved in the industrial system as their opponents. They were as numerous among the new class of Forsytes as Liberals, if not more so. And they might have quoted the record of their press and politicians to prove their loyalty to that class quite as well as to prove themselves the champions of the rights of labor.

During this period—at the turn of the century—their greatest achievements on behalf of labor were their Workmen's Compensation Acts (1897 and 1900). The Primrose League made much of the Act of 1897 in the industrial areas as an example of the work of the Conservatives in behalf of working class interests. It was somewhat embarrassed, however, by

standing that they will buy provisions, etc. of their employers. It was similar to the American system of company houses, company scrip, etc.

36 Some of these Acts had not been passed when this propaganda was at its height, but all were on the Conservative program.

37 *Primrose League Gazette*, September 7, 1889.

criticism of the Act by those whose interests lay elsewhere. Grand Council was informed by an agent that much feeling had been aroused in Lancashire by the Compensation Act, many people considering it almost a breach of faith by the Government. (This charge suggests that by this time the Conservative Party was expected to defend the interests of industry quite as much as the Liberal Party, if not more.) Grand Council advised the agent that " Great schemes of social change for a time always upset trade." [38]

The League continued to exploit the Act and its successor of 1900 as evidence of the Conservative concern for the worker. In 1901 the League published leaflets concerning agricultural labor and the Workmen's Compensation Act. Walter Long, who was largely responsible for the Act, told an agricultural habitation that the agricultural laborer had only to make out three cards to receive benefits under the Act.

But by this time the Conservatives were definitely put on the defensive by their opponents. A Liberal leaflet of 1906 entitled " What the Tories have done for Labour " reviewed the Tory record from 1903 to 1905. It accused them of voting against peaceful combination bills, against taxation of land values, against the Miners' Eight Hour Bill: of refusing to amend or extend their Workmen's Compensation Act of 1897; of opposing further protection for railway servants; and of obstructing land reform proposed in the interests of tenants.[39] A Labour pamphlet of 1904 said of the Tory record that though the Conservatives had promised in 1895 to enact thirteen measures of social reform, they had passed only one of any consequence to workers—the Workmen's Compensation Act—and that was turning out to be a gold mine for lawyers.[40]

It is not difficult to reconcile these conflicting claims. The Primrose League propagandists dwelt on the paternalistic leg-

38 *Minutes of the Grand Council of the Primrose League*, July 15, 1897.

39 *Liberal Leaflets and Pamphlets*, 1905-06, Leaflet No. 2061.

40 Glyde, Councillor C. A., *Liberal and Tory Hypocrisy during the Nineteenth Century*. Pamphlets for the People, No. 1.

islation which the Tories had set down to their credit—most of it before 1900. The Liberals and Labourites emphasized the new type of legislation which the Tories had defeated—legislation definitely aimed to increase the power of the poorer class. It must be remembered too that at this time the Conservatives had been in power almost continuously for twenty years. Whatever achievements were made in this time must necessarily be theirs. Therefore the Primrose League could point to Conservative achievements while their opponents could point to Conservative sins of omission. Finally we find that the Primrose League and their opponents were referring to different periods of legislation—the former emphasizing the achievements of the nineteenth century; the latter abusing the Tories for lack of achievement in the young twentieth. In this they were supported by no less a Tory authority than Sir John Gorst.

Yet on the other hand, the Conservatives were subjected to much criticism from their own die-hards for going too far with their social reform, and some of these grumblings found their way into the pages of the *Primrose League Gazette*. We find an article in 1890 describing the criticism of the Government's social reform program from within its own ranks. Some Conservatives denounced the Allotments Act [41] as a " distinctly confiscatory measure "; others charged that the Education Act " promised free education not required by the working classes in their present state of prosperity." The Government had refused protection to workers from " the tyranny of Trade Unionism." No adequate relief had been afforded to Agriculture. The First Lord of the Treasury was censured for " repeating the fallacy that tithes were national property." And the *Primrose League Gazette* reporter ended: " I could add to these counts." [42]

The Primrose League itself never made any direct attack on any of the Government measures. It even claimed credit for

41 This Act increased the land available to workers for cultivation in small plots.

42 *Primrose League Gazette*, August 9, 1890.

the Conservatives for legislation passed by the Liberals during
one of their brief periods of power, notably the Railway
Servants' Act and the Parish Councils Act, which were passed,
the League said, only because they had Conservative support.
The League passed resolutions in February of 1894 thanking
the House of Lords for taking a stand on the Employers' Liability Act and drawing one of its teeth. The League said that
the Lords, " had dared to infuse a drop of liberty into the Bill "
by inserting a contracting out clause, and that " it had gone by
the board." [43] The resolutions passed by habitations indicate
a general agreement on the part of the League with the
Liability Act.

IV

The eight-hour day was a live issue during the last twenty
years of the century. An election couplet of 1892 ran:

> Eight hours work, eight hours play
> Eight hours sleep, and eight bob a day.

During the early nineties the topic provided one of the most
fruitful sources of debate at habitation meetings.[44] Grand
Council instructed Primrose League speakers to stress that its
adoption would mean a negation of individual freedom.[45] Pettifer would tell Tory gatherings that an eight-hour day for rail-
waymen, as for other working class groups, could best be
realized by a rising volume of trade, and so increased dividends,
and then inevitably shorter hours. He made a speech to the
National Union (reprinted as a Primrose League pamphlet)
declaring that if such a measure as the eight-hour day was
really necessary, it should emanate from the trade unions concerned and not from Parliament.

43 *Morning Post*, February 22, 1894.

44 In 1885 the House of Commons had passed such legislation, but it had
been laid aside.

45 *Minutes of the Grand Council of the Primrose League,* December 21,
1890.

The *Morning Post* probably echoed the average Tory reaction to the subject in its editorial on the Engineers' Strike of 1897. " If the men really want to fight their employers," it said, " they may be advised to find more rational ground than an eight-hour day, which spells the decline of this country, and the advance of those foreign states where labour is not so exacting." [46]

Little of the spirit of the ten-hour crusade remained in the Conservative Party leadership. The subject was now inextricably linked in the Conservative mind with a fear of the mounting strength of organized labor as a menace to private capital.

Another contemporary problem was the protection of the community and the workers themselves from the dangers of sweating. Lord Randolph Churchill had drawn attention to the findings of the House of Lords Commission on sweated industry. During the winter of 1888 public interest had been aroused over the conditions accompanying sweated labor in the East End. There was a tendency to attribute sweating to competition from immigrant labor, a charge largely disproved by the investigators for the Booth report. This indignation over sweated labor was reflected at Primrose League meetings during the year.[47]

But the issue which dominated the scene during the eighties and nineties was trade unionism, which many people took to be the beginning of a general social upheaval. Not many decades before Marx had predicted the coming of the socialist state in the near future. A few enthusiastic British Marxists fixed on England as likely to be the first breach in the citadel of capitalism. In the mid-eighties the Social Democratic Federation sprang into prominence with its propaganda for the philosophy of Marx, and it assumed exaggerated proportions in the eyes of

46 July 2, 1897.

47 No legislation was to result from this agitation. Lord Dunraven resigned from the Commission in disgust. Even after the Boer war no legislation was passed to cope with the problem of sweated industries.

those who were fearful of an immediate social revolution. Hyndman, the founder of the Federation, predicted that a popular uprising would come in the year 1889, the centenary of the French Revolution.

The eighties seemed to provide the economic setting. The security of the working class was violently shaken by a series of trade depressions, bringing widespread unemployment in their wake. The depression of 1877 was followed by a boom in 1882, which in turn gave way to one of the blackest depressions of the century, whose trough was reached in 1886. At that time some trade unions reported 23½% of their membership out of work. Among the unskilled, who were not yet organized into unions in any effective sense, the Labour Commission of 1886 found that unemployment was at its worst.[48]

The depression year 1886 was made memorable in January by "Black Sunday." A procession of unemployed marching under the auspices of the Social Democratic Federation found its way barred by the police as it was proceeding to demonstrate in Trafalgar Square. The marchers slaked their excitement by surging into the West End, thereby leaving an indelible impression on many West Enders whose ideas of revolution had hitherto been less concrete. In the course of the next year came "Bloody Sunday", a great mass demonstration in Trafalgar Square, when Cunninghame Graham and John Burns, leading a crowd of unemployed, attempted an attack on the police.

A similar clash with the police occurred in the famous riot of 1888, when the first Marxist martyr fell in England. This tragedy was immortalized by William Morris in the hymn which ends with the stirring lines:

> Not one, not one, but thousands must they slay
> But one and all, if they would dusk the day.

[48] Great Britain, *Final Report of the Royal Commission on Depression of Trade and Industry (Parliamentary Paper), 1886,* Appendix A, 50.

It was the great Dockers' Strike, however, that was to throw the whole question of trade unionism as a workers' weapon into bold relief, and to link for many the "socialist menace" to the respectable trade unionism of the sixties and seventies. When the strike broke out it seemed inconceivable, not only to the ruling class but to the labor leaders as well, that this rabble, this scum of the laboring class, to be seen for weeks winding in a daily procession up from the docks through the West End, could ever hold out more than a few days. That the straggling, uncouth ranks could ever hold firm against the forces arrayed against them seemed fantastic.

After a fortnight, surrender loomed inevitable when suddenly contributions began to pour in from Australia. The contributions for the strikers came from the football clubs, from the Australian Salvation Army and from many other groups. Aid was to follow, equaling that from Australia, from all sections of the British public. By the end of the strike the general public was found to have subscribed over ten thousand pounds while the contributions from trade unionists and socialist groups amounted to some four thousand pounds.[49]

Even such a staunchly Tory party organ as *England* opposed the strike with considerable moderation and qualification, rebuking the absentee dock shareholders for leaving the conduct of affairs to mortgagees, directors and lawyers. After five weeks of processions, Cardinal Manning, as intermediary, carried to strike headquarters terms spelling almost complete victory for the dockers.

Following the successful end of the Dockers' Strike, the Primrose League issued an official statement of its attitude on trade unionism: "One of the most important advantages enjoyed by workingmen is the right of combination to obtain by peaceful means increased wages, shorter hours, and better conditions of labour," the declaration begins, and ends with, " It

---

49 Smith, H. L. and Nash, V., 187, *The Story of the Dockers' Strike*. The United States sent £29. 0s. 4.d; Germany £51. 5s.; Belgium £21. 10s. 4d.; and France £6. 18s. 11d.

ought not to be forgotten that these measures of Justice and of liberty are due to Conservative Governments, which have enabled British workingmen peacefully to protect their own interests by combining together under the protection of the law, and which have rendered it possible for labour disputes to be settled without riot and violence." [50] But a month after the Dockers' strike the *Gazette* was insisting that trade was leaving the port of London as a result of the strike.

A year after the great strike, the Primrose League tried to make its stand on trade unionism clearer, declaring: " The Primrose League as an Association does not set its face against trades unionism, and lays no ban on strikes. So long as the ends of the strike are worthy, the League will go along, but it is opposed to its tyrannous use by unions and to persecution of those not joining. To the strikers it only asks: Is the game worth the candle? " [51]

The League often attacked the trade union as a monopoly, with the closed shop as its ultimate objective. It persistently warned trade unionists to keep away from any tie-up with the socialists. It commended the Trades Union Congress of 1890 for showing workers what it thought of the revolutionary movement. It congratulated the South London tramway workers for making their own agreement with their company, " without troubling Messrs. Tom Mann and John Burns." [52]

A plea for " free " labor, or, in other words, unorganized labor, was not explicitly set forth by the Primrose League, but was often implied in its comment on current affairs in the trade union field. For instance, the *Gazette* said of the Australian strike of 1890, " We cannot condemn the employers for holding out; they are fighting a great battle in defense of free labor." [53]

[50] *Primrose League Gazette*, January 11, 1890.

[51] *Ibid.*, October 3, 1891.

[52] *Primrose League Gazette*, June 21, 1890. Mann and Burns were prominent socialist labor leaders.

[53] *Ibid.*, June 21, 1890.

Of the Trades Union Congress's suggestion that municipal factories and workshops be established for the unemployed it exclaimed that free labor " would be driven into the workhouse at the bidding of the Dockers' Union and Mr. John Burns." [54] In an article on the Tilbury and Gas strikes, the *Gazette* declared itself opposed to tyranny by the unions.

Articles on " The Exclusion of Free Labour," enlarge on this argument. The attempt of Wilson of the Transport Workers' Union at Cardiff to prevent non-union men from signing up for sailing is condemned by the *Gazette*. " Working men must be taught to think for themselves," the *Gazette* remarks, " and the Primrose League can supply them with the information upon which to base their mental processes." [55] Sympathetic strikes were condemned as well as the closed shop. When the Seamen's and Firemen's Union proposed to join the Glass Stokers' Union in 1889 in their fight against the Company, the *Gazette* was vehement in condemnation.

On other grounds, too, the League viewed trade unionism with alarm: it revived the " close Guild idea; " it kept employment from rising; it favored the weaker at the expense of the better equipped worker; and last, a combination of labor might provoke a combination of capital, and in that event labor would be the loser.

Yet the League admitted in 1892 that, as its three main principles were not directly at stake, a position on strikes should be the individual concern of its members.[56] Apropos of the Dockers' strike and of the Scottish Railway strike, a resolution was proposed by the League asking for an inquiry and possibly for legislation by the Board of Trade to regulate hours.

Throughout the winter of 1892-93 in various parts of England and Scotland a series of open meetings to discuss social and industrial questions of the day were held under the auspices

54 *Ibid.*, September 20, 1890.

55 *Ibid.*, February 14, 1891.

56 *England*, March 26, 1892.

of the Primrose League. Such topics as " The Accumulation of Wealth by the Individual," and " The Source of Wealth " or " Problems of Unemployment," " Trade Unionism," " Strikes and Lockouts' " were reported as having provoked a spirited and varied discussion.

Grand Council directed that at these meetings there should be free discussion from the floor and that the meeting should be open, but that the Primrose League representative should always introduce the topic and summarize the discussion at the end of the evening. All references to party or " party cries " were to be taboo during the meetings.[57] It was reported that at one of these meetings in the East End, the audience became so incensed by " the chaff and sarcasm " of the speaker, presumably from the League, that it was necessary to terminate the meeting suddenly by singing the national anthem. This last manoeuvre was reported to have had the effect of causing the socialists to crush their hats down upon their heads and rush outside the hall to wait in the rain for the appearance of the speaker.[58]

An Independent Labour pamphlet of the period, reminding workers that the Conservative workingmen's associations had not succeeded in placing a single worker in the House of Commons, counseled the laborer to " cast off the Primrose Dames and the Liberal Federation " and go in for " the workingman proper." [59]

V

Though the suburbs were spreading far out into the country in the mid-eighties, the great Georgian houses still stood secure in their parks, and the face of the countryside looked much as it had since the early Whig days. Yet in reality a profound

57 *Morning Post*, October 19, 1892.

58 *Primrose League Gazette*, October 31, 1891.

59 *A Political Thunderbolt: A General Election Address to the Men and Women Workers of the Nation*, by Uncle John's Nephew, 90.

change had come over the agricultural life of England. The change might have been evident much sooner had not foreign wars saved agriculture from 1846 onwards. It collapsed in the seventies, a victim to peace and foreign competition.

With a growing realization that the monopoly by Great Britain of the world market was slipping, had come slowly a conviction that the slump in agricultural rents and wages which had set in at the end of the seventies and deepened in the beginning of the next decade, was no passing depression, but in the nature of a permanent condition.[60] The witnesses before the agricultural commission of 1881 had stressed the " dripping seasons " which had preceded that year as a prime cause of the slump, but the witnesses before the Agricultural Commission of 1893-94 admitted that the problem was essentially one of world prices.[61]

Prices for agricultural products were falling constantly from the seventies onwards, except for a slight rally at the end of the eighties, and wheat reached its lowest point for the century in the disastrous year of 1894.[62] That rents were not only off, but falling at a disastrous rate was the burden of the testimony of landlords and farmers before the Commissioners after the seventies.[63] There was a considerable migration of Scotch and

60 Ernle, The Right Honble. Lord (Prothero, Rowland Edmund), *English Farming, Past and Present*, 374-78. Agricultural prosperity had ceased to rise as early as 1862. By 1874 the tide had turned, falling swiftly with a short respite in the last half of the eighties through to the end of the century. Ernle, *op. cit.*, Chapter XVIII.

61 Great Britain. *Report of the Royal Commission on Labour* (*Parliamentary Papers*) Minutes of Evidence, 1893-94, Vol. XXXV.

62 In 1855 the price of wheat was 74/8, its peak for the century; in 1874 it was 55/9; in 1879 43/10; in 1887 32/6 and in 1894 22/10. Climbing slowly, it reached 34/0 in 1898, 26/11 in 1900 and 29/8 in 1905. Ernle, *op. cit.*, Appendix III, 441. Taken from Agricultural Statistics, 1910, Vol. XLV, Part III.

63 The Agricultural Commission of 1894 was told that eight large estates in Essex reported that during the preceding thirteen years their rent had fallen off by 52.6 per cent.

Lancashire farmers into Essex, Hereford and Suffolk to buy farms for speculation. Many landlords before the Commission of 1894 estimated that their land had fallen in value by one half, and some thought that the worst fall in rents since 1869 had occurred in the nine or ten years before 1894.[64] From time to time the *Morning Post* printed announcements of general reductions of rent by Tory landlords.[65]

Marked depopulation of the rural areas occurred between 1880 and 1905. While in 1851 it was estimated that one out of every six males in Britain was engaged in agriculture, in 1881 the number had fallen to one in ten and by 1911 to one in twenty. Census returns show the farm laboring group to have diminished from 1871 to 1901 by about one third.[66]

One could drive fifteen miles through parts of Norfolk without passing a single tenant farm in 1891, according to one observer.[67] A decline of ten per cent in the farm laboring population in Norfolk is reported for the period from 1891 to 1911.[68]

A glance at the prevailing wage rates for agricultural labor over this period explains the exodus.[69] Wages were falling steadily till the end of the eighties. A slight recovery in real wages occurred between 1889 and 1892, but this was followed by a sharp fall. From the middle of the nineties wages rose

64 Great Britain. *Report of the Royal Commission on Agriculture (Parliamentary Papers)*, 1894, XVI, Part III, 284. (Evidence of George Adams).

65 See March 23, 1888, for example.

66 962,348 in 1871; 870,798 in 1881; 780,707 in 1891 and 620,986 in 1901. Ernle, *op. cit.*, Appendix VI, 459.

67 Graham, P. A., *The Rural Exodus*, 11.

68 Springall, L. M., *Labouring Life in Norfolk Villages, 1834-1918*, 122.

69	1872	1882	1892	1898
North and Northwest	17/4	16/9	16/5	16/11
West Midland and S. W.	13/1	12/10	11/10	12/11
Eastern and N. E.	13/2	13/	12/7	12/8
S. E. and E. Midland	14/10	14/1	13/	13/10

—Ernle, *op. cit.*, Appendix IX, 468-70.

slightly as a readjustment to the contracted labor market took place. Migration to the towns or overseas had left a slightly better wage for those left behind.

Measured in pounds and shillings, it might seem that the landlord and the farmer bore the larger part of the burden of the crash of agriculture. But when we look at the wage figures, even after the recovery in the nineties, it is clear that the laborer, living as he did so near to the starvation line, must have suffered most of the three classes involved. In the eighties his condition was no better than the picture painted in Kingsley's " Yeast," written some forty years earlier:

> We quarrelled like brutes, and who wonders,
> What self respect could we keep,
> Worse housed than your hacks and your pointers
> Worse fed than your hogs and your sheep.[70]

So ran the polemic of the philosophical gamekeeper of " Yeast," which he read aloud to the astounded squire. The lines ring through the eighties and nineties.

The Agricultural Commission of 1894 admitted that it could not escape the painful feeling that too frequently and too commonly the agricultural laborers lived under conditions which were both physically and morally unwholesome and offensive.[71] One-and two-room cottages were still common in many rural areas, and the report found the housing situation one of the least satisfactory in the rural picture. Low rents and low prices were, of course, offered by landlords to explain their inability to provide better cottages.[72] Rural housing shared—and more than shared—in the generally very low standard of housing for

---

70 Kingsley, Charles, *Yeast. A Problem.*

71 Great Britain. *Final Report of the Royal Commission on Labour, The Agricultural Labourer (Parliamentary Papers)*, 1894, XXXV, 210.

72 Rents were, of course, low. In parts of Norfolk in 1892 an average cottage rental was 1/; in Wales it was often 6d. It must be remembered that emigration led to a wider choice of cottages.—Graham, P. A., *op. cit.*, 98.

the working class as revealed in the Booth and Rowntree Reports.

To the bad housing, and generally low standard of living was added a new impoverishment of social life. In the seventies the National Agricultural Union had provided a community life in villages where it often existed in no other form. Laborers with their families marched in demonstrations and came together in social gatherings of the Union, united in a common cause which gave meaning and purpose to their otherwise uneventful lives. The collapse of the Union left a void in village life, and the people had to face the long dreary evenings again, as well as a growing economic insecurity.

Much of the support of the agricultural union movement had come from the village artisans and small tradesmen who, as the depression grew, moved to the towns in fairly large numbers. With the loss of this politically conscious element another social and intellectual stimulus was withdrawn. When the agricultural laborers were enfranchised by Gladstone a few years later, and so became of political concern to both parties, a very real gap of political and social importance remained to be filled.[73]

Dubbed by its Liberal adversaries "a League of farm labourers and servant girls," the Primrose League found in the life of the farm laborer of forty years ago a special field for its efforts.

"One of the reasons for the depletion of the villages . . . is the dullness of village life," the *Gazette* told its readers. "Work on the land ceases, as a rule, soon after sunset, and it is not resumed till sunrise. Thus, in the winter there is an interval even for those who have anything to do—which not all have—of, perhaps twelve hours, nine of which, at most, can be spent in sleep. There is nothing absolutely to do but sleep between work and work. There is nothing whatever going on in the village. The farmer smokes and reads the weekly papers

73 See Seeley, E., *Village Trade Unions*, and Springall, L. M., *Labouring Life in Norfolk Villages, 1834-1918.*

and broods mournfully over his difficulties. The labourers cannot afford much smoke, and cannot read with ease and pleasure even if they have anything to read. For all the village inhabitants of every class the slow evening is dullness unutterable; night after night, through the long, dark, cold winter, they all have to sit at home, with no alternative but going to the almost equally dull and far too expensive public-house parlour. Into this state of affairs comes the Primrose League, like a great beam of brilliant interest. It creates a fellowship between rich and poor, between squire and schoolmaster, between vicar and blacksmith, between farmer and labourer." [74]

The League's informal methods were especially well adapted to village life. A love of finery and of dressing up, not peculiar of course to the villager, but often especially strong in him, if judged by his delight in Templar and other decorations, was most effectively satisfied by League badges and clasps. His loneliness disappeared in the congenial warmth of community singing. His boredom vanished in the glow of entertainment suited to his tastes.

The *Illustrated London News* waxed eloquent on the diversion offered by a habitation meeting. " Crowded into a small schoolroom or other public room are farmers from miles around, ' gentlemen's servants from all the Great Houses,' innkeepers, blacksmiths and the families of these as well as the labourers. A concert, a half hour of political oratory, ' extinct ' dances with community singing during the waits, the labourers drift in and out from the nearby Pub, and one leads in ' Hurrah for the Red, White and Blue,' and finally at eleven o'clock, the schoolmaster, who has been the leading spirit, calls home.

" It is, in short," concludes the *Illustrated News,* " a return to Merrie England's traditions for the village folks. But mark! It is politics all the same: Every woman, as well as every man there, will feel a degraded and contemptible traitor if, when the election comes, they fail to work for ' the Primrose Cause.'

74 *Primrose League Gazette,* October 1, 1901.

Who invented this village and city political union of sexes?
He or she deserves a medal of commendative honour." [75]

The Primrose League set up a number of circulating libraries
in villages, and stocked them with Dickens, Marryat, Wilkie
Collins and Florence Montgomery, as well as their own
political leaflets. One such library in Buckinghamshire contained
" books on the Queen, lives of statesmen, Ireland and how
people live there, allotments, books of Parish law, a very amusing pamphlet, the Irish Green Book, and political leaflets." [76]

Workers with the red vans of the Land Restoration League
in 1892 commented: " The old English sports have disappeared,
and in their place you have the Primrose tea-meeting, at which
you may sell your citizen rights for a few slices of cake and a
display of juggling (political and otherwise)." " Education? "
they scoffed, " well, have you not the ' Reading Room ' (carefully closed on your one leisure day) from which the vicar's
wife thoughtfully excludes all papers (e. g. The Church Reformer) which might give offense to her Uncle-in-Law at the
Hall? " [77]

Lord George Hamilton described the Irish Nationalists' successful tactics in agricultural constituencies, their skill in making themselves at home in the local public houses, and so in
making friends easily and gaily with the voters. He said that
their friendly footing with the rural constituents had rather
nonplussed the Conservatives until the Primrose League came
to the rescue.[78]

75 *Illustrated London News*, November 19, 1887. (Reprinted *Primrose
League Gazette*, November 26, 1887.)

76 *Primrose League Gazette*, August 18, 1888. In 1915 only 2.5% of the
rural population had access to public libraries (in contrast to 89% of the
urban population).—*Carnegie Trustees 1915 Report*, quoted by Courtney, J.,
Contrywomen in Council, 88.

77 " About Red Vans," *The Church Reformer*, XII, 161 (1892).

78 Hamilton, Rt. Hon. Lord George, *Parliamentary Reminiscences and
Reflections, 1886-1906*, II, 76.

Until the Primrose League came upon the scene, the *active* political influences in the country were almost exclusively Liberal. Nonconformist preachers and tradesmen, key figures in the villages, were usually Liberal, and the Anglican vicars had less influence with the laborer than the nonconformist. Much of the leadership of the agricultural union movement had come from the nonconformist ministry,[79] and this movement, though it was dying in the eighties, left behind it a tradition of loyalty to the Liberal Party.

An amusing comment on the relationship of church and politics is furnished by a retort made in parliamentary debate, in which Balfour uttered the constant Conservative charge of undue political influence by Irish priests in their constituencies, to which Courtney countered : " The honourable gentleman represents an agricultural constituency in England, and would he not be delighted if he could get the Primrose League parsons to take the smock-frocked labourers to the poll to vote in his favour? " Anglican vicars or Anglican schoolmasters often presided over local Primrose habitation activities, as they did for that matter over Parish Councils, for as a class their general political complexion was Tory.

It is probable that the more feudal nature of rural life made the influence of the Primrose League of much more importance in the country than in the urban districts. There the influence of the classes over the masses was strongest, and there it died most slowly. It was upon this influence that the Primrose League counted most heavily to safeguard Conservative interests and to win votes for the Conservative Party.

So far as active Conservative propaganda was concerned, the League found the rural areas practically virgin soil. The popular Conservative organizations were, and remained, hopelessly inept at dealing with village audiences. The Chief Agent of the Conservative Party, Captain Middleton, complained that

79 Joseph Arch had been a noncomformist preacher, and George Edwards, another agricultural union leader, a Primitive Methodist Reader.

the usual party speaker, confronted by an audience of twenty agricultural workers, opened with a long account of affairs in Ireland, proceeded to a discussion of foreign policy, pausing to touch on colonial federation, and then, with a word or two of abuse of his opponents, would sit down. Captain Middleton sighed as he thought of the comparative responsiveness of town Tory audiences, and even more of the rival Liberal meetings, " where all burst to speak." [80]

The Primrose League recommended a special technique to political speakers and party organizers in dealing with rural audiences. It served as interpreter in the rural areas for the party which claimed to represent the great agricultural interests of the country. Its own organizers were at pains to adjust their political propaganda to the peculiarities of rural psychology. For instance, the term " Estates " as it appeared in the Disraelian motto: " Maintenance of the Estates of the Realm " proved a source of confusion to rural audiences, and of embarrassment to speakers.[81] The difficulty was reported to Grand Council, who had special leaflets on the League's land policy prepared to appeal to agricultural laborers.

Results began to show remarkably early. A contrast in the election returns in 1886 with those of 1885 revealed that the influence of the Primrose League was already beginning to make itself felt. During the parliamentary elections of 1885, the newly enfranchised voters took comparatively little interest in the issues, but when they did vote, on the whole followed the Liberal tradesmen and nonconformist preachers. In the elections of the following year, the agricultural laborers stayed away from the polls in large numbers, stunned by the growing economic dislocation, and feeling nothing but apathy toward the Irish issue. But there were some exceptions where they went

80 Middleton, R. W. E., *A Speech on Organization read before the United Club*, December 5, 1889.

81 *Minutes of the Grand Council of the Primrose League*, May 18, 1893.

to the polls and voted Conservative, having been successfully propagandized by the newly born Primrose League.[82]

As the agricultural crisis grew worse, various sects of land reformers began to present their programs to the agricultural worker. Earlier agricultural unionism had not committed itself to a program of land nationalization, but by the eighties and nineties the single taxers, socialists and the Land Restoration League raised the issue. The red vans of the Land Restoration League rolled through the eastern counties with a double message of nationalization and labor organization, thus linking the ideas of unionism and land reform.[83]

A writer of the period showed how the farm laborer reacted to the two opposite streams of propaganda which were playing upon him. " He hearkens respectfully to the Knights and Dames of the Primrose League, and makes a plaything of the badges they give him. He sidles off to the agitator's meeting, and comes back with the conviction that he is a wronged and down-trodden martyr, yet full of doubts in regard to the advice he has listened to." [84]

The Primrose League's land policy was simple. One of its leaflets read: " The Conservatives want to remove all unjust burdens from the land, so that it may produce all it can and make us more independent of foreign supplies—they want to take away every just grievance in regard to tithes, unfair rates, and the carriage of produce." As to land tenure, " The improved value of agricultural land since feudal times is the property of those who created it, or of those who had acquired the right to it by inheritance or purchase." [85]

Landlordism, League organizers pointed out, was not confined to the Tories, and they cited a long list of Liberal land-

82 Springall, M. L., *op. cit.*, 111.

83 For an account of the activities of the vans in 1890 and 1892, see *The Church Reformer*, 1891-92.

84 Graham, P. A., *op. cit.*, 91.

85 *Primrose League Gazette*, August 15, 1891.

owners. They dwelt at length on the large and increasing proportion of rural distress borne by the landlord and the farmer.[86] They cited the Tory legislation on allotments, housing and small holdings. They quoted from the Tory record such measures as the Artisans' and Labourers' Dwellings Improvement Act of Cross, Home Secretary in Disraeli's last cabinet; the Allotment Act of 1887 (there was an increase in allotments of over 100,000 between 1887 and 1892); the Glebe Lands Act of 1888; an Allotment Act of 1891; the Small Holdings Act of 1892; the Land Transfer Act of 1897; and the Agricultural Holdings Act of 1900.[87]

In addition the Salisbury Government had occupied itself with Irish land reform, and had set down to its credit the Land Purchase Act of 1887. In 1891 another Land Purchase Act was passed when Balfour was Secretary for Ireland. After the Conservative return to power in 1895, they added to their record a Land Amendment Act, a Land Law Act and, finally, the Comprehensive Irish Land Act of 1903.[88] Under this Act more than 253,000 Irish peasants became owners of their own farms between 1903 and 1913.

It was true that the evidence before the Commission on Agricultural Depression in 1894 reported little demand for allotments. In England especially allotments alone seemed weak reeds on which to base hopes for relief. But a Cork habitation of the Primrose League passed a resolution of satisfaction at the Government Land Act in 1897, and added its regret, in view of the provisions of the Allotments Act, " that no ade-

86 An anti-Liberal pamphlet of 1884 lists eight members of the Liberal Cabinet of that date as owning a total of over 120,000 acres, or an average of 15,000 apiece.—Fielding, Thomas, *Radical Hypocrisy; or War, Waste and Corruption, being an Eye-Opener for Working Men and a Plea for Political Honesty.*

87　37 and 38, Vic. Ch. 59　　　55 and 56, Vic. Ch. 31
　　50 and 51, Vic. Ch. 26　　　60 and 61, Vic. Ch. 65
　　51 and 52, Vic. Ch. 20　　　63 and 64, Vic. Ch. 50
　　54 and 55, Vic. Ch. 33

88 3 Edw. VII, Ch. 37.

quate provision is made in the Bill to extend to landlords similar advantages by way of Government loans and other means." [89]

During the nineties the Primrose League came in contact with Lord Winchelsea's National Agricultural Union. Founded in 1892, the Union aimed at uniting the three classes involved in agriculture,—the landlord, the farmer, and the farm laborer, —in a common effort to exert pressure on Parliament in the interests of agriculture, and eventually to form an agricultural bloc in Parliament. The National Agricultural Union was thus in no way a part of the trade union movement. In fact, it helped to keep the trade unions in rural areas dormant during the nineties, and to that extent probably weakened Liberal prospects, and contributed to Tory and Primrose League successes in agricultural constituencies. [90]

Lord Winchelsea addressed Primrose League habitations, and there was some exchange of speakers between the two bodies, and some overlapping of membership. Grand Council officially expressed hearty sympathy with the National Agricultural Union, but ruled that habitations as such might not join it, though their individual members were free to do so. [91]

A story of the election of 1885 written for children by a Primrose Dame [92] tells the tale of how the little son of the Lord of the Manor, Lord Dashleigh, wins the election for the Tory candidate, his uncle, just returned a hero from the Soudan campaign. In spite of much seditious talk in the village of " a cow and three acres," by the neighboring landlord (lately raised to the peerage), the boy persuades one of his father's oldest dependents, Old Gammon, to affix his mark for the Tory candidate with his dying breath. This vote of Old Gammon turns out to be the very one that decides the election!

89 *Primrose League Gazette*, June, 1897.

90 Springall, L. M., *op. cit.*, 102.

91 *Minutes of the Grand Council of the Primrose League*, January 26, 1893.

92 "A Little Primrose Knight," by a Primrose Dame.

Of the death of the old retainer the story says, " His work in the world was over, and he had done it honestly and well; serving the Dashleighs all his life, and even in his latest act, for had not his vote decided the fate of the election, and so saved the district from the subversive Liberals ? "

VI

Since the Primrose League made such a point of submerging its labor appeal in its more general one, it is difficult to estimate or evaluate the role of the League as distinct from the party in popularizing the Conservative cause with the new electorate. Certainly it enrolled a large number of working people under its banner. From a total of nine hundred and fifty-seven in 1884, the numbers of associates or working class members grew by great strides, and by 1891 they numbered nearly one million.[93] In 1901, it will be remembered that out of a League membership of slightly over one million and a half, the associates accounted for over one million, four hundred thousand members.

The Primrose League's most conspicuous achievement was its success in penetrating and taking root in the rural areas. The *Primrose League Gazette* estimated that of its reported membership at least 57% were either agricultural laborers or persons living in small towns.[94]

As in recent years, when a large portion of the working class vote has still gone to the Conservative Party, so in the League's heyday, it was probably its appeals to tradition which won the largest number of adherents to the party which it served. This was especially true in the last part of the nineteenth century, before the rise of the Labour Party, when the social pattern in rural areas still bore the imprint of an earlier age.

After the turn of the century, a dawning of consciousness of class interest on the part of the working class changed the political complexion of England. There were some who ascribed the crushing defeat of the Conservatives in 1906 to a neglect

93 See Appendix III.
94 June 30, 1888.

of social reform, and to a fatal obliviousness to the rising political power of labor. Sir John Gorst and other Conservatives ascribed the disastrous election to the failure of the party to occupy itself during its long lease of power with such crying evils as unemployment, sickness, bad housing, and malnutrition. These evils were brought home to imperialists as well as to social reformers by the Report on Physical Deterioration of 1903, which exposed the numbers of working class recruits turned down as physically unfit for military service in the Boer War.

" Since the death of Mr. Disraeli," Gorst wrote after the 1906 débâcle, " the leaders of the Tory Party have been always too weak to protect the interests of the workers against any fixed determination of the capitalists." [95]

The ensuing years proved Gorst a true prophet. From that time onward the working class looked first to the Liberals, and then to the Labour Party, to realize their new practical objectives. Housing, nutrition, old age pensions, sickness insurance, and the minimum wage were the issues of the day, and the splendid vagueness of the Primrose League was superseded.

The time had come when neither the traditional appeal of the party, nor the propaganda technique of the Primrose League could win the majority of working class votes. For the very strength of the League's appeal depended on the reverence for tradition, and the impulse to escape reality into a world brilliant with aristocracy and titles and fêtes in great parks. When these emotional forces yielded to the new working class objective, the League's ability to dramatize them lost its value. There was, to be sure, a renaissance of Conservative strength in the two decades between the two great wars, but the Primrose League's part in it was negligible. It was the child of the Victorian era, and in no phase of its activity is that fact more evident than in its outlook, implicit and explicit, on the class issue.

95 Gorst, Sir John E., *The Children of the Nation. How their Vigour and Health should be promoted by the State,* 221.

CHAPTER VI

"THE MAINTENANCE OF THE IMPERIAL ASCENDANCY OF GREAT BRITAIN"

I

LORD SALISBURY was widely quoted in the press for his tribute to the Primrose League during the Boer War. Addressing Grand Habitation at Albert Hall in May, 1900, he declared, " There is no incident in the history of opinion so striking as the sudden change which has taken place in the latter half of the century in the view which people of the country take in regard to the Empire which they possess. But the strange thing is—if you call it strange," he continued, " that this remarkable change in public opinion is almost absolutely synchronous with the birth and development of the Primrose League." [1]

As after-dinner oratory this comment no doubt hit the mark, but as cool history it would seem to slight the imperialistic leadership of the patron saint of the League. There is no need to begrudge the Primrose League its full honors in turning the balance of public opinion in favor of the Empire, when we acknowledge the equally decisive role of Beaconsfield—and the events of his day—in first awakening the British people to the significance of their imperial position. If we study the signs of the times, we shall probably place the low-water mark of imperialistic sentiment in the late sixties rather than the mid-eighties. From that point on, a rise in the tide can be observed.

In the sixties the Manchester School was in its heyday. The signing of the Anglo-French commercial treaty seemed to indicate that Britain was looking to the best markets and richest sources of supplies for trade expansion rather than to those regions where sentiment might be cultivated to the purchasing point, and raw materials nursed in the hothouses of imperial

1 *Times*, May 9, 1900.

preference agreements. Goldwin Smith's public letters[2] had a profound influence in that decade, reflecting as they did a strong conviction in official and colonial circles of the comparative unimportance of the British colonies to the mother country. Alexander Galt, who was in London in 1866 in connection with the drafting of a constitution for the Dominion of Canada, wrote, " I cannot shut my eyes to the fact that they want to get rid of us." [3]

The creation of the Dominion itself raised the issue in Canadian minds. The union of the several colonies into a single political entity laid the foundation for a greater economic as well as political independence. It set up a formidable power which might be used to resist British aspirations as well as to forward them, unless the interests of both parties were to be served by a policy of cooperation, which of course proved to be the case. There were those who took the federation as a defensive alliance against the United States, though only a small body of public opinion in Canada at that time actually favored annexation to the neighbor to the south. At any rate, Canada's new position was open to a wide variety of interpretations, thus throwing the whole question of imperial relations into the public arena.

The New Zealand question,[4] arising in the late sixties, likewise proved a sounding board for imperial and anti-imperial sentiment. The colonists there were much troubled by attacks from the Maori natives, who believed that the colonists had acquired their lands illegally, and sought to take them back by force. The British Government had been withdrawing its forces from the colonies since 1862, and turned a deaf ear to the demands by the colonists that withdrawal be delayed until their position was secured. When the colonists asked for the guaranty

2 Goldwin Smith, Regis Professor of Modern History at Oxford, was an arch anti-imperialist, and expressed the views of radical separatists in letters which appeared in the *Daily News* in 1861-63.

3 Skelton, O. D., *The Life and Times of Sir Alexander Tilloch Galt,* 410.

4 Folsom, A., *The Royal Empire Society,* 29-30.

of a loan of a million and a half for defense purposes, the Gladstone Government refused it in a note which practically said that Britain had never wanted a colony in New Zealand anyway. The *Spectator,* Liberal and staunchly imperialist, warned that this presaged a dismissal, not only of New Zealand, but of other parts of the Empire as well.

By the late sixties a climax of anti-imperialist sentiment had been reached. Gladstone won the election of 1868 on purely domestic issues; scarcely any allusions to colonial questions were made during the campaign.[5] But that same year saw a turn of the tide. The press began to give more attention to colonial matters; the movement for state-aided emigration got under way, and the Royal Colonial Society was founded. The New Zealand issue stubbornly refused to be forgotten, and the Government's refusal to guarantee a defense loan awakened some spirited opposition at home. The following year the Government softened toward the New Zealanders and agreed to guarantee the loan. " Ministers have changed their policy," the *Spectator* commented on this decision, ". . . and have changed it for the best of all reasons,—because they had begun to discover that their line was not the line of the people of England." [6]

The growing imperialist sentiment among certain influential people led to the formation of the Royal Colonial Society. Its objects were " to facilitate the interchange of experiences among persons representing all the dependencies of Great Britain; to afford opportunities for reading papers, and for holding discussion upon colonial subjects generally, and to undertake scientific, literary and statistical investigations in connection with the British Empire." [7] It made no direct bid for

5 Schuyler, R. L., " The Climax of Anti-Imperialism in England," *Political Science Quarterly,* December, 1921, 544.

6 *Spectator,* May 21, 1870, 632.

7 Folsom, A., *The Royal Empire Society,* 49. Perhaps one of the most direct results of the early work of the Royal Colonial Society was the founding of the Imperial Federation League, in which the Society played a part. For the Royal Colonial Society, see Folsom, A., *op. cit.*; Bodelsen, C. A., *Studies in Mid-Victoriam Imperialism,* 205-14; Boose, J. R., *Memory Serving.*

popular following, but tried to create sentiment in favor of the Empire. It was a strictly non-partisan body from the first. One of its prime movers, Sir Frederick Young, was also an enthusiastic sponsor of the movement for state-aided emigration.

This movement attracted both working class and well-to-do followers. Many of the early imperialists were its enthusiastic supporters, such as Sir Frederick Young, C. W. Eddy, Edward Jenkins, Lord Carnarvon, Sir John Gorst, and J. A. Froude. To such men the movement promised to consolidate and strengthen the ties of Empire through increased colonization from the mother country. To the workers it offered relief for the immediate economic distress at home, so keen at the end of the sixties. Over one hundred thousand workers signed the petition presented to the Queen in 1870 which declared that its signers had " heard with alarm that Your Majesty has been advised to give up the Colonies."

The movement was considered radical in many quarters, and one can imagine that the average manufacturer was deeply concerned at the prospect of the depletion of his labor supply, in spite of the tempting suggestion of the expansion of his overseas market. The *Times* branded the movement as downright communistic. And indeed it might be regarded as a demand by the working class for its share of the benefits of imperial expansion.

As imperialism was by no means a purely upper class movement, it was likewise in no sense a purely Conservative Party movement. Though it was crystallized in the course of its attack on the Gladstone ministry, it united widely varying political elements in that attack. It enlisted the support of many Liberals and of prominent colonials as well.[8] Its ablest literary ally was the radical *Spectator*. And we have seen that it made a strong appeal to the working class, though on purely domestic issues

8 Edward Wilson, R. Torrens and P. F. Labilliere were Australians; Edward Jenkins had spent much of his life in Canada; while Macfie was a Liberal, Torrens an independent Liberal.

the Gladstone program seemed to have a more logical appeal to them.

It was Disraeli, of course, whose leadership brought imperialism into its full flower, though the opposition grew more determined as the cause waxed stronger. In his famous Crystal Palace speech in 1872 Disraeli attempted to graft the new imperialistic spirit on to the older Tory concern for social legislation. These two issues were not destined to travel a parallel course in Tory political history. In fact, they were to be more like Plato's two yoked steeds whose plunging and rearing in opposite directions threatened at times to throw their driver from his seat. Except in the case of Chamberlain and a few others, it was rarely that an ardent advocate of both causes was to be found in the same person.

Nevertheless imperialism became the paramount political issue in the course of the seventies; to that extent Disraeli triumphed. After the acquisition of the Suez Canal shares, it was no longer possible for England to lose her colonies simply because she had forgotten their existence. Imperialism figured largely as an issue in the election of 1880. The defeat of the Tories that year was in part a defeat of their imperialist policy. As prominent an imperialist as Lord Carnarvon wrote of this election, " It is indeed a revelation . . . Imperialism (though there is a true as well as a false imperialism) has not answered." [9] Gladstone in the Midlothian campaign of that same year had insisted that the Liberals were called on to ward off the disastrous effects of Tory centralized control on colonial ties with the mother country.[10] Yet it was after this same election that a Liberal statesman said that after this recoil from the rising tide of imperialism, the country was not likely to have another such recoil for a generation.[11]

9 Hardinge, Sir A., *The Life of Henry Howard Molyneux Herbert, The Fourth Earl of Carnarvon*, 1830-90, III, 49.

10 Knaplund, P., *Gladstone and Britain's Imperial Policy*, 145.

11 Rendel, Lord, *Personal Papers*, 149.

After 1884 the increased electorate itself contributed to the rising enthusiasm for the British Empire. " It is evident," the *Morning Post* warned its readers in 1884, " that the uneducated factors in the new electorate will be particularly alive to the impulse of the moment. In support of this we may quote the example furnished by what has ironically been called the Music Hall of Politics. During the excitement of 1878 it was abundantly evident that a keen and even combative patriotism pervaded the lower strata of society. Radical speakers and writers sneered very much at it in those days. It is none the less certain that they have let loose a vast quantity of the same feeling which had hitherto been without effectual means of expression. In these two considerations lies, then, we believe, the key to the conduct of the new elections." [12]

The educated classes, on the other hand, were profoundly stirred by a book which appeared in 1883. This was *The Expansion of England* by John Robert Seeley, Professor of Modern History at the University of Cambridge. Seeley interpreted modern English history in terms of colonial expansion, and linked the fate of England with the fate of the Empire itself. He maintained that the acquisition and loss of the first British Colonial Empire was the most important fact in modern English history, and that the colonies which she now held were an integral part of England herself. His thesis was not new, but it was a complete exposition of the concept which was taking shape in the mind of the British public at that time, and it became the book of the decade. Eighty thousand copies were sold within two years of publication, it was claimed, and the book was widely reviewed, and constantly referred to in the contemporary press. [13]

12 *Morning Post*, December 12, 1884.

13 Bodelson, C. A., *op. cit.*, 149-176. For other literary influences on the imperialist movement see Hill, Winifred, *The Overseas Empire in Fiction* and " The Literary Inspiration of Imperialism," *Scottish Review*, 1900, XXXV, 262.

A year later, the Imperial Federation League [14] was formed under the presidency of W. E. Forster. The League attempted to formulate a concrete plan for federation, but failed conspicuously in this aim, and contented itself with calling public attention to the need for federation.[15] It took part in arranging the Colonial and Indian Exhibition of 1886,[16] and in other ways contributed to the growing interest and understanding of overseas Britain among the people of the mother country. Garvin, in his life of Joseph Chamberlain, holds the League responsible for spreading " a respectful though vague sense of the greatness of the subject." [17] But diversity of opinion within its ranks as to the form which federation should take, as well as failure to agree on the question of a preferential tariff, prevented the League from doing more than urge Colonial Conferences to take up these matters. These same factors likewise led to the disruption of the League less than ten years after its birth.[18]

14 For the origin of the Imperial Federation League, see Labilliere, F. P., *Imperial Britain* (which can be used almost as a primary source) ; as well as Folsom, A., *op. cit.* For additional material on the organization and history of the Imperial Federation League, see the following: Adams, G. B., " The Rise of Imperial Federation," *American Historical Review*, Report 1894; Bodelson, C. A., *op. cit.;* Cheng, S. C. Y., *Schemes for the Federation of the British Empire*; Crewe, The Marquess of, *Lord Rosebery*; Hardinge, Sir A., *op. cit.*; Reid, T. W., *The Life of William Edward Forster*; Saunders, E. M., *The Life and Letters of the Right Hon. Sir Charles Tupper*.

15 " Kindred Societies Past and Present," *United Empire Journal*, 1915, VI.

16 Bodelson, C. A., *op. cit.*, 209; *Imperial Federation Journal*, January, 1886.

17 Vol. III, 178.

18 *Imperial Federation League Journal*, August 1, 1891. In one of his last letters, W. E. Forster had written, " Our Federation movement is gaining great strength—the idea possesses men's minds; but we might throw it back greatly by any premature plan."—Reid, T. W., *Life of the Right Hon. William Edward Forster*, II, 526. After the demise in 1893 of the Imperial Federation League, three separate organizations carried on various aspects of its work. The United Empire Trade League, founded in 1891, sought to carry on the cause of preferential trade. A military section of the Imperial Federation League, was formed in 1894. The British Empire League, founded two years later, though in practice mostly concerned with trade questions,

By far the most important work of the Imperial Federation League was the calling of the first Colonial Conference in the Jubilee Year 1887. Here for the first time the premiers of the self-governing colonies met together, thus establishing a precedent which has done much to keep the Empire alive until the present day. It is interesting to note today that at this first conference in 1887 Lord Salisbury told the delegates that its purpose was " to form neither a general Union nor a Zollverein, but a Kriegsverein—a combination for purposes of self-defense."

By the end of the eighties the cause of the Empire had triumphed. In spite of the dire prophecies of the opponents of imperialism, Canada had not joined the United States. Dominion subjects indeed appeared to be as much imbued with a romantic nostalgia for the homeland as with a desire for independence. Moreover, the English people, realizing that their industrial and commercial position was no longer impregnable, gave more attention to the colonies, and were prepared to make concessions to them. Such a situation as that in New Zealand in the sixties would have been impossible by the end of the eighties. On the one hand, enormous progress in transportation and communication made the representation in London of far-away Dominions increasingly feasible, and on the other, the same far-away regions were, to that extent, more open to the danger of attack from other European powers.[19] At the same time European and American nationalism, both growing more militant, no doubt played their part as well.

was concerned with the general idea of federation. The Duke of Devonshire, presiding at the Eastbourne Branch of the British Empire League in 1899, declared the League continued the work of the Imperial Federation League's interest in the colonies, " eliminating only that part of its work which had reference to any constitutional or political changes to be brought about in the connection between ourselves and the colonies."—*Morning Post,* May 1, 1899.

19 The first continuously successful Atlantic cable was laid in 1865-66; the Australian cable in 1872, while the Suez Canal was completed in 1869.

II

It remained for some one to develop the latent dramatic possibilities of imperialism. No group or organization was quite so fitted for this task as the young Primrose League, and no other subject afforded quite such an outlet for its histrionic talents. The League was concerned with creating a magnificent enthusiasm for Empire rather than with the petty details of political federation and economic cooperation. Unlike the Imperial Federation League, it never tried to formulate a concrete program for federation. Unlike the Royal Colonial Society, it avoided detailed study of the new problems which arose as the Dominions emerged as political entities. In the field of imperialism, as elsewhere, the League avoided issues, and presented its ideas with that simplicity which is so essential to the popular cause.

The Khartoum disaster, occurring almost at the moment of the League's birth, provided a rallying point for imperialist sentiment. Years later Lord Salisbury was to remind Grand Habitation that the League had strangled two serpents in its infancy—Majuba and Khartoum, and that there had been a reaction in public feeling, first over Majuba and then over General Gordon during the years 1881 to 1885.

General Gordon's expedition to Khartoum [20] in the early part of 1884 was watched with intense interest by the British public, and indeed by the whole of Europe,—by every one, it seemed, except by the British cabinet. A successful uprising of the fanatical Mahdists the previous year had left a series of Egyptian garrisons on the Nile dangerously exposed, and Gordon had been dispatched after considerable delay to rescue them. Gordon apparently did not carry out his original plan, which was to evacuate Khartoum, but tried to hold the city and the Nile valley with the aid of Zobeir Pasha, an Egyptian leader. While the Gladstone Cabinet in London debated whether to extricate Gordon from the difficult position into which he had

20 Allen, B. M., *Gordon*, 113.

manoeuvered himself, the Mahdists surrounded him and laid siege to Khartoum.

The Primrose League, then in its infancy, was profoundly stirred by the fate of General Gordon, and clamored for a more spirited overseas policy on the part of the Gladstone Government. Colonel Burnaby, one of the earliest members of the League, was closely associated with the expedition from the first, and served as a special link between the League and the Khartoum incident throughout the period.[21] Wounded at the battle of El Teb in February, 1884, in the service of the Egyptian Government, Burnaby received the Soudan Medal from the Khedive. He returned to England and made a speech at the inaugural banquet of the League, denouncing the Government for its desertion of General Gordon.[22] The League took up the challenge. On May 3rd, 1884, a Precept was issued to all the habitations enjoining them to hold protest meetings and thereby secure signatures to a petition protesting against the " abandonment." [23]

Meanwhile, the Government was too deeply immersed in the Reform Bill to take any action to rescue Gordon, and he held out longer than any one had believed possible. Wolseley's expedition was sent belatedly in August, and Burnaby went out to

21 Maurice, Maj. Gen. Sir F., *The Life of Lord Wolseley*, 201, 205 n. Colonel Fred Burnaby was the hero of a horseback ride through Asia Minor in 1876, and his account of this exploit, " The Ride to Khiva," went through eleven editions. The son of a clergyman, after leaving Harrow he had gone into the Horse Guards. Standing six feet ten inches in height, and strong enough to lift two ponies off the ground at once, his picturesque appearance and personality made him a popular figure in society, and in the Blues in the seventies. As a young man he had joined the Carlist forces in Spain, and in 1882 he crossed the Channel in a balloon called " The Eclipse." When he was killed at Ablu Khan while on the expedition endeavoring to rescue General Gordon at Khartoum, he was forty-two years old. See Duff, L. B., *Burnaby*; Wright, T., *The Life of Colonel Fred Burnaby*.

22 *The Primrose League, Its Rise, Progress and Constitution. By one of the Staff*, 10.

23 *A Short History of the Formation of the Primrose League. Corrected and Revised by the Founders*.

join it in January of 1885. Twice this desert column, called by Von Moltke " a band not of soldiers but of heroes," marched to attack at Jakhut, and at the Wells of Ablu Khan, while the situation in Khartoum grew hourly more critical.[24] On the second and last trip the British force, made up of the Heavy Camel Corps, and the Naval Brigade, was surrounded and attacked by dervish forces. Though the British drove back the dervishes, and the result was a British victory, at the end of the engagement Colonel Burnaby lay dead with an Arab spear driven through his body. On January 28th the expedition arrived at Khartoum, only to find that the city had fallen two days before, and that Gordon had been killed.

The fall of Khartoum evoked a tremendous burst of indignation at home. Gordon and Burnaby became symbols of British heroism sacrificed by an indifferent Government. Poets sang of Gordon's valor, and the press denounced the Government for its desertion. Even twenty years later the camel harness used by Gordon in the campaign was one of the most popular relics on view at Madame Tussaud's.[25] *Punch* described Burnaby as " a latter-day Palladin, whom death had affronted so often before." In many ways, he personified the novelist's hero of the end of the nineteenth century, as well as that of the early Primrose League.

The League not only joined in the outcry; it kept the indignation at boiling point through the ensuing years, when it might otherwise have subsided. Resolution after resolution at habitation meetings in 1885 condemned the Government for its vacillation in the rescue of General Gordon. When the news of Gordon's death reached England, Abbey habitation passed a resolution ending : " and this meeting trusts that every legitimate pressure will be put on the Government to force them to adopt such a policy as will vindicate the honour of England, avenge the

24 Maurice, Maj. Gen. Sir F., *op. cit.*, 199.

25 Madame Tussaud and Sons Exhibition — *Catalogue of Pictures and Historical Records*, 1901.

Khartoum disaster, and be satisfactory to the people of the nation."

For many years after the disaster, the Conservative press as well as the Primrose League, continued to be preoccupied with the fate of General Gordon. Newspapers featured serials on Gordon, and prize contests for the best poem on such subjects as " The Meeting of Wolseley and Gordon at Khartoum," or " The Death of Colonel Burnaby." [26] On each anniversary of General Gordon's death his statue in London was decorated. Habitations continued to sponsor an endless series of benefits for Gordon Memorial Charitable Funds. In fact, Grand Council found it necessary to issue an official notice to habitations that they were prohibited from using any part of their regular funds for these memorial funds.[27] A tableau depicting the death of General Gordon and announced as " Defeat " was a frequent and popular number at habitation entertainments.

The Afghanistan frontier crisis,[28] following on the heels of the disaster in the Soudan, began to compete with it in popular interest and to draw off some of the excitement over the death of General Gordon. Resolutions at habitation meetings began to couple condemnation of the Government's Khartoum policy with condemnation of its policy " in bringing this country face to face with a terrible war with Russia " and to speak of the " disastrous course of affairs in connection with the Afghan frontier following upon the lamentable events in Egypt extending over the past two years." [29]

About a decade later, the dramatic success of Lord Kitchener in Egypt was to revive the memory of General Gordon for the British public as well as to stimulate renewed interest in Egyp-

26 *England*, January, 1885.

27 *Minutes of the Grand Council of the Primrose League*, November 15, 1888.

28 Gladstone, reversing the policy of Disraeli, had ordered evacuation by British troops from that mountainous and warlike state in 1881.

29 *Morning Post*, March 31, 1885.

tian affairs. After the rout of the Italian military force at
Adowa in 1896 by an Ethiopian army, so profoundly shocking
a defeat to the whole European world, the long planned recon-
quest of the Soudan under Kitchener was set in motion. This
campaign was designed, also, to relieve the pressure on the
Italians.

As the British advanced up the Nile, Soudanese resistance
collapsed at Dongala and then the British force won a decisive
battle at Abbara River and by September, 1898, were outside
Omdurman. With a loss of about ten thousand fighters, the
Soudanese dervishes fell back and the British entered the city.[80]
After the capture of Omdurman, Kitchener pushed forward until at last Khartoum was reached. The fall of Khartoum appeared to the British public in the light of a vindication of
General Gordon's disaster as well as a stirring and colorful
campaign.

London crowds and visitors from the provinces during the
autumn of 1898 made special trips to Madame Tussaud's to
gaze at the new wax group depicting the death of General Gordon over a decade before, and at a representation of Lord
Charles Beresford's attempt to rescue General Gordon on the
steamer Safieh. A portrait model of Captain Marchand, the
French hero in Egypt, now faced one of General Gordon in
the main salon. To commemorate the fall of Khartoum, Madame Tussaud exhibited models of General Gordon, Colonel
Stewart, Colonel Burnaby, Lord Hartington (who had delayed
sending relief to General Gordon), and even of the Mahdi.[81]

A tremendous demand arose at this time in Primrose habitations for lectures and lantern slides on the Soudan, and this
continued for two or three years with almost undiminished
volume. A new lantern lecture on Egypt was prepared especially
for the League in 1899 by a Mr. Kemp, M.P. A chapter of the

30 For a graphic description of the Battle of Omdurman, see *A Roving
Commission*, Chapters XIV, XV, by Winston Churchill, who as a war
correspondent, was an eye witness of the battle.

31 Madame Tussaud & Sons, *Catalogue, 1897*.

Knights Imperial reported in 1900 that four lantern lectures on
" Our Career in Egypt and the Soudan " had been in demand
during the year. The *Gazette* suggested to habitations as an attractive title for a popular lecture, "A Double Desertion—
Gordon and Ulster." The tableau " Defeat," depicting the fate
of General Gordon, was now followed by a sequel called " Vindication," the orchestra crashing into the strains of the national
anthem as a tableau showing Kitchener at Khartoum was revealed by the parting curtain.[32]

In 1898, when Lord Salisbury addressed Grand Habitation
on imperialism, the magazine *Truth,* taking Lord Salisbury to
task for his fiery speech, made him reply in his own defense—

You must not forget that the task I essay is often uncommonly hard,
Indeed, if at times I seem in spite of my best a bit of a jingo to be,
Let me add this significant piece of advice—
Blame the Primrose League—do not blame me.[33]

III

Yet it was the Irish question which really awakened the
League to full life. To the far-seeing British imperialist of the
eighties, the Home Rule issue was more than an issue of loyalty
to the Empire. If Ireland were to prove to be another America,
the consequences for England might be far more serious, economically and strategically. On the one hand, British landholders had a vested interest in Ireland, and that interest was
threatened by the Home Rule movement. On the other, British
military and naval strategy demanded that the Irish coast be
kept inviolable from any foreign power, and that Irish naval
bases remain at the disposal of the British navy.

32 Undoubtedly the Fashoda Affair of the same year, when the tension
between England and France over their respective stakes in the opening up
of Africa for a time looked dangerously like the prelude to war, served to
rivet popular interest more firmly on overseas expansion, as well as to whip
up nationalism in both countries. See Riker, T. W., "A Survey of British
Policy in the Fashoda Crisis," *Political Science Quarterly*, 1929, XLIV, 77.

33 *Truth,* May 12, 1898.

When the Home Rule issue rocked the country, splitting the great Liberal Party, and revolutionizing political alignments everywhere, it began to monopolize the attention of the Primrose League. The Imperial Ascendancy of Britain was menaced, and the League rallied its forces to the defense. In fact, this dominating issue probably was responsible for the tremendous growth of the League from 1886 to 1891, when its membership topped the million mark.[34] *Reynolds'* was moved to exlaim, referring to Charles Stewart Parnell, " I think in his horoscope he has counted without the Primrose League." [35] Within the League itself the Irish issue awakened an interest in the Empire as a whole, which was to be carried over with increasing momentum into the struggle for Empire in South Africa and its accompanying flurry of interest in home defense.

Ceaselessly the League campaigned against Home Rule. Vans to distribute anti-Home-Rule literature and leaflets; posters, lantern slides, lectures, skits at habitation entertainments; the distribution of " loyal " Irish newspapers in English villages; drafts of anti-Home-Rule petitions circulated by habitations,— all these monopolized to an overwhelming degree the activities of the English habitations during the late eighties. Lecturers and organizers were sent to Ireland itself and habitations established there.

Early in 1886 Grand Council sent to habitations specimen petitions against Home Rule, which the *Gazette* reports as meeting with almost totally successful response.[36] *St. Stephen's Gazette* during that year published a series of colored cartoons on " Irish Outrages " which a friendly commentator finds, with some degree of truth, to have some of the characteristics of Gillray's cartoons. They were arranged in a series and were in much demand at habitation entertainments, where they were shown with a magic lantern.[37] A League organizer delivered lectures

34 For figures on the growth of the League, see Appendix III.
35 *Reynolds'*, April 24, 1887.
36 *Minutes of the Grand Council of the Primrose League*, February 3, 1886.
37 *St. Stephen's Review*, July 5, 1886.

all over England, illustrated by these lurid pictures of outrages perpetrated by the Irish Land League against farmers and landlords. Dr. Tyndall Robertson, after a trip to Ireland for the League, reported great activity during 1887 in Dublin, though he found the League unknown in northern Ireland.[38]

Posters issued with the approval of Grand Council were much used by habitations in aid of their work. A large and highly colored poster entitled " The Reign of Terror in Ireland " was said to have caused considerable comment in Birmingham during Gladstone's visit to that city.[39] Characteristic posters on the Irish question showed scenes of the 1798 rebellion; wild-eyed terrorists applying flaming torches to ricks; and other illustrations of mob rule at its most melodramatic and unbridled.

When some troops in barracks in Cork refused to stand at attention during the playing of " God Save the Queen," and there was a report that royal standards were being mutilated in Ireland, the *Gazette* was moved to vehement protest. A banner inscribed simply with the word " Mitchelstown," commemorating the Irish riot of 1887, hung for years behind the speakers' table at the annual banquet of the Primrose League.[40]

At one time the *Gazette* ran a competition for the best suggestion for a magic lantern slide series on the Irish question. The winning series ran as follows: (1) John Bull holding out his hand to Erin, who is looking downcast. (2) Erin looking up into John Bull's face and placing her hand in his. (3) John Bull once more united in peace with Erin with Britannia in the

38 *Minutes of the Grand Council of the Primrose League,* November 17, 1887.

39 *Primrose League Gazette,* December 15, 1888.

40 During the trial of O'Brien, the Irish Nationalist leader, a crowd of 8,000 persons had collected at Mitchelstown in County Cork. A scuffle broke out between the police and the crowd, on which the police opened fire, killing three persons. The County Inspector and five constables were brought to trial, but no verdict against them was sustained. The watchword " Remember Mitchelstown," coined by Gladstone, was more often used by Home Rulers. But the Primrose League appears to have thought that the memory reflected more shame on the Home Rulers than on the authorities.

background. (4) An Irish farm in the days of prosperity. (5) The same farm in the days of the Land League. (6) The interior of an Irish farmhouse in days of prosperity. (7) The same in days of the Land League. (8) The terror of Moonlighting. (9) Cattle maiming in Ireland. (10) View of a general meeting of Loyalists in Belfast in 1888. (11) Resorts used by tenants willing to pay rent. (12) Two flags, the Royal Standard and another with no harp. (13) Justice, Law and Order. (14) Lord Salisbury with Balfour on his right and on his left Hartington, and (15) Lord Beaconsfield encircled by a wreath of primroses.[41] A correspondent of the *Gazette* in 1890 suggested facetiously a slide of " Mr. Parnell and the fire escape." [42]

Skits written and acted by local Primrose talent, with such titles as " The Pig, the Paddy and the Patriot M. P." were put on by the Chevening habitation and enlivened other habitation programs during the late eighties and early nineties. Irish landlords, farmers and tenants spoke up and down England at habitations. Individual landlords would defend conditions on their estates, or describe the misery of Irish rural life in contrast with English. In a Welsh habitation a spirit slate was actually pressed into service. To the question, " What do the Welsh people think of the Parnell Bill now before Parliament? " (August, 1888) the spirit slate obligingly replied in Welsh, " The people of Wales wish the Commission to bring out the truth, the whole truth and nothing but the truth."

It was reported to League headquarters that many English rural audiences had been under the impression that " Home Rule " meant a plan to end competition for the English worker from cheaper Irish labor by sending Irish immigrants back to Ireland, while others were surprised that a talk on " Unionism " did not touch on the Workhouse Union.[43]

41 *Primrose League Gazette*, January 19, 1889.

42 *Ibid.*, December 20, 1890.

43 *Ibid.*, October 1, 1892. The word "union" was associated in people's minds with the British Poor Law System.

Occasionally the routine resolution against Home Rule met with a rebuff. In one instance, Grand Council asked a habitation in Wales to explain the extraordinary fact that it had passed a resolution *in favor* of Gladstone's Irish policy. The explanation was that local radicals had managed to swamp the habitation meeting. In some places the tactics of the colliers proved a match for Grand Council.[44] The *Morning Post* described a habitation meeting in Leicestershire, where a Mr. F. de Lisle, F.S.A., rising to address the audience on Home Rule, was greeted by a phalanx of colliers who managed to keep up a steady barrage of cheers for Gladstone, Parnell, Davitt, Bagshawe and Morley, amidst which Mr. de Lisle, with commendable endurance, concluded his speech an hour later.[45]

During the eighties and early nineties, leaflets were sown broadcast by the League on all aspects of the Irish question. Over three million leaflets, all apparently on Home Rule, were distributed in one year.[46] Although the Ladies' Grand Council was advised in 1888 that pamphlets on Ireland were not so much in demand as formerly, yet the same report ended by urging that these pamphlets be continued. " So long as crime is rampant there, the demand for pamphlets dealing with its details is persistent." [47] As late as April of 1893, Grand Council ordered five thousand extra Home Rule pamphlets, as well as issuing fourteen different leaflets on the Parnell Commission.

The League offered at special rates leaflets issued by other anti-Home-Rule organizations. These leaflets bore such titles as " Parnellism and Crime," or " The Vandalism of the Irish Loyal and Patriotic Society." One thousand copies of the Irish Unionist Alliance leaflet: " Should Ireland have Home Rule? " were ordered in 1893.[48] John Bright's speech at a Unionist din-

---

44 *Minutes of the Grand Council of the Primrose League,* March 17, 1887.

45 *Morning Post,* May 13, 1886.

46 *Ibid.,* May 30, 1890.

47 *Minutes of the Grand Council of the Primrose League,* July 12, 1888.

48 *Primrose League Gazette,* June 17, 1893.

ner was printed by the Primrose League as campaign literature, and widely circulated. A pamphlet entitled " Remember Mitchelstown " presented Mr. Gladstone's change of front on the Quirke murder, and Mr. Balfour's answer in two parallel columns.[49]

Hartley Greenwood, an organizer who had been especially successful with Primrose League audiences with his magic lantern lectures on Ireland, was much ridiculed in *Truth* for his attempts to parry heckling over the Piggott exposure.[50] He declared in a speech in Derbyshire that of Piggott's two conflicting statements, one had been made on oath, and the other " alleged " to have occurred in Labouchere's house. " This oxy-hydrogen Tory Ass! " exploded Labouchere. And in the pages of *Truth* he retorted that this " alleged " conversation was buttressed by the oaths of three witnesses and clinched, moreover, by Piggott's suicide.[51]

Hartley Greenwood endeavored to defend the authenticity of the Piggott letters by pointing to the fact that Parnell was a co-respondent in a divorce suit.[52] Liberals accused Primrose League lecturers of brazenly telling rural audiences that Pig-

---

49 Some of the titles of the Home Rule pamphlets were: Irish Home Rule, What it Means to Working Men; Mr. Pease, M.P. and Mr. John Dillon, M.P.; Home Rule plus Vengeance; Mr. Chamberlain on Ulster and Home Rule; What would they do with it?; Mr. Gladstone's figures; a Speech by the Rt. Hon. John Bright, M.P., August 5, 1887; A " Boycotted " Family; An Eye Witness at Mitchelstown; England for the Irish; Radical Complicity with Crime; John O'Connor, M.P.; and a series called Tyrants of the National League, some numbers of which bore the titles: Murdered on Duty, Shaking hands with their victim before murdering him; " Boycotting," Outrage on Defenseless Animals, Cutting the Hair and Tarring the Head, " If a man were to break your head... " " Englishmen and Scotchmen should know . . .," etc. *Primrose League Gazette,* October 1, 1887.

50 Piggott sold to the *Times* certain documents subsequently proved to be forgeries, which pointed to the complicity of Parnell in the Phoenix Park murders. Parnell vindicated himself completely in Court, and Piggott fled to Spain and there committed suicide.

51 *Truth,* April, 1890.

52 *Ibid.,* December, 1890.

gott's forgeries had never been proved conclusively, and charging that Labouchere had bribed Piggott to commit suicide (presumably for a promise of support for the Piggott children).[53] According to *Truth*, Greenwood charged that agents of Parnell were occupied in blowing up Metropolitan Railway trains, helping the Boers against England, giving aid to Arabi Pasha in Egypt and to Riel the Canadian rebel leader, and finally that these same agents were involved in the deaths of both General Gordon and Colonel Burnaby.[54]

The Primrose League carried its campaign into Ireland itself. A visiting secretary was dispatched by the League to Ireland in 1885,[55] but the *Morning Post's* weekly columns of habitation news and progress reflect little interest in the Irish question during that year. By 1890, however, several large habitations in Ireland were included in the roster for the year. Naturally these habitations flourished only in those centers where there was a considerable Anglo-Irish population. A habitation at Belfast achieved a membership of over two thousand under the leadership of the Marquis of Londonderry. Dublin City, with its large enclaves of English residents, boasted at least three habitations—Blackrock, with 2,207 members, Rotunda Ward with 2,250, and St. Stephen's or Beaconsfield habitation, the oldest in Ireland (founded in 1885), with a substantial membership. Dublin County had several large habitations as well.[56] There were also habitations in Tralee and in Tipperary, with a membership of more than two thousand each, two in Galway, each numbering over a thousand, and the Castle Townshend habitation in Cork with a membership of 1,841. By 1887, the *Gazette* declared that nowhere was the League functioning more vigorously than in Ireland, and any one reading its pages might have

---

53 Thorold, Alger L., *The Life of Henry Labouchere*, 366.

54 *Truth*, July, 1890.

55 *A Short History of the Formation of the Primrose League; Corrected and Revised by the Founders.*

56 Primrose League—Roll of Habitations, 1890.

got the impression that no Irishman wanted to break the union.

Cork, Tralee and Dublin seem to have been the most conspicuously successful of the Irish habitations. In Galway, over 1,000 sat down to tea at a League meeting: at the Corn Exchange in Cork, an equal number " with great excitement " sang "Arise and Swear they shall not tear the shamrock from the rose." [57] During 1893 the Dublin City and Dublin County Primrose League organizations were congratulated by the *Gazette* for their part in the general elections of that year.[58]

In Ireland the middle and professional classes rather than the upper classes were the supporters of Primrose League work.[59] The Irish peasant was never attracted to it. It was reported to Grand Habitation that of twenty-two Irish Peers only five were Primrose Leaguers. Tralee habitation asked the central organization for financial help, since its 700 members, it declared, were mostly shopkeepers and tradesmen who " were all good haters of the National League, but all impoverished." [60]

The Irish National Land League came in for considerable attack by the Primrose League, perhaps in reprisal for odious comparisons made by the Liberals between the boycotting practices of the two organizations. Contrasting the " true nature of the Land League with that of the Primrose League," the *Gazette* ran a serial with the title, " Love will find out the way, or the Story of Two Leagues." Sir James Marriott, speaking to the Primrose League in 1888, told a story of a district visitor inquiring of an Irish moonlighter with a cracked head and a black eye how he was getting on, only to be answered, "Oh sir, Oi'm getting on well, Oi'm a primrose." [61]

English habitations sometimes contributed small sums of money to Irish charities and the Wimborne habitation was

57 *Primrose League Gazette*, January 18, 1887.

58 *Ibid.*, July 30, 1893.

59 *Morning Post*, April 19, 1890.

60 *Ibid.*, November 5, 1888.

61 *Ibid.*, April 22, 1891.

moved to send potato seed " to help Mr. Balfour's noble work." [62] An'editorial in the *Morning Post* even found a similarity between the early careers of Mr. Balfour and of the Primrose League in Ireland, since both started, it pointed out, under a suspicion of dilettantism.[63] The *Primrose League Gazette* printed such advertisements as "A loyal Irish Lady recommended for the position of companion or Lady Housekeeper." [64]

Sir Edward Carson, later famous as the leader of the Ulster rebellion, in the days immediately preceding the first World War, told the press that he had not felt it necessary to join the Primrose League since he was " fireproof against Home Rule." [65]

The Primrose League found itself cooperating against Home Rule with other organizations in the field. The Irish Unionist Alliance with its 71 associations in Ireland (out of a possible 101 constituencies) provided speakers for habitations. Grand Council, however, discouraged cooperation with the Orange League, and protested when a habitation advertised a joint meeting with an Orange lodge,[66] the famous Irish Protestant organization. A letter to Grand Council asking, " Do Orange principles coincide with the principles of the League? " was answered with a firm " No," and a definite statement that cooperation with the lodges was against the principles of the Primrose League.[67]

From time to time, the Irish Loyal and Patriotic Union provided speakers for habitations. Although habitations might not affiliate with the Union, individual members were urged to do so.[68] A representative was sent by the Primrose League to the

62 *Ibid.*, December 23, 1890.

63 *Ibid.*, July 25, 1889.

64 March, 1899.

65 *Morning Post*, January 26, 1894.

66 *Minutes of the Grand Council of the Primrose League*, February 14, 1894.

67 *Ibid.*, October 18, 1894.

68 *Primrose League Gazette*, December 6, 1890.

Council of the Irish Unionist Alliance, but no formal affiliation was allowed. Undoubtedly, there was much overlapping in membership between the Primrose League and the Irish Loyal Patriotic Union.[69] Irish Loyalist Liberals were, of course, encouraged to join habitations, and Liberal anti-Home-Rule speakers were much featured.[70] Members of the Ulster Anti-Repeal Association were directed, however, to get permission from Primrose League agents in their district to attend League meetings, and these agents were warned to be chary with their permissions.[71]

A religious issue was involved in the Home Rule question. Liberals accused the Tories of arousing nonconformist prejudice against Catholics, and appealing to fear of a Catholic domination of Ireland. Cardinal Manning wrote Lady Dorothy Nevill on May 3, 1886, " Many thanks for your note, which tells me what I did not want to know, and does not tell me what I do want to know. I know that Catholics are not excluded, but I have been informed that the Primrose League or its habitations, or its members circulate anti-Catholic and Protestant fly-leaves.

" I am anxious to refute this, as I have staked my character on your being a League of Innocents." [72]

Lord Salisbury, addressing Grand Habitation at Covent Garden in 1891, told the League, " In the Primrose League we gladly accept the cooperation of all who wish to maintain the acknowledgment of religion in this land. But by religion we mean that which points at and teaches the lesson of holy things and brings a voice of the world beyond. We do not mean the contrivances by which the preachers of religion may have the larger share of secular success. I have great reverence for the

69 *Ibid.*, June 20, 1891.

70 Richard Bagwell, the historian of Ireland, for example, was a much featured speaker.

71 *Minutes of the Grand Council of the Primrose League*, February 3, 1887.

72 Nevill, Lady Dorothy, *Reminiscences*, 287.

lawn sleeves and crozier of an Archbishop, but when I see behind the crozier the familiar features of Mr. Schnadhorst my reverence disappears." [73]

Dr. Bagshawe, Roman Catholic bishop of Nottingham, forbade his flock to join the Primrose League, stating, " It is intrinsically dangerous for Catholics to expose themselves to strong influences affecting the Church, religion and public morality of heretics, Freemasons, and Orangemen." [74] He warned the clergy that if any Catholics had participated in the League within the limits of the diocese, or should persist in disregarding his prohibition against founding or promoting habitations or attending League meetings, they would not be absolved unless they should renounce for the future such disobedient conduct. At the same time, however, Dr. Clifford, Roman Catholic Bishop of Clifton, told his parishioners that they might join the Primrose League and other organizations of a similar nature " provided they be equally loyal to the Queen, true to the Constitution, and not opposed to religion or morality." [75] Apparently Dr. Bagshawe's position was not endorsed by authority in Rome.

Grand Council found it necessary to remind habitations that they " have no right to exclude anyone on the ground of religious belief, provided such persons have signed the necessary declaration and otherwise complied with the requirements of the statutes." [76] There was some trouble over a habitation in Ireland which persisted in opening its meetings with prayer, presumably of an Anglican character. Finally the General Committee of Grand Council was forced to recommend the withdrawal of this habitation's warrant.[77]

73 *Morning Post*, April 22, 1891. Schnadhorst was the foremost organizer of the National Liberal Federation. He was closely identified with urban machine politics and with the Birmingham Radicals.

74 *Ibid.*, March 15, 1886.

75 *Ibid.*, March 29, 1886.

76 *Ibid.*, April 21, 1886.

77 *Minutes of the Grand Council of the Primrose League*, April 14, 1887.

Later on the League was often charged with being pro-Catholic.[78] Mr. Lane Fox, who worked for the League for many years as its executive officer, was a devout and prominent Catholic, while the Duke of Norfolk, a Primrose League Chancellor and a great power in the League, represented the powerful Catholic anti-Home-Rule group.

Alfred Morris, who toured Southern Ireland for the League during the autumn of 1893 to give heart to scattered Unionists, reported that speaker after speaker at meetings in Southern Ireland would rise to describe himself as a Catholic resolved at any cost to defeat the policy of separation.[79]

Reverberations of its anti-Home-Rule campaign reached the Primrose League even from overseas. A letter to the *Gazette* signed " Prospector and Miner, native of Bath, Somersetshire, England," and mailed from Diamond City, Meagher County, Montana Territory, U. S. A., opened, " I take the liberty of sending a mesage across the mountains and across the sea to apprise you that there are English-Americans who fully appreciate the noble work of the Ladies of the Primrose League in their untiring canvassing for success and unity and against the Irish National League, which is nothing but intimidation backed by Irish-American dollars." [80]

England considered that one of the League's greatest contributions to the anti-Home-Rule cause had been a tour made by one of its agents, a newspaper man, through Australia, in the wake of the Home Ruler, John Dillon.[81] The agent dogged Dillon's footsteps, issuing a constant stream of propaganda to the Australian press.

After nearly a decade of incessant Home Rule discussion, people grew weary of the issue. In 1893, the *Gazette* reported

78 *Primrose League Gazette,* August, 1903.

79 *Minutes of the Grand Council of the Primrose League,* October 5, 1893.

80 *Primrose League Gazette,* June 23, 1888.

81 April, 1890.

that leaflets on labor questions vied with those on the Irish question in popular demand.[82] As early as 1887 a resolution in the minutes of the National Union of Conservative Associations declared that the Union looked forward to a British parliamentary session since " the House of Commons and indeed every place of public meeting in the whole country has been saturated with purely Irish affairs during the past half dozen years." [83] Yet the following year Lord Salisbury devoted almost his whole speech in Covent Garden to Home Rule. The *Morning Post* later likened Salisbury, on the Home Rule question, to an expert removing the surface paint from an old master to find the original.[84]

In 1901 Balfour said that he had heard that Irish members of Parliament contemplated boring the country into the passage of the Home Rule bill this time. In 1905 the *Primrose League Gazette* referred to a woman member as " one of the few earnest workers of the Primrose League now left in Ireland." [85] And in January of the following year the *Gazette* found it necessary to charge campaign workers to remember to keep Home Rule to the fore.

IV

At a Devonshire habitation tea party in the nineties, after the regulation resolutions on Home Rule and congratulations to the Duke and Duchess of York on the birth of an heir, the Duchess of Buckingham and Chandos rose to confess impulsively that, after visiting the colonies, she had come to the conclusion that it was not right for Parliament to spend so much of its time on the Irish question, " whilst England has such interesting colonies to legislate for." [86]

82 *Primrose League Gazette*, February 25, 1893.

83 National Union of Conservative and Constitutional Associations, Minutes of Conference, 1887.

84 April 20, 1893.

85 *Primrose League Gazette*, June, 1905.

86 *Morning Post*, August 12, 1893.

The League could never have been accused of neglecting the remoter parts of the Empire, even at the height of its enthusiasm for the Irish question. Through its contacts with overseas groups, through lectures at habitations on imperial federation, often delivered by speakers furnished by the Imperial Federation League, and through the establishment of Primrose habitations in the Dominions, the Primrose League became the outstanding popularizer of imperial unity. Leaflets on " Our Colonial Empire " were distributed, and magic lantern lectures entitled " Our Colonies," " Our Glorious Empire," and " The British Empire, its Trade and Commerce," touched up and modernized from time to time, ran during the eighties and nineties at habitation entertainments. Nearly all these lantern slides were reported to be still in constant use in 1897.[87] Magic lantern exhibitions were often accompanied by patriotic singing by the audience, and were followed by a lecture on the colonies.

On Primrose Day in 1887 an elaborate fireworks piece was set off : A cluster of primroses as it burst gave way to an illuminated portrait of Lord Beaconsfield, which in turn faded to reveal a dazzling national emblem surrounded by the mottoes : " Union is Strength " and " Peace with Honour ; " and finally emerging in the center appeared the emblems of the four Dominions, the tiger, the ostrich, the kangaroo, and the bison. It was noted officially that the last word to disappear was " Honour." [88]

Direct contact with the Dominions was established through the League's own branches [89] in various parts of the Empire. Almost as soon as the League was born, habitations sprang up in the Dominions, and in other British possessions.[90] Contact

87 *Minutes of the Grand Council of the Primrose League,* January 29, 1897.

88 *Morning Post,* April 20, 1887.

89 English habitations were not allowed to establish daughter branches in the colonies.—*Minutes of the Grand Council of the Primrose League,* January 2, 1887.

90 In 1890 six were listed in India : Thazipur, Dacca, Calcutta, Benipore, Farhoot, Madras ; and one each in Cyprus, Valetta, Mauritius, British Honduras, and Malta.

with "native" populations sharpened the social conscience of the overseas habitations, and inspired the members to shoulder the White Man's Burden with the cheerful sense of duty which might be expected. The aims of the Malta habitation, for instance, were stated as follows: " To instruct the poorer classes (who are very ignorant) in the relations existing between England and Malta, the benefits which the Colonies and dependencies derive from the Mother Country, and the value of electing members to the Malta Council who will cooperate with the English Government in directing and ruling the interests of the Island of Malta." [91]

As a matter of fact, there was never any great growth in membership of these overseas habitations, and they seem never to have played any special part in Primrose League affairs. In recent years the League has felt that dominion nationalism has made a rather too delicate situation for the central organization to handle. Presumably the League has feared that these habitations may become involved in dominion politics even if they adhere to a strictly " imperial " program.[92]

V

It is a truism today that an Empire of the seven seas requires a navy dotting those seven seas. Yet it was not until the nineties that Britain awoke to that fact.

Popular interest in the navy had been in abeyance since the fifties. It was not until 1895-96 that the expenditure for the

---

91 *Morning Post*, May 18, 1887.

92 In 1893 Grand Council was petitioned for a warrant for a habitation by a group of Englishmen in Baltimore, " who were very anxious to express their devotion to the Crown and their detestation of Fenianism and all its kindred atrocities."—*Primrose League Gazette*, July 1, 1893. The petitioners pointed out that there were English and Irish organizations flourishing in the United States just as there were, for example, German organizations in Great Britain. Grand Council rejected the petition on the grounds that the establishment of habitations on foreign soil was contrary to its Constitution.—*Minutes of the Grand Council of the Primrose League*, July 27, 1893.

navy equalled that for the army.[93] The great Jubilee Naval
Review off Spithead of 1897 attracted widespread foreign as
well as domestic attention.[94] Two incidents in 1888 and again
in 1893 marked a growing popular interest in the fleet. The
first of these crises had resulted in Lord George Hamilton's program for a greater navy. A collision at sea between H. M. S.
Camperdown and H. M. S. Victoria in 1893, sinking one of
the ships and gravely disabling the other, impressed the public
with the urgent necessity of possessing more battleships. Reinforced by a secret technical naval report, this popular concern
was given recognition in the adoption of Lord Spencer's " New
Squadron " of 1894.[95]

The American Admiral Mahan's " Influence of Sea Power
Upon History " published in England in 1890, had attracted
wide attention and made a profound impression. Mahan's visit
to England in 1893-94 was almost a triumphal tour and he was
received with much enthusiasm, both by the public and by the
naval authorities.[96] Spenser Wilkinson's " The Command of
the Sea " appeared in 1894 and was a British repetition of
Mahan's argument for a strong navy as a keystone of national
defense. Various articles by Admiral Colomb had been published in book form which restated the conclusions of Admiral
Mahan on sea power in its application to Great Britain.[97]

93 Langer, W. L., *The Diplomacy of Imperialism*, II, 420.

94 An advertisement of a *Book for Baby Patriots* in the *Primrose League
Gazette*, November, 1890, prints a sample verse which runs:

> N is for Navy
> We Keep at Spithead
> It is a sight that makes foreigners
> Wish they were dead.

95 A Cabinet split over naval expansion in which Gladstone found himself
in a minority against the First Lord of the Admiralty, Lord Spencer, had
been a contributing cause of Gladstone's final resignation in 1894.

96 Taylor, Charles C., *The Life of Admiral Mahan*, Chapter VII.

97 *Naval Warfare, its Ruling Principles and Practice Historically Treated*,
1891.

There was a growing apprehension that Britain's command of the sea might be challenged, and there were even suggestions in the popular press that the island fortress might prove to be something less than impregnable. A Russian book called "Russia's Hope, or Britannia no longer Rules the Waves" had appeared in an English translation in 1888, and was widely read. Russia's large naval appropriation in the late eighties did not escape British attention. The British Naval Act of 1889 was, in part, a reaction to the Russian naval program, as well as to the impending Franco-Russian Alliance.

Serials appeared in the newspapers before the end of the century which pictured the lurid details of a German invasion. Books painting gruesome pictures of foreign invasion were popular in England in the nineties. One of these accounts has a preface which ends "for the French are laughing at us, the Russians presume to imitate us, and the day of reckoning is at hand." [98] The *Morning Post* tried to arouse its readers by asking them to suppose that the French had discovered "a diving torpedo boat" in which case the British Navy would be able to furnish little protection, since the French could land 75,000 completely equipped soldiers, quickly capture London and so have the Empire by the throat.

There seems to be conclusive evidence that even before 1904 England was genuinely apprehensive about German naval expansion in the sense that she feared the weight of German sea power thrown into a continental alliance against her. [99] A prize of £25 was offered by the *National Review* in conjunction with the Navy League for an essay of not over 10,000 words which would furnish "a forecast of the probable effect upon the United Kingdom of an indecisive war against two first class

[98] Amongst these was Colomb, P. H., *The Great War of 189-*, published in 1894. This is an account of the landing of armed Russian and French forces on the English coast, and the siege and the subsequent capture of Manchester and Birmingham. German and Italian soldiers aid the Russian and French invaders.

[99] Langer, W. L., *op. cit.*, II, 427.

Powers, it being borne in mind that ocean cables would probably be cut before war was declared, and that the price of bread would rise to at least one shilling per loaf." [100]

The Navy League was launched in January, 1894. Its primary purpose, as declared at the inaugural meeting, was to secure " The Command of the Sea " [101] Among its subsidiary aims it listed " To call attention to the enormous demands that war would make upon the Navy," and, more specifically " To secure the appointment of a single professional adviser, responsible to the Cabinet, upon the maritime defense of the Empire." The meeting resolved to place this program before public men and before members of Parliament in particular. The League, of course, disclaimed any political affiliation, and described itself as " a non-party organization detested by the Mandarins of both Front Benches."

The Primrose League's interest in a larger navy antedated the founding of the Navy League. In fact, the *Spectator* found some cold comfort in this fact when the realignment of political factions in the wake of the Home Rule issue threw it into the same camp with the Primrose League. Eyeing its new ally rather ruefully, it tried to reassure its readers—and perhaps it-

100 *National Review*, February, 1898.

101 For the formation of the Navy League, see: *Pall Mall Gazette*, October 16, 1894, and the following Navy League pamphlets: *The Four Average Englishmen*; *Formation of the Navy League* (no date) ; *What We Ask of You*, 1896; *The Colonial Press and the Navy League*, 1896 ; *The Navy League Journal* (the first volume of which appeared July, 1895), and also the *National Review*, January, 1902; *Spectator*, January 12, 1895; *The Times*, June 1, July 5, October 19, November 23, 1895.

For the platform and programs of the Navy League, see the following League pamphlets: *The Navy League*, 1896 ; *The Navy League*, 1898 ; *The Navy League Guide to the Coronation Review*, 1902; *The Navy League Annual*, 1907-08. Annual reports may be found in the *Journal of the Navy League*, and are also reported at some length in the columns of the *Times*.

Further information on the Navy League may be found in the following: Elliot, A. R. D., *Life of George J. Goschen*; Gaus, J. M., *Great Britain, A Study in Civic Loyalty*; Langer, W. L., *op. cit.*, II, 654; Wilkinson, H. S., *Thirty-Five Years*, Chapter V.

self—by reminding them that after all the League was responsible to some extent for the current interest in the naval
program.[102]

As a matter of fact, the League had earned better than this
grudging tribute, and the next decade saw a growing interest
in the issue, which was sometimes presented hand in hand with
the pleas for support of the Empire. In 1889, habitations passed
resolutions expressing satisfaction in the outlay for the navy,
" as tending to improve the trade of the country and this district." [103] A series of Primrose lantern lectures helped to pre-
pare the ground for more direct Big Navy propaganda, and
kept it fertile for the acceptance of increasing navy appropria-
tions. A lantern lecture on " Our Glorious Empire " circulated
in rotation with one entitled " Our Army and Navy," and both
ran through the nineties with scarcely any falling off in
popularity.[104]

A lantern lecture, " Our Imperial Navy," was another great
favorite for habitation evenings. One can picture many a small
habitation in January of 1894 listening to the vicar read these
lectures, accompanied by lantern slides shown on a sheet at the
end of the room, and then all present joining in the chorus of
such a song as " Man the Fleet." [105]

Speakers such as Lord Charles Beresford, a prime mover in
Primrose League as well as in Navy League circles, Henry

102 *Spectator*, May 25, 1889, 701.

103 *Morning Post*, September 14, 1889.

104 The lecture on " Our Army and Navy " was advertised in the *Primrose
League Gazette* of July, 1896, as containing the following slides: A portrait
of the First Lord of the Admiralty; Lord Salisbury; the Duke of Saxe-
Coburg-Gotha; the Duke of York; the Duke of Cambridge; Lord Wolseley;
the Duke of Connaught; The Great Harry; the Spanish Armada; Nelson's
Victory; Britannia training ship; a map of the world; Gibraltar; Hong
Kong; Life on board ship; Various battleships (all the latest); Display at
Aldershot; Recruiting Types of various regiments; also H. M. the Queen's
portrait; and a list of suggested music and songs suitable for the lecture
was furnished.

105 *Primrose League Gazette*, January, 1894.

Wyatt and other Navy League speakers, constantly addressed habitations under the auspices of the Navy League. At the end of one Navy League lecture at a Primrose local meeting three boys sitting in the front row were reported to have enlisted in the navy. Slides of Trafalgar Day celebrations were shown, and the day marked by special ceremonies at many habitations.[106] (It was said that the Leamington habitation refused to celebrate out of courtesy to France!)

VI

Borthwick, in introducing Lord Salisbury in 1896, had expressed a desire to see every Englishman " a self-contained warrior " with his horse, his bicycle, his motor car and his rifle ready for defense." Liberals scoffed at the speech. *Truth* ironically remarked that all should remember " that the defense of the country is (as Lord Salisbury has informed us) primarily the business of the Primrose League." [107]

In his annual speech to the League in 1900, Salisbury urged his audience to embark on a program of home defense, and to foster rifle clubs. " In the work which we have before us," he said, " the problems which we will have to solve and the dangers which we will have to meet in external affairs will occupy a considerably larger place than they have done in the periods of the century that has passed by." [108]

Under the stimulus of the war in South Africa, the League was already showing considerable interest in the question of home defense. In a circular issued on the subject in April, 1900, it urged drilling and patriotic teaching in schools, and rifle prac-

106 On the anniversary, through the efforts of the Navy League, the Nelson monument in Trafalgar Square was garlanded with flowers and the square used as a center for the London celebration. Four to five pages of the *Times* were devoted to listing donors of wreaths. Nelson's flagship at Portsmouth was decorated with laurel, and she ran through her old signals for the occasion. Even the grave of one of Nelson's pursers near Rochester was not forgotten.

107 May, 1900.

108 *Times*, May 10, 1900.

tice and training in tactics and scouting. Habitations were urged to cooperate with local organizations in the interests of defense.

Several habitations made specific proposals for the defense program. The Dunstable habitation criticized it on the ground that the only true defense for Great Britain lay in naval protection from an armed foreign landing force. Headquarters replied that this was beside the point, " as the Navy cannot be everywhere, and a sudden and unexpected invasion was by no means impossible." [109]

Boys' brigades were fairly popular in agricultural areas, and lectures on home defense and rifle competitions were the order of the day for Primrose Leaguers. Grand Council directed that Rifle Clubs formed of Primrose League members should not bear the name of the League, and wherever possible, should be affiliated with the National Rifle Club.

Meanwhile, the League continued to emphasize the importance of the regular army. A lantern lecture, " The British Army and Some of Its Exploits," written especially for habitation audiences, had been in demand since 1896. Many a lecture or magic lantern talk before a habitation was punctuated by the singing of such martial songs as " The Old Brigade " and " The Lads in Red " by the entire audience. Mr. Horace Wyndham, introduced to its readers by the *Gazette* as having himself served seven years in the ranks, prepared a lantern lecture for the League in 1899 called " The Everyday Life of the Soldier." In 1902 a new lecture on the army which had been submitted to the War Office for approval, was in great demand among the habitations.[110]

These patriotic activities in England had their counterparts on the continent. A number of societies sprang up in France and

109 *Morning Post*, April 14, 1900.

110 Three series of lantern slides on the army were provided simultaneously by the League—one called " The Army " (running for one hour and in sixty slides) and the others called " The Army and the War " and " The Transvaal War " (both running over an hour and each composed of ninety separate slides).

Germany pledged to the greater glory of the homeland, and its possessions beyond the seas and, in some cases, to strengthen the forces maintained to defend them. Some of these organizations concentrated on pure nationalism, such as the French League of Patriots; [111] others, like the Pan German League, devoted themselves as well to propaganda for a greater overseas empire. In both countries there were societies which were primarily concerned with the newly acquired colonies, such as the French Colonial Union, and the German Colonial Society.[112] A wave of naval enthusiasm swept over Europe in the nineties;

111 The League of Patriots (Ligue des Patriotes) was founded in 1882 by a group of Frenchmen who were profoundly stirred by the defeat of their country in the Franco-Prussian War. Guided by Paul Déroulède, although suffering a partial eclipse as a result of the Boulanger affair, the League of Patriots flourished during the Dreyfus period. The League concentrated its attention on "the amputated frontier" rather than on the colonies. For the foundations and history of the League of Patriots, see *La Ligue des Patriotes, 1882-1925; Le Livre de la Ligue des Patriotes:—Extraits d'articles et de Discours*, 1887; *Paul Déroulède* par un Professeur d'Histoire; *La Glorification de Déroulède à Metz*, October 16, 1921; *Patriotes en Paris.* (These pamphlets are available at the office of the Ligue des Patriotes in Paris); Poignant, Georges, *La Ligue des Patriotes*, 1923; Tharand, J. and J., *La Vie et la Morte de Déroulède*, 1925 and Hayes, C. J. H., *France, A Nation of Patriots*, 209-211. On the fly leaf of *La Ligue des Patriotes 1922-1925* can be found the later platform of the League.

112 After the stagnation in French imperialism in the last half of the eighties, two societies concerned with the French colonies, the French African Committee (Comité de L'Afrique Française), and the French Colonial Union (L'Union Coloniale Française) were organized in 1891 and in 1893 respectively. The latter was a clearing house for information between commercial interests concerned with colonial trade and the Government at Paris. For the origin and work of the French African Committee, see *L'Afrique Française*, May, 1932, and for the French Colonial Union, see *La Depêche Coloniale*, November 30, 1903; *Bulletin de l'Union Coloniale Française*, February and March, 1903; Bell, Sir Hesketh, *L'Union Coloniale Française, Its Aims and Functions*, Reprint from *Times* (no date given).

In 1887, the German Colonial Society was organized. Indignation over the Zanzibar Treaty led to the founding of the Pan German League in 1890. For these German societies, see Langer, W. L., *The Diplomacy of Imperialism*; Townsend, M. E., *Origins of Modern German Colonization*, and *The Rise and Fall of Germany's Colonial Empire*; Wertheimer, M. S., *The Pan German League.*

navy leagues were formed in France [113] and Germany and other countries, but the German Navy League was destined to be the most conspicuous of all.[114]

VII

The *Morning Post* ascribed to the Primrose League a highly significant connection with the public reaction to the Boer War. Its editorial on Grand Habitation of 1900 told its readers that " it is not the war in South Africa that has created the policy of the League, but it is rather the policy of the League that is transfiguring the South African War. In the programme of the League, war will only have begun when peace is proclaimed at Pretoria." [115] "A superfluity of encomium " is how the *Pall Mall Gazette* characterized the above sentiments, and the *Daily News* remarked that it had always labored under the impression that orthodox Tory thought ascribed the rise of modern imperialism to Lord Beaconsfield. The *News* concluded with the query, " Will Chamberlain like this? " [116]

Even in 1889, in the midst of their preoccupation with Home Rule, Primrose League speakers had touched on South African affairs. They compared Gladstone's policy with that of Disraeli

113 The French Navy League (La Ligue Maritime et Coloniale) was formed in 1899. For the founding and purposes of the French Maritime and Colonial League, see *Les Services Rendus à la Cause Nationale par le Ligue Maritime et Coloniale Française*, 1937; the official *Journal* of the *Ligue Maritime et Coloniale Française, Mer et Colonies*, November, 1936, *Ligue Maritime et Coloniale Française; Seul Programme Officiel de la Grande Semaine Maritime Française, 1905; Navy League Journal* (British), March, 1899 and January, 1902.

114 The German Navy League first appeared in 1898, the year of the Reichstag Naval Bill. Within six years, it was to boast a membership of over a million. For the history and activities of the German Navy League, the following may be consulted: Hurd, A., and Castle, C., *German Sea Power;* Schoenberg, A., *Um den Twopowerstandard; Englische Flotten-Politik, 1880-1895; Times*, December 27, 1904; and the *Navy League Journal* (British), February, 1899, October, November and December, 1901.

115 *Morning Post*, May 10, 1900.

116 *Daily News*, May 10, 1900.

or Salisbury, who was in office at the time, to the great dis-
advantage of Gladstone, of course. The following year they
contrasted Salisbury's handling of the Portuguese question with
Gladstone's South African policy and Majuba Hill—a compari-
son which suggests that their audiences already knew what to
think about these matters. As early as 1890, a speech by a
blinded veteran from South Africa led to a habitation resolution
against further encroachments by the Boers.[117]

The Imperial South African Association was founded in
1896. Its objects were " to uphold British supremacy and to
promote the interests of British subjects in South Africa with
full recognition of Colonial self-government." [118] Lord Charles
Beresford, Lord Bathurst and others prominent in the Primrose League, were among those included on the general committee. From the year 1897 speakers were furnished to habitations by the South African Association, and they were permitted
by the League to show slides and give " historical lectures."

Interest in South Africa, however, got under way slowly.
Even after the war began, it failed somehow to monopolize
public attention. At first the *Times* printed only one or two short
paragraphs of military news in the midst of endless columns of
diplomatic and political reports. But gradually, during 1900,
these military items grew, until the diplomatic and political news
had changed places with the military, and finally the war was
almost completely filling the daily press.[119] *The Daily News* and
The Daily Chronicle, at first opposed to the war, went over to
the Government camp, leaving the *Morning Leader,* the *Star,*
and the *Westminster Gazette* alone of the great dailies still in
opposition. Popular interest is shown by the fact that Conan
Doyle's " The Great Boer War," criticized by anti-war journals
as giving only the official version, went through sixteen editions
during the war.

117 *Primrose League Gazette,* February, 1890.

118 Imperial South African Association, *The British Case Against the
Boer Republics.*

119 See Doyle, A. C., *The Great Boer War,* 58.

The all-pervading war spirit swept the music halls, and thence throughout the country on a wave of jingo songs. One typical song, composed by the Hon. Sybil Amherst, began: "Victory! Victory! Give it to them well!" Another favorite ran:

> Take off his muzzle
> And let him have a go!
> Shall the Boer or Briton rule—
> That's what we want to know.
> There's only one dog in this game
> And *that's* John Bull.

The Primrose League carried the fever to its members and audiences. Martial spirit was aroused at rural habitations by recitals of "The Light Brigade" or by the singing of such rousing songs as "Soldiers of the Queen" and "Tommy Atkins." Maskelyne's animated photographs of the Transvaal were very popular. Sometimes a midshipman from H. M. S. Powerful would be invited to tell his experiences at Ladysmith.[120]

There is some evidence that the interest in the war among Primrose habitations was not quite spontaneous. In some districts the war was forced to compete with the usual social features of habitation programs. During the winter of 1900 many habitations reported only the usual round of teas and sports. Lantern slides, however, began to show views of Ladysmith, portraits of General Buller, Lord Roberts, Baden Powell, Kitchener, scenes of British attacks under fire on Boer positions, views of armored trains, Kaffirs, "trekking" and Maxim batteries as well as of Majuba Hill and others of the same nature.[121]

---

120 London was deeply stirred when the bluejackets from Ladysmith marched through the densely packed streets, hauling their famous siege guns behind them. They proceeded to Lloyd's in the City (the financial district of London), where they were served tea by members of the Exchange, who acted as waiters for the occasion.

121 *Primrose League Gazette*, February, 1900.

Recitations of Kipling's "Absent Minded Beggar" became a regular item on habitation programs, and pennies tinkled in a steady shower into war relief contribution cups all over the British Isles. Many resolutions of congratulations on the successful raising of the siege at Mafeking were passed by League habitations.

A typical meeting during the war would hear a lecture by a South African Association speaker, followed by all present singing "Soldiers of the Queen," or "The Bold Menelaus," or "The Two Flags," or "In the East and West there's trouble brewing," and then there would follow the inevitable recitation of "The Absent Minded Beggar" and a collection for war charities. Finally, a resolution would be passed "that this meeting emphatically approves of the action of the Government in seeking to secure political equality for all white men south of the Zambesi and expresses the earnest hope that after the war the Transvaal and the Orange Free State will be constituted British Colonies." [122]

Resolutions were passed such as the one which attributed the war to "the invasion of our colonies at Natal and the Cape," or resolutions supporting Milner in any steps which he might find necessary to redress the grievances of fellow Englishmen. Of course bloodthirsty appeals to nationalist feeling were made from many public platforms besides those of the League. [123]

Many Primrose Dames went out to South Africa as volunteer nurses, a movement which critics labelled "The Plague of Women." Labouchere amused himself by suggesting that "The Flinty-Hearted Beggar" be substituted at "Primrose League orgies" for the Absent Minded one, and that the song be dedicated to the British taxpayer.

---

122 *Morning Post*, December 7, 1900.

123 For samples of speeches and songs of this type during the Boer War, see Hobson, J. A., *The Psychology of Jingoism*, Part I, Chapter II, 33-34, 38, 39; Part II, Chapter II.

In the course of a single month, November, 1899, the League had distributed over one hundred thousand leaflets on the situation in South Africa.[124] A series of leaflets published by the Primrose League in collaboration with the central Conservative office during the first year of the war, bore such titles as " The Boers in South Africa;" "Grievances of the Outlander;" " Milner's Message;" " Why we are at war;" " Why the Boers are fighting us;" " Complaints of the Transvaal" and " The Boers outside Pretoria." In 1902 some new leaflets were issued by the League entitled, " Charges of Barbarism;" "A Bishop's Answer;" " Our Army in South Africa."

A typical Boer War pamphlet printed on one side of a medium-sized handbill reads, " Why are we at war with the Boers? To protect our fellow subjects from ignorance and oppression; to maintain the authority of our Queen and country; for equal political and civil rights for all and to lay the foundations of a lasting peace." [125]

Another Primrose League leaflet, entitled " The Object of the War," contained an extract from a letter from a British soldier at the front which said, " The only thing we are afraid of is that Chamberlain with his admitted fitfulness of temper, will cheat us out of the war, and consequently of the opportunity of annexing Transvaal and the Orange Free State."

The League took no part in the bitter criticism of the Government for the mismanagement of the war, though that criticism was by no means confined to the Opposition. Even the *Morning Post* attacked the Government sharply early in 1900 for its incompetent prosecution of the war in South Africa. Lane Fox, the Chancellor of the Primrose League, when interviewed as to the League's position on the attack, replied that the *Morning Post* was in no sense the official organ of the Primrose League, and that he personally felt that criticism of a ship's commander in the midst of a storm was most ill-advised.[126]

124 *Morning Post,* November 30, 1899.
125 Leaflet No. 221.
126 *Primrose League Gazette,* February, 1900.

The Hammersmith Knights passed a resolution giving their hearty and unqualified approval of " the recent policy of Lord Salisbury (our president) and Her Majesty's Government in regard to South Africa; and also its unanimous admiration of the spirited action of the Right Honourable Joseph Chamberlain in the course he has pursued, in the face of untold difficulty and the most virulent opposition, and for the unflinching courage with which the Right Honourable gentleman has upheld the honour and interests of Great Britain against her enemies, whether at home or abroad." [127]

With the surrender of the main Boer army, the interest at home shifted to the question of peace terms. Any suggestion of a peace which might leave the Boer republics independent was anathema to the die-hards, and they feared it might obtain support with that large section of the public with whom the war had been unpopular from the first, and to whom its gross mismanagement in the early months seemed to confirm their objections.

This was the sort of issue on which Primrose League methods and leadership were at their most effective. With a General Election impending, the League raised a hue and cry for annexation. On September 24, 1900, it issued a Precept to its members which was released to the press and ran as follows: " It is right that on the eve of this important election, Grand Council should issue a word of advice to the members of the Primrose League. Our principles are at stake—on the result of this election will depend the unity and strength of the British Empire. The menace of the South African Republics to our Imperial position in the world is not yet a thing of the past. The battle has been won, but the future settlement has to be made. The Government requires the support of the nation to ensure a lasting and permanent peace ... It is not sufficient to call yourselves Imperialists. Show by your actions, by your work and your votes at the most momentous period in the history of our Race, that you will have

127 *Ibid.*, November, 1899.

no hesitation, and no compromise. Our policy is just and our cause is righteous. Defer any consideration of side issues, and fight the election for Empire and Liberty." [128]

The Government won the election of 1900 but the issue of peace terms continued to be the bone of contention. In the spring of 1901, the League held its general meeting as usual. Preceded by a gay array of white, gold, green and red banners, Lord Salisbury was described as marching with " bowed " head to the dais in Albert Hall. Some said this was because, on the previous day, the Chancellor of the League had publicly chided Lord Salisbury's Government for having shown signs of making a patched-up peace.

But Grand Habitation adopted the following resolution : " The members of the Primrose League in Grand Habitation assembled, recognize with the highest satisfaction the growth of the Imperial sentiment as exemplified by the assertion of British supremacy in South Africa." [129]

A year later, in his address to the League, Salisbury reviewed the war. Of the Boers he said, " They chose to dispute our rights without a vestige of a ground for doing so." In answer to John Morley's charge that if the Tory Government in 1899 could have foreseen the results of its own policy in South Africa, it would have repudiated its own program, Lord Salisbury said that though he looked forward to a daughter colony in South Africa, he would refuse to be responsible for a settlement that would leave a loophole for any man to renew the conflict, " or to challenge the complete supremacy of our sovereign." [130]

VIII

In commenting on the striking change since the seventies in the interest of the British public in its Empire, Lord Salisbury

---

128 Primrose League Precept, Sept. 24, 1900. See *Minutes of the Grand Council of the Primrose League*, Vol. XIII.

129 *Primrose League Gazette*, June, 1901.

130 *Times*, May 8, 1902.

said: "Of course it would be too much to say that this great change in national opinion is the work of the Primrose League, but moral causes and moral effects always interwarp with each other and if it be true, as I believe it is, that the Primrose League is a child of that great reaction, it has itself powerfully influenced the opinions from which it sprang and has strengthened the force by which its birth was originally caused. These two results are a great entry in the annals of time for an organization which has not existed twenty years." [131]

The end of the war in South Africa marked the climax of imperialist sentiment. A reaction in favor of social reform was to follow similar to that of 1880. Whether the Primrose League had helped to postpone that reaction ever since the eighties, when social unrest was so evident, and the demand for reform so loud, is a matter for speculation. Certainly the League reached its climax at the same moment as the enthusiasm for Empire.

It was undoubtedly in its reaction to imperialism that the Primrose League most fully realized itself. It is hard for a later generation to recapture the exuberance of a period when the British Empire, spanning continents and seas, appeared to be as eternal as it was splendid. Indeed the abundant emotion and the crusading spirit evoked by the vision of a far-flung empire, might be said to have been appropriated later by the anti-imperialist cause.

Majuba Hill, Khartoum, Mitchelstown, Ladysmith and Mafeking are all forgotten names. Yet in its prime the Primrose League hurled itself with all its crudity and vigor into the heat of all the controversies aroused by them.

In one respect, the outstanding success of the Primrose League in upholding its platform of "The Maintenance of the Estates of the Realm" as well as that of "Imperial Ascendancy" is worth comment. A great section of the public of a full grown political democracy chose to cling fast to its traditional

131 *Morning Post*, May 10, 1900.

leadership. To do this it was necessary to rely not only on the lingering charm of title and ancestral trapping, but to present election issues in a form at once simple and stirring.

To the Conservative Party, the Primrose League offered not only the strength of its widely recruited and well organized body of workers, but it presented the Conservative slogans—A Great Empire, the safeguarding of existing institutions, the establishment of a true union of classes—shorn of the worn and shoddy trappings of ordinary party politics.

The *Pall Mall Gazette's* leading article on the sixth anniversary of Primrose Day [132] might have been written with equal truth on the twentieth: " Much as we deplore the malign influence of the Evil Minister whose favorite flower the League has adopted as its emblem, and mischievous as we believe its political activity to have been, it must still be frankly admitted that it has done, and is doing, better work than almost any political association now in existence."

132 April 18, 1889.

APPENDICES

APPENDIX I

It may be interesting to Primrose Leaguers, as showing how future circumstances can alter and develop primary ideas, if there are here set out *verbatim* the resolutions of the first meeting of the Council, held November 17th, 1883, together with the original statutes then promulgated.

RESOLUTIONS

1. That a political society be and is hereby founded under the title of the 'Primrose Tory League.'
2. That * * * * constitute the Ruling Council of the League, and have power to establish branches in all parts of the British Empire.
3. That the objects of the League are the promotion of Tory principles—viz. the maintenance of religion, of the estates of the realm, and of the 'Imperial Ascendancy of Great Britain.'
4. That * * * * be the first Grand Councillor, and that in the event of any vacancy in that office the Ruling Council have power to fill the same.
5. That the form of admission to the League and the powers of the various branches shall be determined from time to time by the Ruling Council.
6. That the motto of the League be 'Imperium et Libertas,' the seal 'Three Primroses,' and the badge 'An Imperial Crown encircled by Primroses.'

ORIGINAL STATUTES

I. The League will be governed by the Ruling Council. In case of any vacancy the Ruling Council within the space of three months shall select a fresh Councillor.

II. The President of the Council will be called the Grand Councillor. His appointment will last for three years. He will be assisted by three Executive Councillors, to be elected annually.

III. There shall be a Central Office for communications, with a Registrar.

IV. In every town and district in the United Kingdom where there are thirteen Knights of the League a Habitation can be established by a warrant from the Ruling Council. The warrant shall be marked with the mark of the Grand Councillor, stamped with the seal of the Order, and testified by the Registrar. Every Habitation shall have a number assigned to it by the Ruling Council, by which it shall be always designated.

V. Every Habitation shall be governed by a Ruling Councillor and three Executive Councillors, who shall regulate the admission and initiation of Knights. It is not necessary that the Ruling Councillor of a Habitation should be a member of the Ruling Council. Every Member of the League shall have a number at the time of enrolment, which shall appear on his warrant.

VI. Every Habitation shall keep a roll of its Members. The name of every Member initiated shall be immediately sent for enrolment to the Registrar in London, together with a fee of one crown, which shall include the tribute for the first year. A Diploma of Knighthood shall thereupon be sent to the Ruling Councillor of the Habitation containing the name of the new Knight, marked with the mark of the Grand Councillor, stamped with the seal of the League, and testified by the Registrar.

VII. The annual tribute of each member to the funds of the League shall be a half-a-crown, payable on the 19th April (Primrose Day). This amount will be remitted by the Ruling Councillor of each Habitation annually to the Secretary. Each Habitation will regulate the local tributes of its Members. The Diploma of each Knight shall be stamped annually by the Ruling Councillor on payment of the tribute.

VIII. Every Knight shall pay his own tribute, and shall himself pay for any refreshment consumed by him in the Habitation, whether occasional or at a banquet.

IX. The Knights shall be divided into two classes — Knight Companions and Knight Harbingers. After probation of one year a Knight Harbinger may be promoted by the Ruling Councillor of his Habitation to the rank of Knight Companion, and his warrant shall be stamped accordingly. Members in holy orders shall be designated Knights Almoners. Knights Almoners shall rank with Knights Companions. Seniority of Knighthood shall govern the precedence of Knights in the several grades.

X. In all towns and districts under a Habitation one or more Knights shall be assigned to sub-districts. Such sub-districts shall not contain more than one hundred houses. It will be the duty of such Knights to promote to the best of their ability the doctrines of the League throughout their sub-district, to obtain information as to the views and position of each inhabitant, details useful for registration, and to make reports on these and other subjects of importance at the meetings of the Habitation. During any public election the Habitation will meet every evening, each Knight bringing a report of his proceedings during the day. Monthly reports of the Habitation, and during election time daily reports shall be forwarded by the Ruling Councils of the Habitations to the Registrar.

XI. Every Knight shall be entitled to wear the badge of the order attached to a ribbon. The ribbon of a Councillor shall be all primrose; of a Knight Companion or Knight Almoner, primrose on violet; of a Knight Harbinger, primrose centre with violet borders. The badges must be worn by Knights at all the meetings of Habitations. On Primrose Day all members of the League shall wear a bunch of Primroses.

XII. Any Knight or Councillor who during an election has been found guilty of any corrupt or illegal practice shall be degraded and expelled from the League. His name shall be erased from the roll of the Habitation and from the roll of the Ruling Council, and the reason of such erasure shall be entered on the books. The same course shall be adopted in the case of any Knight or Councillor divulging the secrets of the League or acting in a manner unbecoming a Knight or gentleman.

XIII. No Knight not a member of a Habitation shall be admitted to any meeting except on the responsibility of two Knights, members of the Habitation. There shall be no strange guests at any banquet, and stranger Knights shall be required equally with members to pay for their own refreshments.

XIV. The Ruling Council may withdraw the warrant of any Habitation.

XV. Every communication from the Ruling Council to the Habitation shall be called a Precept. It shall be headed by the word ' Precept,' shall bear the seal of the order, the mark of the Grand Councillor, and shall be testified by the Registrar. Every communication from a Habitation to the Ruling Council shall be termed a " Representation," whether originating with the Habitation or in answer to a Precept. It shall bear the stamp of the local seal, which shall be the same as the seal of the Ruling Council, together with the number of the Habitation. On the receipt of a Precept a meeting of the Habitation shall be summoned within two days, for the purpose of considering it and returning an answer to the Registrar, and as far as possible complying with the requirements of the Precept.

XVI. Every Member on his initiation shall make the declaration hereto annexed and signify his adhesion to the bye-laws of the League by subscribing his signature to a copy thereof. He shall also sign his name in a book to be kept for the purpose.

FORM OF DECLARATION

This obligation may be administered to any person by a member of the Ruling Council or by a Habitation, which shall be responsible to the Ruling Council for his fitness.

XVII. The Ruling Council and the Habitation shall conform to all the requirements of the law regulating societies of this character.

XVIII. Gentlemen wishing to become Knights of the League must, until further steps be taken, apply in writing to the Registrar, accompanying their application with a fee of a crown and a reference. They will announce their readiness to subscribe to the statutes and ordinances, and to take the declaration. No applicant can be accepted except upon the approval of the Ruling Council. In case of non-approval the fee will be returned. No application will be received by the Registrar from any town or district where a Habitation has been constituted, but the applicant will be informed to whom he can apply in the town or district of his residence. The Ruling Council may reward either by Diplomas of Honour, or the presentation of special badges or clasps, any distinguished services rendered by Knights.

XIX. The Ruling Council shall be entitled to receive monies both from the Habitations and from individuals, to be spent for the advancement of the purposes of the League. An account shall be kept of receipts and expenditure, and such account shall be annually audited by chartered accountants. Any Ruling Councillor of a Habitation may at any time have access to the Auditor's report. These rules can be altered or added to by the Ruling Council.

APPENDIX II

ORDINANCES OF THE LADIES' GRAND COUNCIL
(*Primrose League Gazette*, January 2, 1899)

1. There shall be a Ladies' Grand Council of the Primrose League which shall meet once every year.

2. Any Dame of the League may become a member of the Ladies' Grand Council if proposed and seconded by two members. The annual subscription is one guinea, due on January 1st, in addition to the usual fees to habitations of the League.

3. No member of the Ladies' Grand Council shall issue any circular, leaflet or pamphlet, or other publications with the imprint of the League, which have not been submitted to, and approved by, the Grand Council.

4. Members of the Ladies' Grand Council are warned that 'they cannot make use of the machinery of the League (e.g. meetings, committees, circulars) for collecting money for any purpose whatever outside the objects of the League as defined by statutes.

5. Any member who has not paid her subscription for three years will be considered to have resigned her position as a member of the Ladies' Grand Council.

EXECUTIVE COMMITTEE OF THE LADIES' GRAND COUNCIL

1. There shall be a President and four Vice-Presidents, who shall be appointed by the Executive Committee of the Ladies' Grand Council, and who shall hold office during life or until resignation.

2. A retiring President or Vice-President may be appointed by the Executive Committee of the Ladies' Grand Council to be an extra President or Vice-President.

3. There shall be an hon. sec. and an hon. treasurer appointed by the Executive Committee, who shall hold office during life or until resignation.

4. There shall be 15 members of the Executive Committee besides those named above, who shall retire in rotation every 3 years, but are eligible for re-election. The election to be by

ballot, voting papers sent to all members of the Ladies' Grand Council a fortnight before the annual meeting, when the result of the election will be announced.

5. All vacancies which occur during the year shall be dealt with at the annual election.

6. Any member of the Ladies' Grand Council is eligible for the Executive Committee, provided she is proposed and seconded by two members, one of whom must be a member of the existing Executive.

7. Until the complete list of candidates for election is laid before the Executive Committee, members of the committee shall not be allowed to pledge themselves to propose or second any candidate. The list of candidates in question shall be laid before the Executive Committee between March 1st and 15th or the hon. treas. and hon. sec. cannot propose or second any candidate.

9. Canvassing by letter or circular is not allowed, and the election of any member of the Ladies' Grand Council transgressing this rule shall be void.

10. The D. P. of the habitation which wins the Champion Banner shall be co-opted a member of the Executive Committee for a year from the date of meeting of the Grand Habitation. If there be no D. P., the R. C. shall select the lady who is to represent the Champion Habitation.

11. In all matters not herein mentioned, the members of the Ladies' Grand Council shall conform to the rules laid down for guidance of the League, and should any difference of opinion arise as to the interpretations of the above, a reference should be made to the Grand Council.

(Signed) S. SALISBURY, *President.*

Revised at a meeting of the Ladies' Grand Council Executive Committee on Friday, the 24th of June, 1898.

Sanctioned as amended by the Grand Council this 29th day of June, 1898.

GEORGE LANE-FOX, *Vice-Chancellor,*
Primrose League

APPENDIX III

(From the reports of Annual Grand Habitations in the
Primrose League Gazette and the *Morning Post*)

THE PRIMROSE LEAGUE

Year	Knights	Dames	Associates	Total	Habitations
1884	747	153	57	957	46
1885	8,071	1,381	1,914	11,366	169
1886	32,645	23,381	181,257	237,283	1,200
1887	50,258	39,215	476,388	565,861	1,724
1888	54,580	42,791	575,235	672,616	1,877
1889	58,180	46,216	705,832	810,228	1,986
1890	60,795	48,796	801,261	910,852	2,081
1891	63,251	50,973	887,068	1,001,292	2,143
1901	75,260	64,906	1,416,473	1,556,639	2,392
1910	87,235	80,038	1,885,746	2,053,019	2,645

The total number of new members enrolled in 1905 was 33,590
(*Times*, May 5, 1905).

APPENDIX IV

1883 Lord Randolph Churchill	1895 Lord Politmore
1884 Lord Abergevanny	1896 Lord Harriss
1885 Sir William Hardman	1897 Lord Glenesk
1886 Viscount Folkestone	1898 Duke of Marlborough
1887 Lord Harriss	1899 Duke of Marlborough
1888 Lord Harriss	1900 Viscount Curzon
1889 Earl of Amherst	1901 Viscount Curzon
1890 Earl of Radnor	1902 Earl of Powis
1891 Lord Borthwick	1903 Lord Willoughby de Eresby
1892 Sir William Marriott	1904 Gerald Loder
1893 Earl of Abercorn	1905 Duke of Norfolk
1894 Lord Borthwick	1906 Duke of Norfolk

APPENDIX V

The Truth about the Education Bill

(*Primrose League Gazette*, October 1, 1902)

No matter what the Liberals say, the Education Bill is not a Tory attempt to destroy Board Schools nor to hand education over to the parsons.

It does not destroy a single school, but, on the other hand, it will improve those now in existence, and will also establish many new schools.

It does not hand education over to the parsons, because it puts all schools under the control of the local authorities.

The Bill hands the Government Education Grant to the County Councils, and certain Borough and Urban District Councils, and gives them power to levy an education rate, instead of the Board School rate, for the support of secular education in all schools.

It is true that Church and Nonconformist schools will benefit by the education rate, but only for secular education, and in the same proportion as other schools.

As for religious teaching, all that the Bill does is to leave Churchmen and Nonconformists the right they have always had of giving their own religious instruction in the schools they have built and maintained. This is fair play, and does not cost the ratepayer one penny.

It is false to say that Conservatives are no friends to education. Remember it was a Conservative and Unionist government that gave free education, and has since given increased money grants, reformed the Education Code, and in other ways done all they could to promote and improve education.

The Education Bill is a fair and honest attempt to improve education by legislating for—

> Economy in expenditure
> Better training for teachers
> Better local control
> Better buildings
> More chances for clever children
> Better management, and
> Increased efficiency all round.

APPENDIX VI

How Shall I Vote?

A Leaflet for Agricultural Labourers and Working Men

(*Primrose League Gazette*, July 20, 1889)

The working classes in town and country have now obtained, mainly through the Conservative and Unionist party, the largest share in the government of the nation.

Lord Beaconsfield's Reform Act of 1867 gave votes to the artisans in the towns: the Franchise Acts of 1884 and 1885, which were passed by the joint consent of both parties, gave the labourers in the counties their votes; and Lord Salisbury's Local Government Act of 1888 has given them a share in the choice of the County Councils. The working classes, therefore, owe their votes more to the Conservatives than the Liberals. How can they use these votes best for the happiness and prosperity of the country?

Here are a few reasons why this object can be best attained by supporting the Conservative and Unionist candidate.

Peace. — Without peace the country cannot be prosperous. Lord Salisbury has kept the country for three years at peace with all the world. Mr. Gladstone was five years in office and had a war every year. (Transvaal, 1881; Egypt, 1882; Bechu-analand, 1884; Soudan, 1884; Nile Expedition, 1884).

These wars cost us many hundreds of British lives and many millions of British money, and brought nothing but discredit and disaster. Remember Gordon and Majuba Hill!

Retrenchment.—No government is to be trusted which does not economize the public expenditure. Mr. Gladstone spent over eighty-seven millions a year in governing the country. The Conservatives have managed to do it at a yearly average of eighty-one millions.

Mr. Gladstone put on seven millions of extra taxes while he was in power. The Conservatives have reduced the taxes by more than two millions a year. They have also given three millions extra to relieve the local rates, and have saved a million

and a half in interest on the National Debt, besides reducing the
debt itself by over twenty millions.

Good finance is the essence of good government, and its effect
is seen by the revival of trade. Our exports and imports are
sixty-six millions more than they were in 1885; the deposits in
saving banks have increased by thirteen millions; and the cargo
traffic carried by sea has increased by nearly five million ton.
This is one result of having a good administration.

Reform. — Besides preserving peace and practising economy,
the Conservatives have carried many useful reforms. For instance:

The Local Government Act gives control over local affairs to
the representatives of the people in the counties.

The Coal Mines Act protects the miner by reducing the risks
of employment to the lowest possible limit.

The Railway Act prevents unfair rates on farmers' produce.

The Merchandise Marks Act prevents foreign' swindlers from
palming off inferior goods as English.

The Technical Schools Bill will help the British workman to
acquire skill to compete with the foreigner.

The Allotments Act has encouraged private owners to provide
cheap land for labourers' allotments, and enables the public
authorities to acquire land for the same purpose if it is wanted.

The Margarine Act stops the fraudulent sale of foreign substi-
tutes under the name of butter.

The Irish Land Act enables Irish farmers to become the owners of the land they cultivate, by payment of a reduced rent for
a fixed number of years.

These are a few of the measures which are due to Lord Salisbury's government, and many others of equal value have been
introduced. Mr. Gladstone can show no such record of useful
legislation in the same time.

So much for the past: what about the future?

The leading object of the Conservative Party is to preserve
what is best in the established institutions of the country.

Ireland.—We only want one Parliament for the United Kingdom. We are against separation in any form. The Irish have
no right to separate Parliament any more than England, Scotland or Wales. It would lead to civil war in Ireland and con-

sequent ruin to trade and commerce, while it would only satisfy for a time those who are rebels against British Rule. Two millions of loyal subjects of the Queen in Ireland protest against Mr. Gladstone's proposal to set up a separate Parliament and Government, and nearly all the most intelligent and prosperous classes in the country are against it.

The policy of the Conservatives is to put down all *interference with the freedom of individuals,* either by boycotting, outrage or murder, such as has prevailed in the past. They want every man to be free to buy and sell, to hire and let land, and to carry on his business in comfort and security. At the same time they wish to make Ireland prosperous by improving the roads and railways, draining the bogs, encouraging the industries and fisheries, and preventing injustice either to landlords or tenants.

The efforts of the Government have almost stamped out agrarian crime, and have relieved over 4,000 of the poorest classes from the tyranny of boycotting and the necessity for police protection.

The outcry about evictions is intended to throw dust in the eyes of the people. No farmer need pay an unjust rent; he can always appeal to the Land Court to fix a fair rent. The landlord is bound to compensate him for every improvement he has made. If the farmer is unable to pay the fair rent, common justice requires that he should give up the land to its owner, and when the courts of law order this to be done, every government is bound to lend troops and police to support their decrees. Mr. Gladstone, when in office, frequently sent soldiers and police to assist at evictions, and when appealed to to stop them he replied that he could not possibly do otherwise. Home Rule would not prevent a single eviction, unless an Irish Parliament were to abolish rent of every kind.

Education.—The Conservatives want to extend education, but they insist that it shall be combined with religion. There can be no such thing really as free education. It must be paid for somehow, and if the present voluntary schools were abolished, as the Radicals want to do, every working man in the country would have to pay far more than he does now.

The Land.—The Conservatives want to remove all unjust burdens from the land so that it may produce all it can and make us more independent of foreign supplies. They want to take away every just grievance in regard to tithes, unfair rates, and the carriage of produce, *but it is utterly untrue to say that they wish to put a tax on corn, or raise the price of bread.* No Conservative statesman has ever proposed it: every member of the government has declared against it.

The Defence of the Country.—The Conservatives want to see the country strong enough to resist all attacks. With that view they have voted money to build 70 new ships of war, so that our navy may keep the command of the sea, which is essential to our prosperity and even safety. The Radicals, while admitting the danger, objected to spend the money necessary to remove it.

The above are a few reasons why working men, in their own interests, would do well to support the present government. They do so most effectively by giving their votes to the Conservative and Unionist candidate at any election that may occur.

APPENDIX VII

Candidates nominated for election to the Grand Council at Grand Habitation. Sixteen to be elected.

(Primrose League Gazette, May, 1905)

The Duke of Abercorn, K.G. — Chairman of the British South Africa Co. President of the Irish Landowners' Convention, and greatly helped in making the Irish Land Bill possible. A Past Chancellor of the P. L.

The Earl of Amherst—Was M. P. for West Kent 1859-68 and for Mid Kent 1868-80. Has been Lieut. and Capt. Coldstream Guards. *Served in Crimea.* A Past Chancellor.

F. Cave Maitland, Esq. (Hammersmith No. 293) — R. C. Hammersmith Habitation, one of the oldest on the Roll. Is on the Political Committee of the Constitutional Club.

Colonel W. T. Dooner—For some time Chief Staff officer at Royal Engineer Barracks, Chatham. Alderman of the City of Rochester Council. R. C. Rochester (Cecil) Habitation. Good speaker.

John Goddard, Esq.—One of the keenest and most generous supporters of the League in Sussex. Has been a valuable attendant at Committees and Grand Council during the past year.

Captain the Hon. R. Greville, M. P.—Represented Bradford since 1896. Late Captain 1st Life Guards. Has been a Vice-Chairman of Grand Council.

H. Percy Harris, Esq., L.C.C.—Leads the Moderate party of the L.C.C. in their efforts to keep down growing expenditure. Has been a Whip and Deputy Chairman of the L.C.C. Has done good work for his party.

Sir R. T. Hermon Hodge, Bart. M. P.—Elected M. P. for Henley, Oxon. 1895. Lieut. Col. in Oxford Hussars. Created Baronet 1902. Has been Vice-Chairman of Grand Council during past year. Popular platform speaker.

The Earl Howe, G. C. V. O. — Lord Chamberlain to H. M. The Queen. Formerly Treasurer of H. M. Household. Was M. P. for Wycombe, Bucks 1885-1900. Past Chancellor of the P. L.

The Earl of Jersey, G.C.M.G. — Was Governor General of New South Wales 1890-93. Chairman of Light Railway Commission. Was fine athlete in his youth. Chief partner in Child's Bank.

The Earl of Malmesbury—Capt. 3rd Batt. Hampshire Regt. Was married last month. Was elected L. C. Councillor for Stepney last election but resigned his seat.

The Duke of Marlborough, K. G.—Under-Secretary for Colonies since 1903. Was Asst. Military Secretary to Lord Roberts in South Africa; Paymaster of the Forces. Married Consuelo, daughter of Mr. W. K. Vanderbilt. A Past Chancellor of the League.

Robert T. Marlin, Esq.—Has spoken on many Conservative and Primrose League platforms throughout the country. Sings an Irish song better than any man living.

The Rt. Hon. Sir Fred Milner, Bart. M. P.—Has sat for Bassetlaw, Notts. since 1890. Is a " determined opponent of Home Rule for Ireland, Wales and Scotland". Was M. P. for York City from 1883-1885. Good platform speaker and writer.

S. Roberts, Esq., M.P.—Elected for Ecclesall Division, Sheffield, 1902. Lord Mayor of Sheffield 1900. Director of Cammell & Co., Armour Plate Manufacturers, and chairman of Sheffield Banking Co. Is a barrister, but does not practise.

Sir John Rolleston, M. P.—Elected for Leicester 1900. Is a surveyor, and was President of Surveyors' Institution in 1901. Director of the Leicestershire Banking Co.

Col. Royds, C. B., M. P.—Has represented Rochdale since 1895. Chairman of Rochdale Canal Co. and William Deacon Bank. Created C. B. 1902. Late Colonel Com. Duke of Lancaster's Own Yeomanry.

Edward Terry, Esq.—Well known actor. Has been R. C. Baines Habitation for many years.

Viscount Turnour, M. P. — Elected for Horsham Division, Nov. 1904. Eldest son of Earl of Winterton. Lieutenant in Sussex Yeomanry.

Col. Sir Howard Vincent, K.C.M.G., M.P.—Has sat for Central Sheffield since 1885. Founder and Hon. Secy. of United Empire Trade League. One of the original members of the Grand Council.

The Marquis of Winchester—Lord Lieut. of Hampshire. Premier Marquis of England and hereditary bearer of Cap of Maintenance.

The Marquis of Zetland, M. P. — Lord Lieutenant of Ireland 1889-92; previously Lord-in-Waiting. Takes great interest in the League's progress in Yorkshire.

APPENDIX VIII

Primrose League Gazette, July 2, 1900

HOME DEFENSE

" What you have to provide is the means of learning the handling of rifles, placed in the hands of every man within reach of his own cottage. If he has not to travel away he will learn—not with any great expenditure of time, and with scarcely any expenditure of money—he will learn to emulate the skill and the fame of his ancestors many centuries ago, who by their practice in archery first raised this country to its high level of military glory."—

LORD SALISBURY, at the Albert Hall,
May 9th, 1900.

This important problem becomes easier of solution as the question is more clearly understood.

The answers of habitations to the request for suggestions show that the country at large is willing to do its duty.

Politics should be carefully avoided in this national matter.

The Habitations of the Primrose League should not spend their Primrose resources nor give prizes from habitations.

Their first object should be to support the Government in furthering the movement which aims at the maintenance of Empire, and perfecting of the Army.

Their next business is to promote by their influence every and all schemes having for their object to develop the military spirit and individual efficiency of our countrymen for national defence.

To support the Government in making the Army as efficient as the Navy.

To further the improvement of the Yeomanry and Militia.

To urge the development and to perfect the equipment of the Volunteers.

To assist the formation of Rifle Clubs in every parish, and the teaching of the use of the rifle to the youth of the Kingdom.

Habitations should not proceed upon cut and dried rules, but should act on their own special opportunities.

Evidently some will be able to secure, e.g., Rifle Ranges and a standard of efficiency, which, when once acquired, will kindle that spirit of emulation which has always proved a moving power.

Care must be taken to avoid all interference with existing institutions.

The Primrose League must only seek by its organization to help the national aspiration for the security of the Heart of the Empire.

Lord Salisbury, who knows, has made it clear that the one danger which the Volunteers rose to defend our shores against still exists, and that to repel that danger, the youth of the nation should be efficient in the use *of the rifle, the spade, the cycle, or the horse, and the first principles of tactics, scouting, and discipline.*

We shall have many instructors when the Army comes home, and every district in England will be able to avail itself of the lessons which our returning soldiers can impart with the knowledge which comes from experience.

Any information that may be required by individual habitations for the purpose of carrying out these suggestions will be sent on application to the Primrose League Office, 64 Victoria Street, London, S.W., putting on the envelope " Home Defence."

GLENESK,

Chairman of Committee on Home Defence,
June 28th, 1900

APPENDIX IX

(Primrose League Gazette, August 27, 1892)

Dorchester (S. Oxon) Habitation (No. 832)—By invitation of Mr. Williams Wynn, of Howbery Park, Ruling Councillor, a very successful fête was held in the extensive grounds of that place on the 11th inst. The day was brilliantly fine, and there was a very large attendance; both of members of the Habitation, and others who were invited by Mr. Williams Wynn. The register having just been revised, it is satisfactory to state that the Habitation now numbers nearly 500 *bona fide* members; a large increase having taken place during the past year. An excellent entertainment was furnished by Mr. Clarence's troupe from London; but the most prominent feature of the fete was contributed by eight young ladies in pretty Primrose costume, who danced " The Singing Lancers " charmingly, and were called upon three times to repeat the dance. Tea was provided by Mr. Shewal, of the Livesay, Reading, to which all sat down under the presidency of the energetic Wardens—Mr. Pochin, Mr. Blunt, Mr. Wodehouse (hon. secretary), Miss E. Ruck-Keene, Miss Foster, Miss Hedges, assisted by other ladies. The above named had all been recommended to receive promotion or clasps; and about six p. m. the members being gathered in front of the Terrace, which forms a natural platform, the silk banner of the Habitation was duly displayed behind the chair of the Ruling Councillor, and Mrs. Williams Wynn in a few gracious and pleasant words bade the Habitation welcome, including in her address the members of the Little Milton Habitation, who were present by invitation. The various decorations being handed to her by the Hon. Secretary, she pinned each of them on with some happily expressed words of compliment. Amongst those who were summoned to receive promotion was a working man, the Sub-Warden of Benson, who had the good fortune to be decorated with the Hon. Knights' Badge and Diploma. Mr. B. Tubb, of Warborough, in a short speech explained the then political situation, begging all to renew their efforts, for, though the cause was lost for a time, yet matters might be considered as only in abeyance, and with zeal and hopeful perseverance the true friends of the country would soon return to power. A very pleasant day was brought to a close by dancing to the music of the Dorchester Band.

BIBLIOGRAPHY

I. PRIMROSE LEAGUE

Arbuthnot, G. A. (Ed.), *The Primrose League Election Guide,* 1914.

Lane Fox, George, *The History of the Primrose League,* 1890.

The Primrose Banner, 1886?

The Primrose Bud. Vol. 1, January, 1926.

The Primrose League. *Habitation Ready Reference Register,* 1888.

The Primrose League. *Handbook,* 1929.

The Primrose League. *Its Rise, Progress and Constitution.* By one of the Staff, 1887.

The Primrose League. *Junior Branch Annual Meeting,* 1930.

The Primrose League. *Junior Branch Annual Meeting.* April 29, 1936.

The Primrose League. *The Ladies' Grand Council. Why Should One Join the Primrose League,* 1908.

The Primrose League. *Leaflets:*
1) Miscellaneous Collection, British Museum.
2) Miscellaneous Collection, Conservative Party Reference Library, St. Stephen's Chambers, Westminster, London.
3) Miscellaneous Collection, Library of London School of Economics.
4) Series, Primrose League Office, 54 Victoria Street, London, 1884-1905. (Incomplete).
5) Primrose League Gazette printed many of the Primrose League Leaflets in toto in its columns.

The Primrose League. Minute Books of the Grand Council of the Primrose League. Vols. II-XV. 1883-1906. (Manuscript).

The Primrose League. *Pocket Diary,* 1935.

The Primrose League. Roll of Habitations, 1887. (Manuscript).

The Primrose League. *The Roll of Habitations,* November, 1888.

The Primrose League. *Roll of Habitations,* 1890.

The Primrose League. Roll of Oldest Working Habitations. July, 1937. (Manuscript).

The Primrose League. *A Short History of the Formation of the Society.* Corrected and revised by the Founders. (Minute Book Vol. I), 1886.

The Primrose League Gazette, 1887 to date.

The Primrose Record, September, 1886.

II. CONTEMPORARY PAMPHLETS, PROCEEDINGS, REPORTS, ETC.

Acland, Sir Thomas Dyke. *The County Teachers and Liberal Policy.* Two Addresses to Tenants of Allotments in Devon and Somerset. 1884.

The Address of Mr. X. Y. Z., M. P., to the Electors of East Anglia. Southend, 1885.

American Historical Association. Annual Report. 1901.

The New Conservatism, 1884.

Bottomley, J. H. *The Conservative Brief Against the Gladstone Administration,* 1884.

Broderick, Hon. George C. *Unionism: The Basis of a National Party.* An address delivered at the first meeting of the Oxford University Unionist League, December 1, 1888.

Causes of Conservative Failure in Perthshire. A Letter to Col. Moray by James Rankin. 1886.

Chambers, George F. *Eastbourne Working Men's Conservative Association.* A paper on Organization. January 25, 1885.

Churchill, Lord Randolph. *Plain Politics for the Working Classes.* Letter to Mr. J. Speech, Blackpool. January 23, 1884.

Compatriots' Club Dinner, April 26, 1907.

Conservative Agents' Journal.

Conservative Catechism, 1886.

The Conservative Policy of the Future, 1894.

Conservative Radical, 1883.

Conservatives. *An Appeal from the New Conservatives to the Old,* 1888.

Hill, A. S., *Conservative Political Handbook,* 1885.

The Constitutional Yearbook, 1885, 1888, 1891, 1892, 1894, 1897, 1898, 1905.

The County Council Year Book. Vol. I, 1891. Vol. II, 1892.

Crickmay, H., *A Reply to Midlothian,* 1884.

De Ricci, J. H., *Conservatism and the People.* Leicester Conservative Association, 1883.

De Ricci, J. H., *Unconscionable Agitation,* 1884.

De Ricci, J. H., *The Welfare of the People.*

Empire Union, Leaflets, 1900.

Tracts on Trade, Finance and Statistics. Prospectus of Fair Trade League. 1881.

The Fair Trade Policy. A letter to the Earl of Derby. 1882.

Female Suffrage. A letter from the Right Honourable W. E Gladstone, M.P., to Samuel South, M.P.

Fielding, Thomas, *Radical Hypocrisy, or War, Waste and Corruption, being an Eye-Opener for Working Men and a Plea for Political Honesty,* 1884.

G. to R. Caucus Premonitions. A letter to Lord Brabourne. 1884.

Glyde, C. A., *Liberal and Tory Hypocrisy during the 19th Century,* 1904.

Hamber, H., *An Impeachment of Party Government, with a Plea for National Administration.*

Herbert, A. E., *Organization Without Opinion,* 1882.

Hamilton, A. H. A., *Past and Present Schisms of the Liberal Party.* Oxford, 1888.

Hodge Podge, *Gladdy and Dizzy, or the Rivals,* 1884.

Home Defence, with Special Reference to the Volunteer Force. By an old Adjutant. 1900.

How Shall Catholics Vote at the Coming Parliamentary Election? By His Eminence the Cardinal, Archbishop of Westminster.

Hutton, Barbara (Mrs. Alexander), *The Primrose League Lady's Letter and Reference Book with Mottoes,* 1886.

Hyndman, H. M., *England for All,* 1881.

Imperial Federation League. Report of Adjourned Conference and of the First Meeting of the League, held November 18, 1884. 1885.

Imperial Federation League. Expression of Opinion on the Federation of the Empire. 1885.

Imperial Federation League. The Record of the Past and Promise of the Future. October, 1886. Special Report.

Imperial Federation League. Fifty Years' Progress. Special Number of *Imperial Federation.* 1886.

Imperial Federation League. The 5 Best Essays on Imperial Federation submitted to the London Chamber of Commerce for their prize competition and received for publication by the judges. 1887.

Imperial Federation League. Synopsis of the Tariffs and Trade of the British Empire. 1888.

Imperial Federation League. Speeches delivered at a Public Meeting of the Halifax, Nova Scotia Branch of the Imperial Federation League, June 4, 1888.

Imperial Federation League. Sequel to Synopsis. 1889.

Imperial Federation League. Second Annual Report of our Commercial Bulletin, with the Report on the Maritime Trade of the United Kingdom in 1891 and Reprints of Monthly Articles in *Journal of the I. F. L.* Abstracts for 1889-1891.

Imperial Federation League. Second Annual Report. Report on Marine Trade in 1891.

Imperial Federation League. Second Report on the Imperial Federation League. 1892.

Imperial Federation League. Report of Special Committee. Proceedings of the Council. Epitome of Press Opinions upon the Report. 1892.

Imperial Federation League. Roll of Members. 1892.

Imperial Institute. Bulletin. Vol. II, 1904. Vol. III, 1905.

Imperial Federation League. Colonial Office Pamphlets.

Imperial South African Association. The British *vs.* the Boer Republics. Imperial South African Association.

J. A. P. Lord Beaconsfield, M.G., *His Writings and the Primrose League with a History of Primrose Day,* Nottingham, 1913. Second Edition.

League of the Empire. Report of the Negotiations for Amalgamation with the Victoria League. 1909.

League of the Empire. General Report. 1904-05.

League of the Empire. The Interchange of Teachers. Issued under the Authority of the General Committee. April, 1934.

League of the Empire. Report of the Federal Conference on Education. 1907.

League of the Empire. The Interchange of Teachers. First Conference on Education called 1907.

League of the Empire. Report of the Interchange of Teachers' Scheme. 1907-1923.

Liberal Publication Department Leaflets, 1883-1905.

Liberal Programme in a Nutshell or Reasons for supporting Liberal Candidates. Liverpool Liberal Federal Council. Liverpool, 1892.

The Liberal and Radical Year Book, 1888.

Liberal Unionist Pamphlets. Nos. 1-38. No. 52, What the Congested Districts Act does for Ireland. *Times,* July 23, 1891.

Lies and Replies. An Exposure of Some of the Common Gladstonian Fallacies—Being a Reprint of 40 letters from Rt. Hon. A. J. Balfour, M.P., and from his Secretary, George Wyndham, Esq., M.P. 1892. Liberal Unionist Association.

London. Vol. IV, 1895.

The Position of the Liberal Unionists. By the Editors. Reprint of *National Rev.* No. 54, August, 1887.

Middleton, R. W. E. *A Speech on Organization.* The United Club. December 5, 1889.

Morton, Charles A., *An Indictment of the Party System.* Address at Bath, February 28, 1927.

National Fair Trade League, Leaflets.

National Liberal Federation. Proceedings in connection with the Eighteenth Annual Yearly Meeting of the Federation held at Huddersfield, March 25, 26, 27, 28, 1896.

National Liberal Federation. Annual Meetings, 1877-1905.

National Liberal Federation. Proceedings attending the formation of the National Liberal Federation with Report of Conference. Birmingham, May 31, 1877.

National Union of Conservative and Constitutional Associations. The Constitution and Rules of the National Union of Conservative and Constitutional Associations and of its Provincial Districts. Adopted at a special conference of the National Union held at the Westminster Palace Hotel, May 15, 1886 and revised at the Oxford Conference, November 22, 1887.

National Union of Conservative and Constitutional Associations. The Constitution and Rules adopted at special conference, July 27, 1906. Amended at annual conferences, Birmingham, 1907, Cardiff, 1908, Manchester, 1909 and Nottingham, 1910.

National Union of Conservative and Constitutional Associations. Election for Council leaflets. 1897.

National Union of Conservative and Constitutional Associations, Minutes of Conferences, 1883-1905. (1888, 1889, and 1893 missing). (Manuscript).

National Union of Conservative and Constitutional Associations, No. 287. The Conservative and the People. Newcastle. Conference of National Union Resolutions.

National Union of Conservative and Constitutional Associations. The Platform as a Conservative Agency. A Paper read at Conferences of Conservative Associations of Northern Counties. Durham, October 10, 1882.

National Union of Conservative and Constitutional Associations. Political Tracts. 1884.

National Union of Conservative and Constitutional Associations. Programme of Proceedings. 1894-1905. (1895 missing).

The Navy League. Volumes of Early Reprints, Leaflets B6-Y1.

The Formation of the Navy League, 1887-1889.

The Navy League. A Collection of Pamphlets. 1895.

The Navy League. What We Ask of You. 1895.

The Navy League. Constitution—Suggested Programme for Action. 1895.

The Navy League. A Collection of Pamphlets issued by the Navy League. 1895.

The Navy League. Reports. 1895-1905.

The Navy League. The Colonial Press and the Navy League. March, 1896.

The Navy League, August, 1896.

The Navy League. Malta Branch. General Report for the Year 1897.

The Navy League. A Collection of Pamphlets. 1898.

The Navy League. Another Collection of Pamphlets. 1898.

The Navy League Guide to the Coronation Review, 1902.

The Navy League Annual. Ed. Allan H. Burgoyne. 1907-08.

The Navy League Annual, 1907-1908.

The Navy League. The Navy League of Canada. Montreal Women's Branch. 1918.

The Navy League. The Navy League of South Africa—the Seven Seas. 1920-29.

Nemo., *Political Tracts for the People.* 1885, 1886.

The New Conservatism, 1884.

The New Conservation Programme, 1887.

The Newly Enfranchised. A Dialogue in the interest of the Working Men of Great Britain. Sheffield, 1885.

Noble, John, *Facts for Politicians,* 1892.

Norma, G. W., *Lord Beaconsfield's Ghost,* 1886.

Norma, G. W., *A Political Humbug or half an hour with Lord Randolph Churchill,* 1885.

O'Donnell, Frank Hugh, *Facts for Election.*

O'Grady, Standish, *Toryism and the Tory Bureaucracy,* 1886.

Our Conservative and Unionist Statesmen, 1896.

Pettifer, H. J., " John Bull *vs.* Jonathin, or Free Trade *vs.* Protection," *National Fair Trade League,* 1889.

Pettifer, H. J., *Nuts for Radicals to Crack,* 1903.

A Political Study by a Conservative Radical. *The Future Capital of The British Empire,* 1883.

A Political Thunderbolt, a General Election Address to the Men and Women Workers of the Nation by Uncle John's Nephew. J. Thomas, Secretary of Parcel Post Co.

Primrose—An Elegy in 4 Cantos. Written in Memory of the late Earl of Beaconsfield. April 18, 1884.

Royal Colonial Institute. Proceedings. Vol. XVIII, 1886; Vol. XXIV, 1892-93; Vol. XXXI, 1899.

Home Counties Union. The Rural Elector. Feb. 26, 1890.

The Rural Labourer League, 1894.

S. G. S. Pre Primrose League. Previsions fulfilled. 1886.

Salisbury, Marquis of, *The Conservative Programme,* 1885.

Scriven, C. Scrivener, *The De-Population of our Villages.* An address to the Trade Unionists on the influx of population to Towns.

Sharman, C. H., *Twelve Reasons Why I am a Conservative,* 1887.

Strickland, W. W., *Political Grub Street.* An Appeal from Phillip Drunk to Phillip Sober. Leeds, 1883.

Suggestions for Liberal Organization in Counties, 1886.

Tory Democracy, 1892.

A Plain Tory. Tory Democracy and Conservative Policy. 1892.

Tracts for Manhood.

Tussaud, Madam and Sons' Exhibition. Centenary Number.

Tussaud, Madam and Sons' Exhibition. A Visit to Madam Tussaud's, 1891, 1897, 1901.

The Union and the Unionists, 1892.

Unionist Workers' Handbooks.

Victoria League. First Annual Report (1902), 1903.

Victoria League. Tenth Annual Report, 1910-1911.

Victoria League. Annual Report, 1907-08.

Victoria League. Series of Pamphlets on British Empire.

Victoria League. Summary of work, 1907.

A Whig. The New Conservatism, 1885.

Women's Liberal Federation. Summary of Federation News, 1893-1905.

Women's Liberal Federation. Annual Reports and Council Meetings, 1886-1895. (1887 missing).

Women's National Liberal Association. Quarterly Leaflets, 1895-1906.

A Working Man's Advice. The General Election, 1892.

Young England. Argumentum ad Populum. Tracts for Manhood on Regeneration, Social, Moral and Spiritual. 1845.

III. MAGAZINES AND NEWSPAPERS. (Unless otherwise indicated the numbers consulted are those covering the years 1883 to 1905).

Albemarle.
Association of Conservative Clubs. Monthly Gazette, 1895-96; *Monthly Circular*, 1896-1905.
Bath Argus, April —, 1888.
Bath Chronicle, April 26, 1888.
Birmingham Daily Gazette.
Birmingham Daily Mail.
Blackwood's Magazine.
Bristol Times, April 20, 1885.
Cassell's Family Journal.
Chamber's Journal.
The Church Reformer, Vol. II, 1891, Vol. 12, 1892.
Clarion.
Contemporary Review.
The County and Local Government Magazine, 1890, 1891.
Croydon Express, 1895.
Croydon Guardian, 1895.
Daily Chronicle, 1897.
Daily News, 1887, 1896, 1900.
Daily Telegraph, November, 1929.
Edinburgh Review.
England, 1884-1898.
English Labourers' Chronicle, 1886.
Fortnightly Review.
Gentlewoman.
Glasgow Herald, April 20, 1887.
Illustrated London News, Nov. 19, 1887.
Imperial Federation League Journal, 1886-1893.
Journal of Political Economy, XXXVI, 1928.
Justice.
League of the Empire. Monthly Record, 1904-06.
The Liberal Magazine. Liberal Publication Department, 1894-1908.
Life.
Madame. Supplement, May 25, 1901.
Manchester Examiner.
Manchester Guardian.
Metropolitan, 1888.
The Metropolitan and Provincial Local Government Journal, 1892.
Midland Evening News.
Morning Leader, 1897.
Morning Post.
Municipal Journal, 1899.
National Union of Conservative and Constitutional Associations. Gleanings, 1888-1892.
National Review.

The Navy League Journal, 1895-1905.
Newcastle Daily Leader.
Nineteenth Century.
North American Review.
North British Daily Mail (Glasgow), April 20, 1888.
Pall Mall Gazette.
Pall Mall Magazine.
The Paternoster Review, October 1890.
The People, 1895.
Political Science Quarterly.
Punch.
Quarterly Review.
Review of Reviews.
Reynolds' Newspaper, 1887.
St. James' Gazette, 1883, 1884.
St. Stephen's Review, 1883-1892.
St. Stephen's Review, Presentation Cartoons, 1889, 1890.
The Saturday Review, 1899.
Scottish Review, Vol. 35, 1900.
Scotsman, April 20, 1894.
Sheffield Daily Telegraph, April 20, 1893.
Sheffield Evening Telegraph and Star, April 20, 1892.
The Speaker, 1890-99.
The Spectator.
Standard, 1885, 1886, 1900.
Star, 1888.
Strand.
Times.
Truth.
United Empire Journal, 1915.
Vanity Fair.
Western Mail (Cardiff).
Western Morning News, April 20, 1886.
Westminster Gazette, 1894-97.
Westminster Review.
Wiltshire Telegraph.
Windsor Magazine.
Woman's Herald, 1891-1893.
Women's Suffrage Journal, 1884-1889.
Working Men's Club and Institute Union. *Club and Institute Journal,* 1883-1885.
Yorkshire Herald, April 20, 1891.
Yorkshire Post.

IV. SELECTED BIBLIOGRAPHY OF SECONDARY SOURCES CONSULTED.

Allen, Bernard M., *Gordon and the Soudan.* London, 1931.
Arch, Joseph., *Joseph Arch. The Story of His Life, Told by Himself.* London, 1898.

Aspinall, Arthur, *The Correspondence of Charles Arbuthnot.* London, 1941.

Barker, Ernest, *Ireland in the Last Fifty Years.* Oxford, 1919.

Baumann, A. A. B., *The Last Victorians.* London, 1927.

Beach, Lady Victoria, Hicks, *The Life of Sir Michael Hicks Beach.* London, 1932.

Birrell, Francis, *Gladstone.* London, 1933.

Blease, W. L., *A Short History of English Liberalism.* New York, 1913.

Blunt, Wilfrid S., *My Diaries.* London, 1919-20.

Bodelsen, C. A., *Studies in Mid-Victorian Imperialism.* Copenhagen, 1924.

Boscawen, A. S. T., *Fourteen Years in Parliament.* London, 1907.

Bowley, A. L., *The Change in the Distribution of National Income.* 1880-1913. Oxford, 1920.

Brenner, C. S., *Education of Girls and Women in Great Britain.* London, 1897.

Bright, John, *Letters on Home Rule.* Birmingham, 1892.

Broadhurst, Henry, *Story of His Life.* London, 1901.

Burnaby, Fred, *Ride to Khiva.* New York, 1885.

Butler, G. G. G., *The Tory Tradition.* London, 1914.

Cecil, Lady Gwendolen, *Life of Robert, Marquis of Salisbury.* London, 1932.

Cecil, Hugh, *Conservatism.* London, 1912.

Champion, H. H., *The Great Dock Strike in London.* London, 1890.

Channing, Francis A., *Memories of Midland Politics.* London, 1918.

Churchill, Lady Randolph, *Reminiscences.* London, 1908.

Churchill, Lord Randolph, *Speeches 1880-1888.* London, 1889.

Churchill, W. S., *Lord Randolph Churchill.* New York, 1906.

Courtney, Janet, *Countrywomen in Council.* London, 1933.

Crewe, Marquess of, *Lord Rosebery.* London, 1931.

Crozier, John Beattie, *Lord Randolph Churchill. A Study of English Democracy.* London, 1887.

Davies, M. F., *Life in an English Village.* London, 1909.

Disraeli, Benjamin, *Coningsby.* London, 1871.

——, *Endymion,* London, 1871.

——, *Sybil or a Tale of Two Nations.* London, 1871.

——, *Whigs and Whiggism.* London, 1913.

Doyle, A. Conan, *The Great Boer War.* New York, 1900.

Dugdale, Blanche E. C., *Arthur James Balfour, 1st Earl of Balfour.* London, 1936.

Dunraven, Earl of, *The Legacy of Past Years. A Study of Irish History.* London, 1912.

Eliott, Hon. Arthur D., *The Life of George Joachim Goschen, 1st Viscount Goschen, 1831-1907.* London, 1911.

Elliot, Walter, *Toryism and the Twentieth Century.* London, 1927.

Elton, Godfrey, *England Arise!* London, 1931.

Ernle, The Right Honble. Lord (Prothero, Rowland Edmund), *English Farming, Past and Present.* London, 1927.

Escott, T. H. S., *Randolph Spencer Churchill as a Product of his Age.* London, 1895.

Fawcett, Millicent G., *Women's Suffrage. A Short History of a Great Movement.* London and Edinburgh, 1912.

Feiling, Keith, *Toryism.* London, 1910.

Feis, H., *Europe, the World's Banker.* London, 1930.

Folsom, Avaline, *Royal Empire Society.* London, 1933.

Forbes, Archibald, *Chinese Gordon.* New York, 1884.

Froude, J. A., *Earl of Beaconsfield,* London, 1890.

——, *Oceana: or England and Her Colonies.* London, 1886.

Garvin, J., *Life of Joseph Chamberlain.* London, 1932.

Gathorne-Hardy, A. E., *Gathorne-Hardy, 1st Earl of Cranbrook. A Memoir with Extracts from his Diary and Correspondence.* London, 1910.

Gaus, John M., *Great Britain; A Study of Civic Loyalty.* Chicago, 1929.

Gorst, Harold E., *The Earl of Beaconsfield.* London, 1900.

——, *The Fourth Party.* London, 1906.

Gorst, Sir John E., *The Labour Question.* 1891.

——, *Physical Deterioration, Its Causes and Some Remedies.* London, 1906.

Graham, P. Anderson, *The Rural Exodus.* 1892.

Grego, Joseph, *A History of Parliamentary Elections and Electioneering from the Stuarts to Queen Victoria.* London, 1892.

Gulley, E. G., *Joseph Chamberlain and English Social Politics.* New York, 1926.

Glasier, J. Bruce, *William Morris and the Early Days of the Socialist Movement.* London, 1891.

Haggard, Henry Rider, *Rural England.* London, 1902.

Hamilton, Rt. Hon. Lord George, *Parliamentary Reminiscences and Reflections, 1886-1906.* London, 1922.

Hardinge, Sir Arthur, *The Life of Henry Howard Molyneux Herbert, 4th Earl of Carnarvon.* London, 1925.

Hardman, Sir William, *A Mid-Victorian Pepys. The Letters and Memoirs of Sir William Hardman.* London, 1923.

Haslip, Joan, *Parnell; A Biography.* London, 1936.

Hearnshaw, F. J. C., *Conservatism in England.* London, 1933.

Hobhouse, L. T., *Liberalism.* London, 1911.

Hobson, J. A., *The Psychology of Jingoism.* London, 1901.

——, *The War in South Africa.* London, 1900.

Holland, Bernard, *The Life of Spencer Compton, 8th Duke of Devonshire.* London, 1911.

Housman, Laurence, *Four Plays of Victorian Shade and Character. Angels and Ministers.* London, 1922.

Hyndman, H. M., *The Record of an Adventurous Life.* New York, 1911.

Jephson, Henry, *The Platform. Its Rise and Progress.* London, 1892.

Jeffries, Richard, *Hodge and His Masters.* London, 1880.

Jeyes, S. H., *The Life and Times of the Rt. Hon. Marquis of Salisbury.* London, 1895-96.

Kebbel, Thomas Edward, *Lord Beaconsfield and Other Memories.* London, 1907.

Knaplund, Paul, *Gladstone and Britain's Imperial Policy.* New York, 1927.

Lang, Andrew, *The Life, Letters, and Diaries of Sir Stafford Northcote, 1st Earl of Iddesleigh.* Edinburgh, 1890.

Langer, W. L., *The Diplomacy of Imperialism.* New York and London, 1935.

Le Quex, William, *The Great War in England in 1897.* London, 1894.

Londonderry, Marchioness of, *Henry Chaplin, a Memoir.* London, 1926.

Lowell, A. L., *The Government of England.* New York, 1921.

Lucas, Reginald, *Lord Glenesk and the Morning Post.* London, 1910.

Lucy, H. W., *A Diary of the Salisbury Parliament.* London, 1892.

——, *Speeches of the Marquis of Salisbury.* London, 1885.

Mallock, W. H., *Memoirs of Life and Literature.* London, 1920.

Marriott, W. T., *The Liberal Party and Mr. Chamberlain.* London, 1884.

Mahan, Admiral, *The Influence of Sea Power upon History.* Boston, 1893.

Manners, Lord John, *England's Trust and Other Poems.* London, 1841.

Maxwell, Rt. Hon. Sir Herbert E., *The Life of the Rt. Hon. W. H. Smith.* London, 1894.

Millin, George Francis, *Life in Our Villages.* London, 1891.

Monypenny, W. F. and Buckle, G. E., *The Life of Benjamin Disraeli, Earl of Beaconsfield.* New York, 1910-1920.

Moon, Parker, *Imperialism and World Politics.* New York, 1933.

Morley, John, *The Life of William Ewart Gladstone.* London, 1921.

Morris, Alfred, *Discussions on Labour Questions between a Conservative, a Liberal Trades Unionist and a Socialist.* London, 1893.

Morris, Homer L., *Parliamentary Franchise Reform from 1884 to 1918.* New York, 1921.

Nevill, Lady Dorothy, *My Own Times.* London, 1912.

Nevill, Ralph (Ed.), *Leaves from the Note-Books of Lady Dorothy Nevill.* London, 1907.

Nevill, Ralph, *The Life and Letters of Lady Dorothy Nevill.* London, 1919.

——, *The Reminiscences of Lady Dorothy Nevill.* New York, 1906.

Ostrogorski, M., *Democracy and the Organization of Political Parties.* New York, 1902.

——, *The Rights of Women.* London, 1893.

Pankhurst, Emmeline, *My Own Story.* London, 1914.

Pankhurst, E. Sylvia, *The Suffragette Movement.* London, 1931.

Paul, William, *A History of the Origin and Progress of Operative Conservative Societies*. Durham, 1838.

Pearson, Hesketh, *Labby*. London, 1936.

Prentice, Archibald, *History of the Anti-Corn-Law League*. London, 1853.

Redlich, J. and Hirst, F., *Local Government in England*. London, 1903.

Reid, T. Wemyss, *The Life of the Rt. Hon. William Edward Forster*, London, 1888.

Robertson, John M., *Patriotism and Empire*. London, 1899.

Rosebery, Lord, *Lord Randolph Churchill*. London, 1906.

Rowntree, B. Seebohm, *Poverty, A Study of Town Life*. London, 1901.

Saunders, William, *History of the First London County Council*. London, 1892.

Seeley, Sir J. R., *The Expansion of England*. London, 1893.

Selley, Ernest, *Village Trade Unions in Two Centuries*. London, 1919.

Sichel, Walter, *Disraeli, a Study in Personality and Ideas*. New York, 1904.

Smith. Goldwin, *A Trip to England*. Toronto, 1891.

Springall, L. M.. *Labouring Life in Norfolk Villages, 1834-1914*. London, 1936.

Steevens, G. W., *With Kitchener to Khartoum*. New York, 1898.

Strachey, Ray, *The Cause. A Short History of the Women's Movement in Great Britain*. London, 1928.

Stubbs, Charles William, *Village Politics*. London, 1878.

Taylor, Charles C., *The Life of Admiral Mahan*. London, 1920.

Thorold, Alger L., *The Life of Henry Labouchere*. London, 1913.

Thompson, George C., *Public Opinion and Lord Beaconsfield*. London, 1886.

Ware, J. R. and Mann, R. K., *The Life and Times of Colonel Fred Burnaby*. London, 1885.

Whibley, Charles, *Lord John Manners and His Friends*. Edinburgh and London, 1925.

Wright, Thomas, *The Life of Colonel Fred Burnaby*. London, 1908.

Wingfield-Stratford, Esmé, *The History of English Patriotism*. London, 1913.

Wolff, Sir Henry Drummond, *Rambling Recollections*. London, 1908.

——, *Some Notes on the Past*. London, 1893.

Woods, Maurice, *A History of the Tory Party*. London, 1924.

Wright, Thomas, *The Works of James Gillray*. London, 1873.

INDEX